UP
FROM
NIGGER

By the same author:

Dick Gregory's Bible Tales
Dick Gregory's Natural Diet for Folks Who Eat:
Cookin' with Mother Nature
Dick Gregory's Political Primer
No More Lies: The Myth and the Reality of American History
Write Me In!
The Shadow That Scares Me
What's Happening
Nigger
From the Back of the Bus

UP
FROM
NIGGER

Dick Gregory

With James R. McGraw

STEIN AND DAY/*Publishers*/New York

First published in 1976
Copyright © 1976 by Richard Claxton Gregory
All rights reserved
Designed by Ed Kaplin
Printed in the United States of America
Stein and Day/Publishers/Scarborough House,
Briarcliff Manor, N.Y. 10510
Excerpts from this book were originally
published in *Playboy* Magazine

Library of Congress Cataloging in Publication Data

Gregory, Dick.
Up from Nigger.

1. Gregory, Dick.   2.   Negroes—Civil rights.
I.   Title.
PN2287.G68A37   818′.5′409 [B]   75-12817
ISBN 0-8128-1832-6

Contents

Illustrations

Preface

I'm really glad about the timing for the publication of this book. This is the Bicentennial year in America; a time for looking back over our past, analyzing the present, and seriously reflecting upon our nation's future. At least, that's what the Bicentennial can and should represent.

The Bicentennial celebration seems to coincide with a national mood of nostalgia. The fifties seems to be a favorite decade for nostalgic return: "Happy Days" and "Laverne and Shirley" on television, *Grease* on Broadway, and countless record albums that collect the hits of the fifties. In this book I'm inviting you to recall with me the decade just past. Of course, it is a recollection based upon my own experiences. But they were experiences in which all of my fellow Americans were involved simply by virtue of living in America.

So this book has both Bicentennial and nostalgic significance. The Bicentennial celebration has a tendency to focus upon the earliest days of our nation's history. Those Bicentennial minutes each night on TV relive the American Revolution and the activities of the founding fathers. But there is a sense, at least from a Black perspective, in which the decade of the sixties was the real beginning of a serious attempt to implement the intention of the rhetoric of the Declaration of Independence and the United States Constitution. Full implementation is yet further down the line. But there has been a beginning.

The spirit of implementing America's most treasured rhetoric has especially taken hold of the minds and vision of young Americans, both Black and white. For those young readers, this book will be not so much nostalgic reminder as recent history. But it is important for *all* Americans, young and old, to look back over the past decade through the eyes of wisdom and understanding rather than in a mood of malice or resentment. The past ten years have been years of struggle, bloodshed, hostility, and anger, as well as years of courage, dedication, beauty, and important legislative achievement. We should all nostalgically cling to the memory of those years, treasuring them as an important part of our nation's history.

It's always a risky enterprise to try to write autobiographically. Lapses in memory combine with editorial considerations to inevitably omit important names and important events. It certainly is true of this work. So I apologize in advance to the many, many people who have been so important to my life and personal growth, but who will not find their names in these pages. I have tried not to mention names simply for the sake of giving well-deserved recognition. I have merely tried to let recollections and memories flow, and some names and events have fallen into place, just as others have been omitted. I might liken this book to that moment when you are riding on an airplane and you know the plane is going to crash. It is said that your life flashes before you in an instant.

So this book is a flashback. Much of the material reflects the remembrances of Jim McGraw. He ought to be a Republican since, like the Republican party symbol, McGraw never forgets! His total recall is as appreciated now as his presence was back when so many of the events were taking place. And, as always, I am so deeply indebted to Jim Sanders.

I want to express my deep appreciation yet another time to Jeannette Hopkins, who has edited my last four books. As always, she has combined editorial expertise with personal patience and understanding to make this book a reality. Thanks to Sol Stein for being more committed to seeing a project through to its conclusion than rigidly insisting upon deadlines. A special word of appreciation to John H. Johnson, editor and publisher of *Ebony*, who opened his heart and his files to provide photographs for this book. I want to thank Dr. Lewis Quercia, Dr. Gerold Eisenberg, and Dr. Bernard Schecter for getting me through a difficult time during the preparation of this manuscript.

And finally, I want to express my deepest love and admiration to my wife, Lillian. As these pages will document, her commitment and dedication to the cause of human dignity are unsurpassed. And yet she somehow finds the time, energy, and love to be a perfect mother to the ten Gregory offspring: Michele, Lynne, Pamela, Paula, Stephanie, Gregory, Christian, Missy, Ayanna, and Yohance.

1

The White House
and My Emancipation

It was thirteen years ago. Nineteen sixty-three. I came home one cold day in Chicago, and as soon as I walked through the door, my wife, Lillian, said, "You got a letter today from the White House."

I opened the letter and read it. The president of the United States was inviting us both to a White House reception on Tuesday, February 12, Lincoln's Birthday, in celebration and observance of the one hundredth anniversary of the signing of the Emancipation Proclamation.

"We're not going," I told Lillian. "Black folks aren't emancipated yet. I can't participate in a fraud."

I thought again of my high school days on the race track. I felt the same way about that White House invitation as I would have felt if they had put up a Jim Crow tape just before the final tape, telling Black runners to stop here while the white boys sprinted ahead to the finish line.

Here was a letter of invitation from the White House, asking for an R.S.V.P., but no mention of reimbursement for travel or hotel expenses. I suddenly realized that White House invitations go only to people who can afford to attend!

That wasn't what the Emancipation Proclamation was all about.

But I could tell that Lil wanted to go. So I agreed on one condition. Since Black folks only have about half their freedom, we would stay only half the time allotted for the reception. It would be my own personal protest. Besides, Lil was almost nine months pregnant. I thought, if we got lucky, maybe the baby would be born in the White House. I'd finally get back at that old silent movie, *Birth of a Nation!*

Lil went out and bought an expensive new dress for the occasion. I remember thinking to myself, "This has to be a one-time outfit. How many times in a woman's life will she be going to a dress-up formal affair nearly nine months pregnant?" We've had eight more kids since then, bringing our total to ten, and somehow the idea doesn't seem so strange anymore.

I decided I'd be prepared to make the best use of my time. I got some Emancipation Proclamation and Abraham Lincoln lines all set to go: "It's nice to be in Washington for the centennial of the signing of the Emancipation Proclamation. We think of it as the colored Magna Carta. Just think of it. One hundred years ago Lincoln freed the slaves. Now if we could just convince Governor Barnett. Of course, down in Mississippi, Governor Barnett has his own ideas about the Emancipation Proclamation. He read about what a practical joker Lincoln was, and now he's hoping old Abe signed it in disappearing ink!"

The big news at the time was President Kennedy's physical fitness program, so I prepared some lines about Bobby Kennedy's fifty-mile hike: "Isn't it funny that Ethel just announced her eighth baby is on the way, and Bobby walked fifty miles? She probably said, 'I don't care where you go, just stay out of here.' But Bobby walked fifty miles in eighteen hours. You got to give him credit— he even sprinted the last few hundred yards. Well, he wasn't exactly sprinting. He was walking down the highway, and one of Jimmy Hoffa's drivers spotted him. But my people are really going for this walking fad. How often do we find something that's both fashionable *and* cheap? I remember when Adlai Stevenson had a hole in his shoe and it was embarrassing. Now it's boasting!

"But we do the craziest things in this country. The Health Department just warned that an Asian flu epidemic was on the way, so we start a walking fad to spread it around. But I have to admit, I can't get too excited about Bobby Kennedy walking those fifty miles. Down South, we walk farther than that just trying to find a restaurant that'll serve us."

I caught the magic spirit as soon as I got to the White House.

All my fellow long-distance runners in the struggle for human dignity were there—Martin Luther King, Ralph Abernathy, A. Phillip Randolph, James Farmer, Whitney Young—and, it must have been "Davis Night at the White House." Sammy was there, and so was Benjamin O. Davis.

There were other familiar voices and faces—Bobby Kennedy, Secretary of Defense McNamara, Secretary of the Interior Udall, Sargent Shriver of the Peace Corps, and Edward R. Murrow of USIA.

The room seemed filled with electricity. Later I would come to realize that it probably was. The room was no doubt wired and bugged. And somewhere in the White House the tapes were rolling. I remember feeling that same special charge I used to feel lining up on the track.

There's something so wonderful and so beautiful about lining up for a big race. When you stand with your fellow competitors, you feel that special electric charge emanating from each body on the line. You feel that sense of oneness—a unity within your whole body and with each runner. As you look down the line, you don't even see the color of your opponent's uniform or the color of his skin. You leave all that for the people in the stands—those who haven't trained, who aren't in condition, who haven't gone the distance.

A joy, a special tranquillity, and a sense of peace takes over as you drink in the beauty of just being there. You smile at your opponents, and they smile in return. You turn to the guys next to you and say, "Good luck, baby," and you really mean that. Then, unconsciously, but also sincerely, you reach out and slap your comrade in competition on the butt. It represents a special sense of comradeship because you know what he has gone through to get into the Big Meet.

A quiet descends. The starter raises his revolver. A shot rings out. The race is on.

I was drinking in the beauty of just being there. Suddenly I heard Lil saying, "Dick, there's the president!"

John F. Kennedy was standing beside me, and I hadn't even realized it.

Still in the comradely spirit of the race track, I reached out to slap President Kennedy on the butt. It seemed like every hand in the room reached out to grab mine! Folks I thought were party guests dropped their cocktail glasses and lunged, and I realized then that they were Secret Service. I still had not been emancipated into a full knowledge of the inner workings of government surveillance. I had really thought all those folks were guests!

The president seemed kind of nervous. He said, "Hi, Dick," and before I could introduce him to my wife, he continued, "Hello, Lil." I went ahead with the formalities, "This is my wife." "Yes, I know," the president answered, "I've talked with her several times on the phone."

President Kennedy said, "Dick, I'd like you to meet the vice president." After introducing me to Lyndon Baines Johnson, he moved on to greet other guests. I remember being overwhelmed at the size of LBJ; the power he exuded made him seem that much bigger. I knew I had to say something. LBJ had just been given the responsibility of overseeing equal opportunity matters, so I said, "It's really good to meet you, and I have a question I'd like to ask. Do you have any colored cowboys on your ranch?"

The vice president sort of tightened up, and all the Black folks within earshot of my question got *really* uptight. Then LBJ smiled and went on to mingle with the crowd. If my government files hadn't already been started, I'm sure they were that night. I'm sure the agents in the room had decided I was a little bit too emancipated, too "uppity." I had made my personal protest in a very different way from the one I had planned. Now I could stay the whole time.

When the reception ended, I had that same old feeling I had at the finish of a big track meet. The excitement and exhilaration were over. It was time now to return to the real world, which is really the unreal world. If everything were fair and just in this country, and as beautiful and natural as it could and should be, it would be normal for all Americans to have that special feeling of kinship with one another twenty-four hours a day. We would all be lined up together in that special comradeship of the starting line.

I lined up beside Jack Kennedy that night, and it had seemed so natural to reach out and pat him on the behind.

2

The Stars and the Starter's Pistol

Show business had become my race track after I left Southern Illinois University, where I was on a track scholarship. The magic of the crowd in a nightclub or concert hall was the same as I had always felt in a stadium. Going over my lines in the dressing room was like warming up before a race. Standing up to perform was like crouching at the starting line. The applause after my introduction was like the starter's pistol.

After the show was over and the tables cleared, the seats emptied, and the crowd gone, I'd have the same feeling I had standing in an empty stadium after a big race. It just didn't seem possible that this empty space could have generated so much excitement, so much electricity only moments before.

Nobody can really go the distance without the help and support of a whole lot of people. The crowd adds that special stimulus. On stage the lighting specialists, the stage hands, the emcee, the waiters, and the ushers all contribute to that special moment.

The most important people seldom get recognition. I remember in high school and college, every good runner always had somebody from the same school to train with, someone who both pushed and supported him and brought out his very best. And the only reward, the only satisfaction, that special person gets is the joy of seeing his partner do his thing in the big meet.

It's the same in show business. Even though I was in the spotlight, I was pulling so much from my writers Jim Sanders and Bob Orben. I couldn't have gone the distance without them. Bob was a sophisticated, experienced, professional writer and he is white. Jim was a young, raw kid, brilliant, bursting at the seams with talent, developing every day as a comedy writer, and he is Black. I just couldn't miss with material salted by Bob and peppered by Jim.

Jim traveled with me, and we became very close. When we'd hit a town, there was no need to go out. We would just sit up in the hotel room and rap about everything. We'd go to the show, back to the room and a few hours sleep. Then we'd wake up early, turn on television, and dissect the news together, reading between the lines and always looking for something funny.

Jim Sanders introduced me to astrology. He would never push it on me. He would just sit down in the hotel room, do his little charts, and tell me about things that were going to happen. And I began to realize that those things did happen!

In November 1963 we were on a concert tour. One night Jim and I were watching the news on television. President Kennedy was in San Antonio, and he was speaking to the crowd in Spanish. Very quietly Jim said, "I've got a feeling something is going to happen to him. I don't think he'll live to see the White House again."

The next night, we were watching the news again. President Kennedy was due in Dallas the following day. Jim said again, "Something's going to happen to him in Dallas." So I decided to play a little game on Jim. We were due in Pittsburgh the next night. I called Chicago and arranged a flight that would get Jim and me to Pittsburgh in time for the concert. The next morning I told the rest of the performers, loud enough for Jim to hear, "I have it on good authority that there's not going to be a concert in Pittsburgh tonight, so we'll catch up with ya'll later. Jim and I are going home to Chicago."

Jim was really worried, thinking I'd taken him too seriously. He timidly suggested that perhaps I should reconsider. I said, "Man, you've been dealing with that astrology. You done said twice that something's going to happen to the president, so obviously there won't be any concert tonight. I don't want to hear no more about it."

We flew to Chicago. In the cab on the way home, I was really enjoying my little game, peeking at Jim out of the corner of my eye. He was still worried about being personally responsible for me blowing the gig in Pittsburgh. But I was playing the game all the way. I told Jim, "Man, I sure am glad you gave me this night off. Do you realize we been on the road for thirty days?"

I was so busy putting Jim on I didn't realize the cab driver was listening to the radio. All of a sudden I thought I heard the words "shot in Dallas." I asked the driver, "Hey, brother, what did they just say on the radio?"

He turned and looked back, and I saw the sadness in his face. "Man, haven't you heard? The president's been shot!"

I was stunned. I looked at Jim. All I could think to say was, "Would you teach me astrology?"

Then I remembered the White House reception. There was the starter's pistol—that shot in Dallas. And I wondered where this race would end.

3

We Had Sown the Wind

I ran into my apartment and turned on all the radios and television sets. I thought to myself, "If someone had been able to tape all the commentary after the assassination of President Lincoln, how valuable those tapes would be today." So I set up my tape recorders and began to do my duty to posterity.

I could think only of all that protection around President Kennedy I had seen at the White House reception. I just couldn't understand how he could be assassinated right under the noses of the Secret Service.

As I listened to the unfolding drama on radio and television, I began to notice a conflict between stories. I'd hear someone being interviewed, and an hour or so later, that same person was telling a different tale.

I started searching for a reason, more out of curiosity than suspicion. I began to notice a thread of continuity. Each person changed her/his story after talking to the Secret Service. Just to make sure, I started playing back my tapes. Sure enough, there was a direct relationship between talking to the Secret Service and changing eyewitness accounts. Instant posterity!

I turned off all my tape recorders. I didn't want to tape a lie. Instinctively I knew the assassination was bigger than the official story. At that time I never even thought of a conspiracy, but I knew there was something more than what I was hearing.

Jim Sanders came by the apartment, and we went to the airport to distribute the gifts I had bought for the other performers on our concert tour. The concert in Pittsburgh had been cancelled, of course, and they were changing planes in Chicago. I simply couldn't convince them that I really didn't know anything was going to happen in Dallas, that I'd only been playing a trick on Jim. So I gave out the gifts and said, "It was a grand tour. I'm just sorry it had to end this way."

During that sad weekend, I learned once again the peace and tranquillity music can bring. Every radio station interrupted regular programming and played music in memory of President Kennedy. Until that time I had always thought comedy—a good laugh—was the greatest relief in times of crisis. But no comedy record could have brought relief to any sane person that weekend.

I've always loved classical music. As a little ghetto kid in Saint Louis, I used to love going to the opera. My friends and I were more than opera buffs. We were experts and critics. Opera allowed even kids on welfare to participate in the best society had to offer. And we loved it. I used to dream of the day I could go to the opera first class, when I didn't have to sit in the cheap seats and, most of all, when I could afford to rent opera glasses. As a kid I could afford the fifteen-cent rental, but the two-dollar deposit priced me and my fellow ghetto critics out of the opera-glass market.

After I made it big in show business, I fulfilled that childhood dream. On a night off between engagements, I took Lil and the kids, Lynne and Michele, to the Saint Louis opera. It was first class all the way! First class on the plane. A chauffeur-driven limousine waiting at the airport. The most expensive seats in the opera house. And, of course, opera glasses.

After the curtain went up, I realized the irony. You don't need opera glasses when you're sitting in the front row! Years later, I had a very special thrill when I walked into the dressing room for the Merv Griffin Show. I looked at the man in the makeup chair, and it was the opera star Jan Peerce! We were guests on the same show. I told him what he had meant to me as a kid, but I'm sure he never realized the magnitude of my appreciation.

Listening to the music that November weekend, I did a lot of thinking. In many ways those hours were a private seminar in questioning the workings of the system. Later I would learn that you don't receive credit for such a course of study! Not even "A" for effort.

I began to realize the deep roots of racism as I never had before. Early reports of the assassination had said that a Black man killed the president. In Detroit a race riot nearly broke out because of that rumor. Racial brawls were avoided only when Lee Harvey Oswald, a white man, was caught.

Racism transcends tragedy. If a Black man had killed President Kennedy, all Black folks would have suffered as a result. But a white man killing the president didn't produce the same reaction—even when that white man was thought to be a Communist. There was no attack upon Communist embassies. Known or suspected Communists were not beaten by outraged white folks. Racism does not disappear even when the hearts of Blacks and whites are equally saddened.

On Sunday, when Jack Ruby shot Lee Harvey Oswald on national television, my private seminar began to develop into a personal crusade of more than a decade. I knew the story was bigger than a lone assassin acting independently. I knew there was something else, like racism, deeply ingrained into the American system, and I had to find out more about it. I had been on the front line of the civil rights struggle. But I knew there was more to it than being called "nigger." That weekend, I began my climb "up from nigger."

Lil and I agreed we just had to be in Washington, D.C., for the funeral. I felt particularly close to President Kennedy. I had met him. He had telephoned to my apartment several times and spoken with both my wife and me. He was closer to me than a president ordinarily is to a private citizen.

The president's coffin rested in the rotunda of the Capitol building for public viewing. And that line of mourners was so long! I was determined not to use my celebrity status to crash that line. Out of respect for President Kennedy, I decided to hold the cause of civil rights in suspension for a moment and stay in my place!

I saw America standing in line that day. Old people, young people, people with babies in their arms, and little kids in carriages. It wasn't a dress-up affair. It was strictly come-as-you-are. People in coats, sweaters, new shoes, old shoes, raw America gathered in grief. Walking to find the end of the line, I noticed that person after person was crying, but most of them were not even conscious of their tears. Nobody talked. If you saw somebody you knew, or were recognized by someone, you simply nodded and went on.

Everyone was on his or her best behaviour. Cars pulled up to let folks out to join the line, but you didn't hear a car door slam or tires screech. Time seemed to be suspended, physical and emotional reactions forgotten. There was no such thing as being tired or cold or hungry. The president was dead. The nation was stunned. The future was uncertain.

It wasn't long before a United States marshal recognized me, and in spite of my reluctance to buck the line, he beckoned to my wife and me. He took us straight into the rotunda. I had such a strange feeling as our turn came to view the coffin. I kept thinking of that game I had played with Jim Sanders. Even Jim never realized it was a practical joke. He was convinced I had known something. And as I filed past the president's coffin, even I began to wonder if my instincts had known something my conscious awareness had not.

The next day, Lil and I went to Arlington Cemetery for the final farewell. The ceremony at Arlington matched the splendor of a White House reception. When the White House sponsors an affair, it is a first-class spectacle, whether the affair is for the living or for the dead. Because America is on display. When the White House throws a party, it is America hosting it. And when the White House conducts a funeral, it is America saying good-bye.

It was chilly that November day. Lil and I were standing way down at the foot of a hill. As I listened to the sad, solemn playing of taps, a strange thing happened. I looked up and saw a cluster of leaves swirling high above my head. The leaves were so high, at first I thought they were birds. I pointed out the strange phenomenon to Lil and said, "I don't know what that means, but it must mean something."

Then I remembered those words of the prophet Hosea I had heard so long ago in church, "For they have sown the wind, and they shall reap the whirlwind."

4

Making Room in the Inn

I couldn't forget that day in Arlington Cemetery. After all, President Kennedy had challenged all Americans to ask themselves what they could do for their country. I knew one thing I could do, that I *had* to do, was to continue to put my career, my body, and my life on the front line in the struggle for civil rights.

There is a strange thing about the course of human events. A beautiful or courageous human action can have the effect of raising the consciousness level of the entire nation. On the other hand, a horrible act often has the reverse effect, and the consciousness level of the nation is dulled.

The assassination of President Kennedy seemed to have a deadening effect, as though a drug had been injected into the main artery of national feeling. The nation was dumbfounded. The tragic circumstances under which Lyndon Baines Johnson became president of the United States seemed to create a moral vacuum and a crisis of conscience. There was a tendency to put protest aside for a while, to give the new president a chance, check out his intentions, and let him chart a clear course for the future.

For a month or so after the assassination, it seemed as though the civil rights movement had been wiped out. There were no demonstrations. Leaders seemed to be caught in a vise of indecision. Something was needed to jar the nation's sensibilities, to free the national conscience from its temporary moral paralysis.

One day I got a phone call from the SNCC kids (Student Nonviolent Coordinating Committee) in Atlanta, Georgia, telling me about a particularly touchy situation there. Although the city of Atlanta had a public accommodations law, it was neutralized and protected from implementation by Georgia state law. State law stipulated that anyone who refused to leave a place of business after having been asked to leave by the owner in the presence of a police officer, could be arrested for trespassing. Every time demonstrators tried to integrate restaurants in Atlanta, they would be arrested under Georgia state law. The city of Atlanta, much like Pontius Pilate, would wash its hands of responsibility. City officials insisted that nothing could be done until the state law was changed.

Lil and I talked about the problem in Atlanta, as well as the need for a dramatic national reminder that the civil rights issue was still very much alive. Lil was pregnant with our twin girls at the time. We decided that the pregnant wife of a national celebrity in jail on Christmas Day, while daddy was at home with the other two kids, Lynne and Michele, would be an appropriate and dramatic Christmas reminder that there was still no room for

Black folks in the inns and restaurants of Atlanta. We decided that Lil should go to Atlanta and get arrested on Christmas Eve. And if she participated in the demonstrations, there was no doubt she would be arrested!

Lil went to Atlanta. She didn't want to go. She didn't want to be away from our other two girls on Christmas. But Lil's humanitarian impulse took over from her motherly instinct. She took part in a sit-in demonstration at one of the Dobbs House restaurants. The white folks didn't let us down! The state law was invoked, Lil and many others refused to leave, and they all went to jail.

I sent a telegram to Lil at the jail on Christmas Eve. It was released to the press on Christmas Day. I said that the kids were all right, but they missed their momma, and I thanked her for being willing to give up her Christmas so that one day all folks in America might have something to celebrate. I added a line which got a lot of coverage in the press, "If they had found as much room in the inn two thousand years ago for a pregnant woman named Mary as the Atlanta police have found in their jail for you, maybe none of us would be celebrating Christmas today."

Lil became a symbolic reminder that the civil rights struggle was not over. Three days later I joined the Atlanta demonstrations. They had grown to huge proportions, with hundreds of people arrested each day.

I had noticed that Dobbs House and Toddle House were on the New York Stock Exchange. I received a sudden inspiration about how to beat the Georgia state law. I bought two shares each of Dobbs House and Toddle House stock. Then I went back to demonstrate.

The manager came over with the required cop as a witness and asked me to leave the premises. I said, "I happen to own stock in this business. Do you?" Of course, I didn't say *how much* stock I owned. It was a great example of how to use an image. Everybody knew I was a big entertainer and assumed I made big money. Their assumptions inflated the value of my stock holdings!

The manager admitted that he wasn't a stockholder. I shook my head and said, "Well, under these circumstances, it appears that I represent more ownership than you do. So I'll have to ask you to leave my premises. Officer, do your duty!"

The manager requested an immediate stockholders' meeting, so we huddled in the corner. He explained the integration problem. There were a number of similar restaurants in Atlanta owned by a man named Charlie Loeb. A Loeb establishment was right across the street. The manager said it wouldn't do any good to integrate his place because white customers would simply boycott and go to the Loeb establishment. I indicated that we'd deal with Loeb after Dobbs and Toddle Houses were integrated.

We won that battle, and the Dobbs and Toddle Houses of Atlanta soon were integrated. But integrating the Loeb establishments was much harder. We met with strong resistance. I wasn't a stockholder, so I didn't have the negotiating power. We kept on demonstrating, going to jail, and it seemed as though we were going nowhere.

One day, while I was in jail, I read a newspaper quote which hinted that Charlie Loeb wasn't the "tyrant" other statements had made him appear to be. As soon as I was released from jail, I decided to try some personal negotiation. I went by Charlie Loeb's house. It happened to be his birthday, and there was a party going on. We went into a side room and I told him, "I've read some statements you've made to the press. I get the feeling there's more to your resistance than shows on the surface. What's the real problem?"

He said, "You're right. There are two problems. I'm getting ready to sell my restaurants, and it's very difficult for me to integrate before I sell. The buyer will think I'm doing it just because I'm getting out."

I could understand that problem, but the second one caught me off guard. Charlie Loeb told me why he had refused to let Harry Belafonte into his establishment. The mayor had brought Harry by after giving him the keys to the city.

Loeb insisted that the incident didn't have anything to do with Harry's being Black. But every time a white person was given the keys to the city, the party was held at the country club. Loeb felt Harry was being brought to his place, instead of to the usual country club affair, because Loeb was Jewish. I wasn't ready for that one! Loeb was on the same side we were. He was protesting discrimination!

We made a deal. We would call off the demonstrations if Loeb would agree to have his restaurants sold within sixty days and would also get city officials to drop all charges against arrested demonstrators. He agreed.

I couldn't help thinking of Lil's contribution. Not only had she helped to open the restaurant counters in Atlanta to Black folks, but she had unconsciously exposed discrimination against Jews. I wondered if that was why there was a no vacancy sign on the Bethlehem inn that night two thousand years ago. Would they have put a pregnant mother out in the stable if she hadn't been Jewish?

5

School Days in New York City

It was an election year, and the civil rights movement was back on the move. I remember a nightclub line I was using early in 1964. "It's been a heck of a day in America—Sidney Poitier gets the Academy Award, boycotts in New York, Boston, and Chicago, the Civil Rights bill, the Clay-Liston fight. Today, U.S. means *us!*"

As I look back, it's hard to believe all the things that happened in 1964. I was in and out of demonstrations, in and out of the country, in and out of nightclubs. It was the year I began hearing the question, "Have demonstrations hurt your career?" It was also the year I developed the answer, "Funny you should ask. I keep asking myself, 'Is my career interfering with my demonstrations?'"

The civil rights movement rebounded into the North in the form of public school boycotts, protesting de facto segregation in the public schools. The school boycott was a particularly potent weapon because of the state and federal aid-to-education guidelines. Funds were appropriated according to a formula based on daily pupil attendance. A successful, long-term school boycott substantially affected the amount of state and federal money that a school system received. As a result, public school officials were particularly intimidated by school boycotts.

Organizing public school boycotts in the northern Black

community was no easy task. Black parents were not tuned into public school involvement because of the struggle to buy food and pay the rent. We didn't have strong Parent-Teacher Associations in the Black community to bring political pressure on school boards and public officials.

Most Black parents were too tired after a hard day's work to think about going to PTA meetings. If they did go, they felt obligated to dress up as though they were going to church. Parents with large families had the additional problem of getting someone to take care of the kids while they were away, and most family budgets couldn't afford the luxury of a baby-sitter. Consequently, most Black parents only went to school when their kids were in trouble or suspended, and even that meant taking a day off from work.

Most Black parents were so glad their kids were going to school in the North that they didn't really relate to terms like "quality education," "overcrowded classrooms," or "inferior facilities." It was difficult to spotlight the problem of northern de facto public school segregation since it involved a crisis in the Black living room as well as in the Black classroom.

In Chicago, we had both an advantage and a disadvantage. School Superintendent Ben Willis gave us an excellent rallying point. His opposition and obstinacy gave us a northern symbol; just as the South had its Bull Conner, the Birmingham, Alabama, police chief. But we also had to struggle against the tightly held grip on politics of Chicago's Mayor Richard Daley. Mayor Daley owned the town, and he had the human resources to try to break the back of school boycott organizing efforts. He used his precinct captains to threaten and intimidate Black parents.

The school kids themselves proved to be the best organizers. We held rallies with the kids at the schools, in churches, and on the street corner. And the kids went home and educated their parents.

Since the kids couldn't vote, Mayor Daley's precinct captains had less control over them.

Of course, critics of the school boycotts condemned us for using the kids as pawns. It was a ridiculous accusation, since the kids, not their parents, were the real victims of the evils of de facto segregation. The lives and minds of the kids were being destroyed, and they had every right to fight back. I frequently cited the story of David and Goliath. If King Saul had listened to voices saying it wasn't right to involve the kids, the men of Israel would have been wiped out. If that story means anything, it is a reminder never to overlook the power and the determination of the kids!

Northern school boycotts produced a new sense of unity in the Black community. They also gave birth to strong new local leadership. The first school boycott in Chicago saw the churches, the NAACP, the Urban League, and all kinds of local groups, Black and white, working together for the first time. Some 200,000 kids stayed out of school. Unwittingly, Chicago city officials helped organize the boycott. They kept talking about potential violence and sent in large numbers of police to "protect" the schools. Black parents who weren't even for the boycott were afraid to send their kids to school.

New local leaders emerged from the epidemic of school boycotts in cities across the nation. Lawrence Landry, Al Raby, and Nahaz Rogers in Chicago. Stanley Branch in Chester, Pennsylvania, the Reverend Milton Galamison in New York City.

During the first part of 1964, I was a frequent visitor to Milton Galamison's Siloam Presbyterian Church in Brooklyn. In February I showed up unexpectedly at his first New York City school boycott and lectured to a freedom school held in the sanctuary of the church. Milton's slogan for the boycott was "quality education through integration," and his protest was intended to pressure the Board of Education to commit itself to a plan and timetable for the complete integration of the New York City public school system. I was really turned on by that New York City boycott. It inspired me to redouble the protest efforts in Chicago.

The freedom schools in New York City were particularly impressive. Everything about New York City is big, but I was awed by the large number of people participating in the boycott and the tremendous amount of organization, coordination, and plain hard work. Milton Galamison's church was filled to the rafters with dedicated, enthusiastic kids. Siloam Church was the first northern Black church I had seen that had become the focal point of community action. It was a church really doing its job, not only blessing the people who came to church on Sunday morning, but also *being* a blessing to the entire Black community in New York City.

Galamison's second school boycott a month later came as a surprise. I was in Chester, Pennsylvania, speaking at a meeting of a new organization of grass-roots leaders in Black communities throughout the country. The name of the group was ACT. The initials didn't stand for anything. It was the whole word. It just meant what it said! I saw familiar faces in the crowd—Lawrence Landry, who led the Chicago school boycotts; Stanley Branch, the Chester, Pennsylvania, activist; Johnny Wilson, from the Princess Anne County movement in Maryland; and Malcolm X. Milton Galamison was conspicuously absent. I wondered why, since he had been an original organizer of ACT.

While I was rushing out to make another engagement, a young white minister caught up to me and asked, "I was wondering if you planned to show up in New York City Monday for our second school boycott. I know you were at the first one." I hadn't realized there was another boycott, but I promised I would be there. The minister mentioned that there was a big night-before-the-boycott rally scheduled for the next evening. I told him to announce I would be there in time for the rally. We exchanged phone numbers, and the minister was to call me the next day with details. As I stuffed the number into my pocket, I noticed the name—the Reverend Jim McGraw.

We never made telephone contact that next day. I guessed at the time of the rally, flew to New York, and headed straight for Galamison's church. There was excitement in the Siloam sanctuary. I took a seat in a front pew and waited my turn on the program. When it came time to take up the collection, the same young white minister I had met in Chester got up to make the fund-raising pitch. He started doing one-liners like Mort Sahl in a clerical collar. The audience loved it. After the rally, I told him, "Reverend, you're somethin' else. I'm going to build me a church in Chicago and put you in it!" I never built that church, but Jim McGraw has been my pastor partner ever since.

I was last. I started off by explaining the difficulty I had getting there. "You know, when I left Chicago, I really didn't know where I was going. I had forgotten the name of Reverend Galamison's church. I got out my Bible, and I didn't find Reverend Galamison or the church mentioned anywhere.

"So I had to rely on human nature. I jumped into a cab with a white cab driver and said, 'Where's that nigger that's raisin' all this hell in New York?' He drove me right to the door of the church!"

I was so turned on by that enthusiastic crowd, I spoke for two hours. The excitement level was so high it seemed to extend far beyond the New York City limits. It felt like a national movement.

The next day I found myself waiting in Milton Galamison's office before the march to the New York City Board of Education offices. I had started my election-year propaganda early, and I was getting a lot of laughs and comments from a "campaign button" I was wearing. It had a picture of a rat with the caption "Elect a Rat for President." Whenever I was asked about it, I would say, "Well, I'm wearing this button so no matter who wins in November, I can say I supported him."

There was such power and beauty in Galamison's office that day. Malcolm X was there when I arrived. Folks were surprised to see him since this was a demonstration to integrate the schools. But by his presence, Malcolm was letting it be known that he was there because the boycott was a people's movement. Above and beyond his social, political, and religious beliefs, Malcolm was saying he was part of the Black community and this boycott represented *all* of "us" against "them." As always, Malcolm was making himself available to the needs and desires of the masses.

All of a sudden the office door opened and a voice announced, "Congressman Powell." Everything stopped! Nothing happened for a moment. Everybody in the room turned around as Adam Clayton Powell swept into the room. He strode over and embraced Malcolm X with a warm, "Malcolm, baby." Congressman Powell filled the office with his presence. He was immaculately tailored in his cashmere coat, smoked an expensive, elegant pipe, the whole works. I must have had Adam's entrance in mind when I did a line about Richard Nixon years later. "You know how some folks light up a room when they walk in? The only time Nixon lights up a room is when he leaves!"

Never before had I seen firsthand the power and magnetism of Adam Clayton Powell. It was hard to believe he wasn't in his own church or even in his own congressional district. I realized for the first time what I would later see all over the country. Adam Clayton Powell was our own Black congressman, no matter where we lived. His district was the Black community of the United States!

It's hard to describe the thrill I had that day. It just wiped me out to be in the same room with two of the most powerful Black men in the history of America. There they were, standing side by side, and even thanking *me* for being there!

Adam and Malcolm each had his own special quality, his own special greatness. In spite of his flair and theatrics, Adam Powell never lost that human quality, that special feeling for the people. Malcolm could never enter a room the way Adam did, but Adam could never stand with the erect dignity of Malcolm. Malcolm was a living denial of that old cliché "clothes make the man." No matter what Malcolm X was wearing, his manhood and his very special human dignity shone through. Kings wear their crowns on top of their heads. Malcolm's crown was on the inside. Malcolm X showed me the difference between a crown and a halo.

We marched to the Board of Education. All along the way to 110 Livington Street in Brooklyn, people would run and join the line when they saw Congressman Powell. His voice drew people like a magnet when he shouted, "Come on and join us!" Malcolm X had wisely declined joining the march, knowing that the press would misinterpret his presence. The press had already labeled him as anti-integration.

We held the rally in front of the Board of Education. As I left the speakers' platform to catch a plane, I looked back and saw the look of success on Milton Galamison's face. His smile told the whole story.

6

Lillian–Tegration

My wife's Christmas message to the nation was fulfilled in our household on March 18, 1964. Lillian gave birth to twin baby girls. We named them Pamela and Paula.

Somehow those two names didn't tell the whole story. So we gave them the middle names "Inte" and "Gration." Together, of course, their middle names spelled out "integration." Their middle names would be a lifelong reminder to Pamela and Paula that, even before they were born, they were in jail with their momma fighting for freedom and human dignity.

Actually, Lil was in jail twice during that pregnancy. The first time was down in Selma, Alabama, in the fall of 1963. Lil was demonstrating in Selma as an indirect result of a personal invitation of Al Lingo, Chief of the Alabama State Police.

Al Lingo was notorious among veteran civil rights demonstrators. Birmingham Police Chief Bull Conner got more press coverage, but Al Lingo almost made Bull Conner seem nonviolent! Lingo rode a horse and carried a bull whip. He would ride into groups of demonstrators, swinging his whip, and had even been known to ride right up on someone's front porch and through the bay window to break up a demonstration.

I had never met Al Lingo, but I had heard a lot of stories about him. One day, I answered the phone at home in Chicago.

"Dick Gregory? This is Al Lingo. I understand a sheriff is not a real sheriff 'til he's tangled with you, boy! When you comin' down?"

"You name it."

"We got somethin' goin' on in Selma right now. Come on down!"

"Can't make it right now. I'm sick. But I'll tell you what I'll do. I'll send my wife down and let you keep her until I get there."

"O.K. That's fair enough. See you soon, boy!"

Lil went down to join the Selma demonstrations and wait for me to recover. Sure enough, the next day I got another phone call. The voice was familiar.

"I got your wife down here in jail, nigger. What you think about that?"

"Good. I've been lookin' for a way to get her out of my hair."

I made a speedy recovery and went to Selma to get Lil out of jail. As soon as I hit town, I met up with Sheriff Jim Clark. We got into the elevator to go up to his office and make arrangements for bail. I never will forget the conversation in that elevator.

Sheriff Clark turned to me and said, "You know, I've arrested a lot of nigger bitches, a lot of nigger whores, a lot of poor white trashy women. But your wife is the first lady I ever arrested. That damn Bobby Kennedy's been sendin' agents in every day to see if she's all right. She's really a fine woman. All she ever wants is cold soda pop. But she'll never drink it unless there's enough cups to give some to everybody else in that cellblock. You really got a good woman."

When we got into the office, I asked Sheriff Clark, "How much bail do you want for her?"

"Two thousand dollars."

"I guess you really do think she's a good woman!"

"How much you got?"

"I got a thousand in my pocket. Is it really necessary to go through all the paper work?"

"Not really."

I pulled the thousand in cash out of my pocket, but I didn't want Sheriff Clark to be able to say I was trying to bribe him. So instead of handing it to him, I threw it on the floor.

He looked at the money and then he looked at me. His southern sensibilities and racial hangups just wouldn't allow him to pick up money a "Black boy" had thrown on the floor. So he made me go the whole bail route.

"Go across the street and tell them boys I said to give you a thousand dollars."

Sheriff Clark was talking about the Elks' lodge, right across the street from the jail. The Black Elks were bootlegging for the white sheriff, so Sheriff Clark kept them right downtown where he could keep an eye on business.

I wrote out a check for a thousand dollars and gave it to one of the brothers. "Sheriff Clark said you'd cash this for me."

I got the rest of Lil's bail money. But that cancelled check never came back. The sheriff had put his money where his mouth was. Out of admiration and respect, Sheriff Jim Clark had put up the bail for his "first lady" of the movement!

The World's Fair Stall-In

Milton Galamison's church was plagued by success during 1964. The next time I returned, it was for the most successful "failure" in the history of the civil rights struggle—the stall-in on the opening day of the New York World's Fair.

The stall-in was the creation of Isaiah Brunson and Herb

Callendar, a couple of sincere, dedicated, determined young militants from Brooklyn CORE (Congress of Racial Equality). Siloam Church became the headquarters, and Milton Galamison's name was frequently mentioned in the mass media as one of the stall-in organizers.

The idea behind the stall-in was to focus public attention upon the ongoing social problems in New York City—segregated schools, the lack of quality education, job discrimination, bad housing, and so on—right in the midst of the billion dollar World's Fair hustle. Those who sympathized with the protest were asked to run out of gas, develop mechanical difficulties, and otherwise stall their cars on the thruways leading to the World's Fair grounds on opening day, creating a massive traffic jam. The World's Fair represented an international circus in the midst of poverty and injustice, and the idea was to close it down on opening day.

The genius of the stall-in concept was that it hitched the bucking bronco of social protest to the multi-million dollar publicity wagon selling the World's Fair. All the news focused on opening day. World's Fair progress reports were given almost every night on national television. People all over the nation, and the world, were wondering how many exhibits would actually be completed by opening day. By hooking the stall-in into the World's Fair publicity, social issues were dramatized which would have passed unnoticed and ignored under normal circumstances.

The idea really caught on. Every night those World's Fair progress reports were coupled with progress reports from the stall-in leaders. The stall-in headquarters looked like a military strategy room, with maps of all the thruways and markers indicating just where the cars would jam traffic. As the stall-in threat was magnified by the mass media, New York City officials felt compelled to appear on national television denouncing it and urging people not to participate. Of course, each appearance by a public official only made the stall-in bigger and gave it more credibility.

All of a sudden the stall-in seemed to be bigger news than the World's Fair itself. People all over the country were hearing about the World's Fair only from the negative reports about social protest. I will always wonder how many people cancelled their plans to attend the World's Fair because of what they saw on television.

Shortly before the day of the stall-in, ACT held a meeting in Washington, D.C. I attended the all-day meeting. A portion of it was devoted to the stall-in. The Brooklyn CORE kids were there with their charts, maps, and statistical projections. They made a very professional presentation. To hear them tell their story, it sounded like the stall-in was destined to be the biggest protest action in the history of the civil rights movement. I decided then and there this was one action I didn't want to miss!

ACT was really a unique organization, although it was a few years ahead of its time. It was strictly grass roots and totally independent. When word went out there would be an ACT meeting, folks didn't worry about where their travel expenses were coming from. They just got to the meeting! ACT performed the important function of bringing together local Black community figures who had not yet been "sanctioned" as "Black leaders" by the press. Through ACT they had an opportunity to exchange ideas, swap strategies, and coordinate programs. The face-to-face meeting was very important. For example, Harlem's Jesse Gray was very important to Black communities all across the nation because he had pulled off the first successful rent strike. Rent strikes were needed in every ghetto.

Everywhere I went people were talking about the stall-in. I started using lines about the stall-in in my performances. "I can just see pictures of the stall-in in the American history books years from now. There'll be captions under the pictures like 'This is the way Negroes looked two weeks before we sent them back to Africa!' "

On opening day of the World's Fair, April 22, 1964, I arrived at Siloam Church early in the morning. The church was filled with organizers and sympathizers who had been there all night. Jim Sanders and I arrived together. Jim McGraw had been there all night. He handed me a phone number to call as soon as I arrived, a newsman who wanted a comment on the day's events. I had just heard on the radio that Lady Bird Johnson had been in New Jersey the night before, and that her car had accidentally stalled on the New Jersey Turnpike. I called the newsman and said, "The stall-in's off to a good start. Lady Bird got things started last night in New Jersey!"

I huddled with Milton Galamison and Jim McGraw to plan our personal participation. Milton and Jim both had cars, but neither of them wanted their cars to be confiscated by the police. They didn't mind getting arrested, but losing their cars was something else! We decided to take along a spare driver in each car. When we stopped the cars, Milton and I would get out and kneel down in front of his car, Jim McGraw would kneel in front of his own car, and the spare drivers would slip in behind the steering wheels. They would offer to move the cars as soon as the kneeling protesters were removed. Of course, we had visions of a traffic jam so big it would be impossible to get the paddy wagons to the scene of the crime.

A cadre of squad cars were parked outside the church waiting for something to happen. At about 10 A.M., we all climbed into our respective cars to hit the stall-in battleground. There were three cars in our group—Milton's, Jim McGraw's, and one other car. In our entourage were the waiting squad cars.

Milton led the parade like a grand marshal. He darted down Marcy Avenue toward the parkway, completely oblivious of minor details like traffic lights and speed limits. The cops behind us could have stopped us anywhere along the way for an infinite variety of traffic violations. But they only had one thing in mind. They were determined to catch us stalling-in.

When our entourage pulled onto the Grand Central Parkway, I really got scared. I thought something really drastic had already happened. The parkway was empty! I could understand cars being stacked up for miles in New York City. But it was terrifying to look ahead for miles and not see any traffic at all.

We had the highway to ourselves. Our three cars were lined up side by side, each car in its own lane, with the cops tailgating close behind. Every few hundred yards there were cops and tow trucks ready and waiting to haul away stalled cars and arrest the drivers. In between the makeshift towing stations were police guards. It seemed like every one of New York's finest was out on the parkway that day. Cops were stationed on the walkway ramps going across the parkway. In addition to the stall-in threat, President Johnson was speaking at the World's Fair opening-day festivities. So there were both stall-in cops and security cops. The parkway was a sea of blue uniforms.

We drove along in formation. Marc Crawford of *Life* magazine was in McGraw's car, and he was really nervous. *Life* had set aside something like fourteen pages to report the stall-in, and Marc had visions of all that empty white space in the magazine.

But the stall-in publicity had obviously worked. Many companies had given their employees a day off to keep them off the highway. It had been announced that many taxi drivers would not be working either. The normal parkway traffic had successfully been eliminated. If there was any stalling to be done on the Grand Central Parkway that morning, our three cars would have to do it.

Milton was having a ball leading the squad cars up and down the parkway. After a while he tired of the chase, and we decided to see what was happening inside the World's Fair grounds. Milton turned off at an exit, started up the ramp, and suddenly stopped. The other cars stopped too. Everybody thought, "This is it!" Marc Crawford jumped out of the car with his photographer. The cops jumped out and ran up to Milton's car. Milton calmly rolled down the window and asked, "Excuse me, officer. Is this the way to the World's Fair?" The cops were caught off guard. They gave us directions, and we went on our way.

We parked our cars in the parking lot and went to the fair. The action was more heated inside. CORE protesters, led by national director James Farmer, were being arrested in large numbers at the New York Pavilion. Pinkerton guards were handling the removal of sit-in demonstrators, and they were not inclined to be gentle. Demonstrators were being dragged and bounced down staircases and turned over to the police. It was an ugly scene.

Jim McGraw and I went back to the parking lot to meet Milton. A squad car was blocking our exit. The hood was up and two cops were fooling around with the engine. The squad car had supposedly broken down, and it was the only stalled car I saw all day.

The press called the stall-in a failure, but in reality the stall-in highlighted the hypocrisy of a racist system. Every day in New York City cars stall during rush hour, jamming up traffic for blocks and miles. Drivers blow their horns, curse, and otherwise display their irritation. But New Yorkers and their elected officials don't denounce those traffic jams the way they did the threat of a stall-in. As long as a car accidentally stalls as the result of a *mechanical* failure, it seems to be all right. But the thought of cars stalling purposefully because of a *moral* failure creates a sense of public outrage!

I probably got more "mileage" out of the stall-in than anyone else involved. It was part of my act for the rest of the year:

"You know I was in New York City the day of the stall-in. I got there early in the morning and was walkin' through Harlem. Right next to a filling station, a cat comes up to me and says, 'Hey, baby, can you loan me three pennies? I want to buy some gas. I'm drivin' to the World's Fair.' I saw another cat drive into the filling station and tell the attendant, 'Empty me up!' I went out to the World's Fair with CORE and all the rest. I was plannin' on going to jail if I had to, until I found out I had to pay two dollars to get in. I don't mind goin' to jail, but I'll be durned if I'm going to pay for it. I understand attendance was so low opening day that the next morning they hung out a brand new sign which said: WELCOME PICKETS!

"But can you imagine how Robert Moses must have felt? He spends a billion dollars on the World's Fair and all people are looking at is *us!* They put so many people in jail opening day, it created the switch of all time, Moses being asked: 'Let my people go!'"

8

Easin' On Down the Road Uneasily

I had another highway encounter in 1964 which I thought would be my last day on earth. Jim Sanders and I had gone into Princess Anne County in Maryland to help out with the demonstrations. We had come all the way from Utah. We had seen television reports of the demonstrations, chartered a plane to Salt Lake City, flew into Washington, D.C., rented a car, and drove to Princess Anne County.

After the negotiations were over, Jim and I started driving back to Washington late at night. We found ourselves in the worst blizzard in the history of snow. As we got to the edge of town, I pulled into a filling station to get some gas. While the attendant was filling the tank, I went to the rest room.

Another car had pulled into the station by the time I returned. A guy who was standing beside his car seemed to recognize me. "Hey, I know you. I've seen you on television." I reached out to shake his hand, but he kept right on talking. "Yeah, you're Dick Gregory! You nigger bastard!" Before I could remember my commitment to nonviolence, I hit him!

I ran back to the car, threw the gasoline money in the snow, and pulled out as fast as the blizzard would allow. Out of the corner of my eye, I saw another car pull in; there were shotguns sticking out of the windows. In spite of my hasty departure, I distinctly heard the words, "Gonna kill him tonight." I was pretty sure it wasn't a friendly gathering of the local chapter of the National Rifle Association.

The chase was on. We hit the highway, trying to make tracks as fast as the snow and ice would allow. But the blizzard held us to about fifteen miles an hour. The car riding shotgun behind me was held to the same pace, unable to close the gap.

Driving was treacherous. At one point I nearly skidded off a cliff. I backed up as quickly as I could and got back onto the highway. Through the rear view mirror, I noticed the car chasing me skid at the exact same spot. Mile after mile, we continued our slow-motion chase through the blizzard. Then I started to fall asleep at the wheel. I had been up for about three days, and my eyelids weren't as scared as the rest of me. I told Jim to keep talking to me, to rub my neck, to do *anything* to keep me awake. I thought of all the things I had been told to do to keep awake. I remembered humming—and fell asleep in the middle of a tune.

Miraculously, we gained a little space on the car behind. We were now about a half mile in the lead. I looked up and saw a welcome sign. The lights of a roadside restaurant. We pulled in, jumped out of the car and ran toward the restaurant. We got to the door, looked up and saw the sign: NO COLORED AL-LOWED. For the first time, I realized what that sign meant. Here I was trying to save my skin, and it was my skin the restaurant refused to serve!

Jim and I stopped dead in our tracks, turned, and ran back to our car. The car chasing us was pulling into the driveway just as we got to the car door. I was trying to get into the car and open the door at the same time, and the car door knocked me down. I jumped up out of the snow, slid into the driver's seat, and took off.

The combination of excitement and fear kept me awake for a

while. Then I started skidding back and forth on the ice and falling asleep at the wheel again. I just couldn't go any further. I asked Jim if he had a driver's license. He didn't. I said, "Can you drive a car, man?"

"Well, I have driven. But I couldn't make it in this blizzard, Greg."

I decided it really didn't make any difference if Jim died with me driving or if I died with Jim at the wheel. So I said, "Jim, you got to drive, man."

We stopped the car. Jim slid behind the steering wheel, and I got into the back seat. As Jim took off, I just knew it was all over for us. If Jim didn't crash, the car behind was sure to catch us. Either way, we were dead.

So I lay back to go to sleep and die. I thought of Lil and the kids. I wished I had spent more time at home with them. I thought of so many things I wished I had done for the kids. Then I drifted off to sleep with death on my mind.

I woke up at the sound of Jim's voice. "Gimme a quarter." I didn't know if we were in heaven or hell, but it must have been pretty much like life on earth.

"Jim, what do we need money for?"

"To get across the bridge."

"What bridge? Ain't we dead?"

"Man, we're here in Washington."

I couldn't believe it. I jumped out of the car, yelling, laughing, and crying at the same time. I fell down and kissed the ground. I got up and said to Jim, "Move over, man. I'll drive from here."

As I drove to the hotel, I couldn't stop chuckling. Here I thought we were arriving at the Pearly Gates, and it was really the nation's capital. It was the one and only time I ever thought of Washington, D.C., as heaven!

Photo by Bela Cseh, courtesy Johnson Publishing Company, Inc.

Show Biz

Courtesy Johnson Publishing Company, Inc.

Above: With Tallulah (1961).

Right: With Freddie
the Freeloader,
Red Skelton (1961).

Courtesy Johnson Publishing Company, Inc.

With Drew Pearson (Christmas 1964).

David Susskind's panel of comics: left to right, Henny Youngman,
Jan Murray, Susskind, Jonathan Winters, Gregory, Zero Mostel.

Photo by Vernon Smith, courtesy Johnson Publishing Company, Inc.

Courtesy Johnson Publishing Company, Inc.

"An Evening with God": with Rev. Malcolm Boyd and
Dr. Timothy Leary (1967).

World premiere: "Sweet Love Bitter," with Mayor John V. Lindsay
and Brahim Ben Benu (1966).

Photo by Paul Schumach, Metropolitan Photo Service, Inc.

Courtesy Johnson Publishing Company, Inc.

Photo by Philippe Pouliopoulos

Pundit and poet: with
David Brinkley of NBC (1964);
and with Allen Ginsberg (1968).

9

Cooling Crowds and Watermelons

I was really beginning to enjoy performing in nightclubs for the first time. The old days were behind me. I was no longer an oddity, a novelty act, the first "Negro comedian" to make jokes about the racial problem in white nightclubs. I had established myself as a stand-up comedian, and I was returning regularly to top clubs like the Blue Angel and Basin Street in New York City, the Hungry i in San Francisco, and Mr. Kelly's in Chicago.

Now I could really enjoy the excitement of show business. I no longer had to worry about making a good first impression on those critics who had come to review my act. I let them write about how much I was improving each year. I enjoyed that exhilarating feeling of coming onstage and taking command of an audience.

I was also growing as a human being, and my act reflected that growth. I didn't restrict myself to racial material. I was dealing with all kinds of subjects, social and political satire at all levels.

Along with having arrived in show business, I felt special pressures because of my civil rights activities. I had to be careful not to get locked into bookings too far in advance. I was in constant demand for radio, television, newspaper and magazine interviews. Most entertainers get the necessary publicity radio and television appearances out of the way during the first couple of days of an engagement. It was different with me. Some shows wanted me as an entertainer. Other shows were more interested in my social and political views. I did interviews all day, between shows at the club, and after the last show was over. And I did them all. I never turned down a request if I could help it.

Between shows at a nightclub, my dressing room was always filled to capacity. Because of my civil rights involvement, I drew audiences of people who didn't ordinarily go to nightclubs—liberal church leaders, politicians, community activists, journalists, college professors, fellow foot soldiers in the battle for human dignity. Most of them would find their way to my dressing room between shows or after the last show. All kinds of people came to see me; folks with problems, folks wanting me to do a benefit, folks who were searching for truth. My dressing room was a combination seminar, counseling center, and speaker's bureau. I might be heavy into a conversation with Murray Kempton or David Brinkley and have to interrupt to answer a request to speak at a Muslim mosque or church youth group, or appear at a community block party.

It was demanding and exhausting. I never knew what it was to rest up for a performance or to rest between shows. Sleep became a luxury, a luxury I could seldom afford, and it took up only a small part of my daily routine. My bed became the back seat of a taxi cab or my seat on an airplane. I learned to live on a series of brief, scattered naps.

An engagement at the Square East, on the fringes of New York City's Greenwich Village, was typical of my blending of performance with social protest. The show was billed as "Dick Gregory Meets the Second City," and I was having a ball. The first half of the show was the New York Second City troupe doing improvisational material. I had the second half to myself.

What a collection of talent in that Second City troupe! Two of the guys later became one of the best comedy teams in the business—Jack Burns and Avery Schreiber. Night after night I watched Jack and Avery develop routines which are now comedy classics—the cab driver, the faith healer, and Avery as a computer. Dick Schaal was another brilliant performer in the Second City troupe. I have fond memories of Dick and his very talented wife, Valerie Harper, now known and loved by millions of television viewers as Rhoda.

By night, I joked about my offstage activities:

"I just read somewhere that half the world's rope supply comes from Tanganyika. I'd always kind of been digging Tanganyika until I read that. I mean, it's bad enough being lynched for four hundred years, without finding out one day that your cousin's been supplying the rope!

"But I'm just so durned glad to be out of jail for a change.

You've never lived until you've seen one of them southern jails. Barbed-wire fence. On top of the barbed wire, broken glass. Outside the barbed-wire fence, an electric fence. Outside the electric fence, a brick wall. Outside the brick wall, guards roamin' around with double-barrelled shotguns, machine guns and man-eating dogs. And with all that protection, I can still get in 'em!

"I just had a trial down in Atlanta, Georgia, not too long ago. That judiciary department down there is second to none. Khrushchev could have sat in that courtroom during my trial, gone back to Russia, and made communism work. I'll say one thing about the judges down there. They're not formal and stiff. They don't wear those black robes or beat on the desk with a gavel and holler, 'Order in the court.' They just light their cross, and you know court is in session!

"I had a heck of a trial in Birmingham, Alabama. I never will forget it. The judge gave me 180 days in jail for parading without a permit. I tried to explain to the jury, 'I'm not with them. I just dig parades.' Don't get me wrong. I didn't mind that all-white jury. It was those sheets! Then the judge said, 'Young man, you don't know how lucky you are. Do you realize that eleven out of the twelve members of that jury are moderates?' Do you know what a southern moderate is? That's a cat who'll lynch you from a low tree!

"So the judge told me, 'I'm not giving you these 180 days in jail because you're a Negro. I just hate comedians.' So naturally I posted an appeal bond. Not that I would ever mind doing 180 days for the civil rights cause. But it's a cold day in Birmingham when them judges are gonna give me 180 days; they only gave Martin Luther King *five* days, and he started it! Do you realize that King could have broke up that whole mess in Birmingham in three days' time? Remember when they put King in jail on Good Friday morning? When they checked that cell block Easter Sunday, he should have been gone!"

By day, those same issues were no laughing matter. During the Second City engagement, I was shuttling back and forth between New York City and Cambridge, Maryland, trying to prevent a potentially bloody race riot. Cambridge had been the subject of nationwide headlines. It was only a little resort town on the eastern shore of Chesapeake Bay, with 4,000 Blacks and 8,600 whites. But one of those Blacks was a woman named Gloria

Richardson, leader of the Cambridge Nonviolent Action Committee and undoubtedly the strongest woman to emerge in the civil rights movement.

Even though Cambridge was small, it was a potent little pocket of white resistance. The battle lines were drawn between the Black and white communities, and the town was under martial law. Four hundred National Guardsmen patrolled the streets under the command of Brigadier General George Gelston. An earlier confrontation between Gloria's marchers and the National Guard had led to violence. The troops shot tear gas into the crowd. Rocks were thrown. Shots were fired. Four guardsmen were injured, including one with a bullet wound. General Gelston had declared a ten-day "cooling off" period during which all mass meetings were prohibited.

Gloria had called and asked me to appear at a fund-raising benefit in the Elks Hall. When I arrived in Cambridge, I discovered that the benefit had been called off. General Gelston had determined that the benefit would be the same as a mass meeting and would therefore violate the prohibition.

I huddled with Gelston and found him to be one of the most honest and fairest men I had ever met. He was sincerely trying to keep the peace in Cambridge and to prevent violence and bloodshed. He also knew that plans were afoot in Washington for the Department of Labor to set up a job retraining program for some 200 unemployed workers in Cambridge. The general was trying to keep things cool long enough for the federal bureaucracy to get the program under way.

The general spoke frankly. "Look, if you have a rally, the white folks will tear up the town. I've got troops in the white section keeping them inside, although we tell them we're protecting them from Negroes."

I asked the general if he thought the federal government was really serious. "If I find out they're not, I'll resign my commission on the spot."

I knew there had to be a mass meeting, if only to let Black folks know that something was happening in Washington. So I asked Gelston, "Is there anything that says I can't do my act? I mean, gathering for entertainment certainly isn't the same thing as a mass meeting. And if it is, all the movies and entertainment facilities in the white neighborhood should be closed up."

The general agreed with my logic. I flew back to New York City to fulfill the obligations of my other career. Gelston announced: "Should there be a request to gather for the purpose of legitimate entertainment or recreation, permission will be granted." Gloria Richardson complied by requesting that I return in three days to perform at the Elks Hall.

In the interim I met Gloria Richardson in Washington, D.C., and we went to see Burke Marshall, one of Bobby Kennedy's men at the Justice Department. He confirmed that the administration was including Cambridge in the poverty program and that a team of investigators from the Department of Health, Education and Welfare was due to arrive in Cambridge the following week. So I had something more than jokes to tell the folks at the Elks Hall!

The big show in Cambridge was a couple of days away, so I had to find another demonstration to fill my free time during the day. A rent strike was being organized in Hoboken, New Jersey. Jim McGraw and I decided to drive across the Hudson River and check it out. We took along another favorite companion in those days—the plumpest, ripest watermelon I could find!

I often used a watermelon as a sort of personal symbol and a private joke. For years, white folks have enjoyed poking fun at Black folks' fondness for watermelon. I reversed the process and made the watermelon a symbol of pride in Blackness. I used to talk about it in my act. "Did you ever see white folks eating watermelon? They just don't know how to do it. They try to use silverware! Now, you know you can't eat watermelon with a knife and fork! You got to grab it with both hands and get your head down in it!"

There was another line that was a surefire laughgetter:

"I've really got to cut my show short tonight. I have to fly out to Kansas City to help out a friend of mine, a white cat who just moved into an all-Black neighborhood. And some Black bigot burned a watermelon on his front lawn!"

I remember early one morning, after I had finished my last show at the Village Gate, Jim McGraw and I stopped by a favorite little spot in Greenwich Village called the Limelight. I had a taste for watermelon. I didn't see it on the menu, so I asked the waiter. No melon!

Clebert Ford, an actor friend of mine, came in carrying his guitar. He was at the Limelight almost every night, singing folk songs and getting everybody else in the place into his act. I said, "Clebert! Wouldn't you like some watermelon?" Clebert grinned from ear to ear.

Jim and I left and walked up Sixth Avenue to Smilers, an all-night grocery-delicatessen. We bought two of the biggest melons ever grown. Then we marched back to the Limelight, carrying the watermelons on our shoulders, singing "We Shall Overcome." Cars screeched to a halt and passengers looked dumbfounded, but we kept on marching and singing right on through the door. We passed out free watermelon to everybody. Clebert says they were sweeping up watermelon seeds around the Limelight for a month!

Another time I booked two first-class seats on a plane back home to Chicago. The tickets were in the names of D. Gregory and W. Melon. No doubt the ticket agent thought I was traveling with a wealthy friend from Pittsburgh. I boarded the plane with my watermelon under my arm. I carefully fastened the seat belt around the melon in the seat next to me and acted like there was nothing unusual. Every time someone would look as though he were getting up the nerve to ask about it, my expression discouraged the question. I guess folks were thinking, "We knew Dick Gregory had a lot of kids, but this is ridiculous!"

We pulled up in front of the St. Matthew's Baptist Church in Hoboken, where an organizational rally was in process. Jim McGraw carried the watermelon inside, propped it up on a chair in front of the pulpit under an American flag, and dressed the melon in dark glasses and a cap. Then he calmly took a seat.

As the minister was making his introductory remarks, the mayor of Hoboken, John J. Grogan, burst into the room. The mayor asked to speak right away so he could make his next appointment. The mayor was a little man with a big voice. He was also given to using gestures to make his point.

As the mayor was shouting that slum housing would be eradicated in the streets rather than in the courts, he banged his fist on the pulpit, toppling the American flag to the floor. He reached down to pick it up, yelling as he bent over, "I apologize for knocking your flag down." As he straightened up, his eyes fell upon the watermelon for the first time. For the next few minutes, the mayor's voice was distinctly softer. Ol' W. Melon commands respect!

On the day of the big show, Gloria Richardson met me at the airport, and we drove by the armory to see Gelston. The general said he was sure I wouldn't try to turn the show into a rally. I told him I would respect the "entertainment clause" but that I had to find a way to make a progress report about the plans in Washington. Gelston understood, but he also reminded me that mass meetings were banned in the white community, and he wanted to be fair to all sides.

As we drove to the Elks Hall, I was thinking how wonderful it would be if a man like Gelston was in charge of civil rights throughout the country. I was determined to be as fair with him as he had been with us.

I began my Elks Hall performance with an announcement. "I first want to remind you that this is a show, not a mass meeting. I'm here today to perform. During my performance, I'm also going to tell you about a dream I had. But, remember, I'm a comedian. Whatever I say, you all must laugh."

"There's one more thing. Performers get paid for their performance. So we're going to take up a collection, and everybody's got to put something into the pot. The charge for members of the press and members of the National Guard is five dollars!"

After the collection, I started my act. I began with strictly comedy. "We've all got problems. You got problems. I got problems. I'm married. My wife can't cook. How do you burn Kool Aid? And raising kids is so difficult these days. My oldest daughter told me the other day she didn't believe in Santa Claus. I said, 'What do you mean you don't believe in Santa Claus—and I'm pickin' up the tab?' She said, 'Dad, you know darned good and well no white man's gonna come into our neighborhood past midnight!' "

After the audience had settled down to laughing, I began to slip in my information. "Now let me tell you about this dream I had. I dreamed I was talking to Robert Kennedy. It was so real, it hardly seemed like a dream at all. Bobby said Cambridge, Maryland, was in the poverty program and that the Department of Labor was going to start a job retraining program a few days from now." The audience laughed, remembering the earlier instructions.

Then I went back to jokes. "I have a lot of reporters ask me if I think there will ever be a Negro president. I tell them, 'We may never get one that looks like it, but I'll be darned if we haven't got one right now that *sounds* colored!' Did you see where Barry Goldwater said the other day, if he were a Negro he didn't think he could be patient? Of course, if Barry Goldwater was a Negro, nobody'd give a damn what he thought!"

At the end of my act, I talked about my dream. "That dream was so real. Bobby told me that HEW investigators would be here next week to look into the problems of Cambridge." The audience laughed. "And when I heard that, I dreamed we called off the demonstrations for tonight." More laughs. "That we went home from here and didn't harass the National Guard, or go into the white neighborhoods." Still more laughs.

Gloria Richardson joined me onstage, and I said, "Gloria, did you happen to have the same dream?" She smiled and said, "Yes, I did." The show was over, and the dream was fulfilled.

General Gelston was at the airport when I arrived to take a plane to New York. He thanked me and I thanked him. He asked me for my phone number. I noticed he was writing the number on the back of his wrist on his skin. He saw me looking. "I do that when I don't have a piece of paper. I guess that's my one advantage."

I turned my hand over and said, "I can write it on my palm."

10

From Moscow to Murder

Even though I was an established star in show business, I still hadn't traveled outside the United States—except for my excursions into Mississippi. I wanted to travel, and I particularly wanted to check out Moscow, Russia. Folks who didn't like what I was doing in the civil rights movement were always accusing me of being a Communist. I figured the least I could do was go to Russia and find out what I was supposed to be.

While playing the Second City engagement, I was asked to speak at a Ban-The-Bomb meeting at Carnegie Hall. The World Peace Study Mission and several other peace, labor, and church organizations were sponsoring the *hibakusha,* survivors of the atomic bombings of Hiroshima and Nagasaki, in a goodwill tour of the United States.

My personal evolution "up from nigger" was heightened by meeting, hearing, and talking with those survivors of that terrible holocaust. I realized that the human struggle was bigger than just civil rights. Human rights and human survival were the real issues. Equal rights have little relevance to the victims of nuclear warfare who are all equally dead.

I decided to join the *hibakusha* on part of their worldwide goodwill mission. My traveling companion was Arthur Steuer. Art had interviewed me for a series of articles on comedians he wrote for *Esquire* magazine a couple of years before. At Second City, Art and I were reunited. He brought a friend of his by the club, Thomas B. Morgan, who was doing an article about me for *Holiday* magazine. Tom had asked Art to pave the way with an introduction.

Art was an invaluable traveling companion and aide. He had a sharp mind, a quick wit, loads of creativity, and enough nerve to make things happen. Art liked nothing better than taking seemingly impossible schemes and bringing them to fulfillment. We were quite a pair!

One night in Paris, Art's urbane sophistication came up against my ghetto instinct. Art had been going to Paris over the years and he knew all the best places. He insisted that I try a great dish at a particular restaurant, assuring me that I'd never tasted anything like it. Figuring Art to be a connoisseur of fine cuisine, I went along.

Art took care of the ordering. Speaking in French, he ordered something under glass. We waited and waited for the main course, nibbling our way through all the prefatory provisions. Fine restaurants in Paris get involved in the whole ritual of eating. Anybody who is ravenously hungry for the main course had better try to find a McDonald's quick-order stand!

The main course finally arrived. Art was all smiles, insisting again, "You will love it. This is the very finest cuisine."

I looked under the glass. I told Art, "I don't know much about international travel or fine restaurants or fancy food. I can't speak a word of French. But I do know one thing. That's a bat under that glass!"

Art thought I was kidding. He repeated the name of the dish in French, but it was obvious he really didn't know what it was.

I called the maitre d' over and he started to address me in French. I said, "You might as well start speaking in English, because I'm going to find out something right now. Whatever this thing under glass is in French, in English, it's a bat! My friend doesn't seem to know that."

The maitre d' smiled, admitted I was right, and proceeded to explain how it was cooked. I wasn't interested in the recipe nor did I sample the delicacy. It might be special cuisine to white folks, but in the ghetto, it's Bela Lugosi.

After leaving Paris, our travels took us to West and East Berlin and then to Moscow. One of my most vivid memories of Berlin is the toilet paper! It made the old Sears Roebuck catalogue seem like Charmin. It reminded me of the wax-paper wrapping you get at a hot-dog stand. I told Art, "If Winston Churchill had ever used the toilet paper here, he'd never have named it an 'iron' curtain. He'd have called it a sandpaper shade. With a boatload of Kleenex, we could win the cold war easily. Just 'soft' them to death."

In East Berlin I attended the peace meeting and listened to German and Japanese delegates talking earnestly about banning the bomb and preventing another world war. They had firsthand experience with being on the losing side of a war. I thought of a comedy line I would use back home to enlist support for world peace in the Black community: "A lot of my friends say, 'Greg, we weren't aware that you're interested in bannin' the bomb,' and I tell them, 'I wasn't at first, until I checked all the Black neighborhoods and found out we ain't got no fallout shelters. We got to ban the bomb—or learn how to catch it.' "

In the Black community, we've known for a long time what it means to be on the losing side. In a nuclear war everybody would be on the losing side, instantaneously losing their rights to "life, liberty and the pursuit of happiness." From that moment on, I became an advocate of human rights, human dignity, and human survival.

After we arrived in Moscow, I soon discovered that Communist Russia was hung up on the same problem as capitalist America—racism. Everywhere I went in Moscow, I kept hearing about the problems at Lumumba University. All the Black African students in Moscow attended Lumumba University. Moscow University was all white. Lumumba University students had been demonstrating in protest over the death of a fellow student. Many students felt he had been murdered because he was dating a white woman. The official explanation was that he froze to death.

I decided to demonstrate in Red Square in Moscow to raise the question of racism in Russia. It would be a lonely witness—just Art and I standing in the middle of Red Square carrying our picket signs. We reported our plans to United Press International. The Moscow bureau reporters were excited and enthusiastic because it was an on-the-spot exclusive with human interest: comedian Dick Gregory and his white traveling companion in a two-man protest against Russian racism. Good headline possibilities: COMIC CALLS COMMIES RACISTS!

That night we were busily at work making our picket signs. A UPI reporter came by the hotel with news from home. Three civil rights workers—James Chaney, Andrew Goodman, and Mickey Schwerner—had disappeared after having been arrested and released in the middle of the night by Mississippi law enforcement officers.

My plans changed immediately. Racism at home was calling me back. I realized how embarassing it would be to be standing in Red Square protesting Russian racism after what had just happened in Mississippi. It was so ironic. Here I was letting the racist Communists off the hook so I could get back home and be called a "Communist" by racists in America.

The three young men disappeared on Sunday night, June 21. I got word in Moscow the following night. I left Moscow at 8:30 the next morning and got to London at 10:30. I arrived in New York at 1:00 and in Chicago at 3:00. That night, Tuesday, June 23, 1964, I was in Jackson, Mississippi, two days after the disappearance.

I went directly to the office of the Council of Federated Organizations. The kids at COFO were sure the three missing civil rights workers were dead. I agreed. Veteran civil rights workers would never have ventured out onto a Mississippi highway at night unless forced at gunpoint. It was obvious that they had been set up for murder. It was also obvious that Mississippi law enforcement officials were responsible for their disappearance.

Some of the COFO kids and I drove to Meridian where Jim Farmer was waiting, having arrived a short time before. I met with Jim, and he was scared. It was a quality he shared with all of the rest of us, but Jim wasn't trying to hide his fear. We agreed to go to Philadelphia where the three young men had been in jail. We went under the guise of a search party, but we were really trying to get a meeting with Sheriff L. A. Rainey. I was sure Sheriff Rainey was responsible for the disappearance.

We assembled a caravan of about sixteen cars and hit the highway for Philadelphia. The Meridian police followed us out of town, and our trail was picked up by local police in the various counties we passed through. Finally we were met by about 150 state police. They stopped our caravan.

I went up front to see what was wrong. The troopers were telling the COFO kids that an investigation was in progress and that we could not conduct a search of our own. That statement gave me a stick to negotiate with. The state police agreed to let Jim Farmer and me and a couple of COFO representatives go on into Philadelphia to meet the sheriff and his deputies, if we would agree to keep the rest of the caravan in the cars until we got back.

At the sheriff's office we were told that everyone was very busy with the investigation and that we could only have thirty minutes of the sheriff's time. We were escorted into an adjacent room where Sheriff Rainey, Deputy Sheriff Cecil Price, the chief investigator of the state highway patrol, the city attorney, and one other person were waiting.

Sheriff Rainey seemed nervous and upset. I could tell he was scared when he called me "Mr. Gregory" and brought me a soda pop. I asked Sheriff Rainey to tell us his version of what had happened. He said he had arrested the civil rights workers for driving seventy-five miles an hour. I pointed out that anyone doing seventy-five miles an hour in that little town would be in another county by the time the car was caught.

All eyes in the room turned toward the city attorney. He nodded. Deputy Sheriff Price said that he, not Sheriff Rainey, had been the arresting officer. "You're right, they weren't going that fast. They were doing sixty-five miles an hour and it wasn't *in* town. It was *outside* of town."

I smiled, "Look, I know you killed those kids." I turned to Jim Farmer, "Let's go. We've got all we need." The sheriff and his crew were visibly shaken. They couldn't believe we hadn't even used up our thirty minutes.

On the way back to Meridian, I said to Jim Farmer, "I've got the wildest idea."

"What's that?"

"You know the only way we're going to crack this thing is with large sums of money. If you'll put up $100,000, we'll break this case in a week."

It was then I found out CORE was broke. I resolved on the spot to do a thirty-day benefit tour to raise money for CORE. The idea of putting up a reward for information leading to the arrest and conviction of the murderers was too good to let go. I was determined to do it myself, although I knew I'd have to reduce the amount of the reward. But I also knew that in this money-oriented society of ours, money talks and people talk for money. I was sure that even a $25,000 reward might get results.

I wanted to announce the reward before leaving Mississippi, but I didn't have the money. I called Hugh Hefner of Playboy Enterprises and asked him to put up $25,000 against my salary at the Hungry i in San Francisco. Hugh agreed immediately, and I announced the $25,000 reward.

I went to Chicago, got the money from Hugh, put it in the bank, and met with my lawyers to draw up the legal stipulations for collecting the reward. Then I flew to San Francisco for the Hungry i date.

I got a $25,000 cash advance after my first show to give Hugh his money. I asked Jim Sanders, who was with me, to get the next plane to Chicago and deliver the money to Lil. Lil would return it to Hugh. Jim asked, "Do I really have to carry all this cash, Greg?" I said, "It's very important, Jim. I promised Hugh Hefner." Jim went back to Chicago reluctantly carrying the $25,000. He was back in San Francisco the next day, glad to be rid of all that money. He kept saying, "I sure was glad to hand that money to Lil."

Just before the last show, David Allen, stage manager at the Hungry i said to me, "I just saw your man walk into the show room with no clothes on." David was always joking around with Jim and me. I said, "Hey, man, I'm tired. Don't play around like that." David repeated, "No, seriously, Greg, I saw little Jimmy Sanders out there in the club with no clothes on." I still didn't believe him.

I walked into the men's room and there, on the floor, was a pile of clothes. They looked very much like Jim Sanders' attire for the evening. I ran into the show room. Sure enough, there he sat, clad only in his drawers!

I grabbed him and took him into the men's room. "Jim, what you tryin' to do to me? This is my gig, man!" Jim just mumbled, "I got the money there safe, Greg."

It turned out that Jim had fallen asleep on the dressing room couch. He woke up and went to the toilet and thought he was home in Chicago. The pressure of having to deliver the money combined with the relief of anxiety that came with a couple of drinks was more than he could handle. But only two people in the whole club noticed Jim's unintentional streaking act—David Allen and me!

The first response to my reward offer came from the FBI. The FBI put up a $30,000 reward—$5,000 more than my offer. To my knowledge, it was the first time the FBI had engaged in offering rewards.

The second response came from a man in Mississippi. He sent me a letter, and later a tape recording, telling who did the killing and where the bodies were buried. He identified the murderers as three Mississippi law enforcement officers, a preacher, and a used car salesman.

I called Bobby Kennedy and asked him to send some FBI agents to my hotel in San Francisco. I told him about the tape and the letter and offered to give him copies of both. Bobby couldn't understand why I didn't just mail the material to him. I didn't want to tell him I didn't trust the FBI and that I felt it was part of this whole mess. So I told Bobby I had promised to return the materials to my informant. Bobby sent the FBI agents to pick up the copies.

Three weeks passed and nothing happened. No bodies were found, and there were no arrests. So I held a press conference. I announced that I knew where the bodies were buried. I told the press that the FBI knew everything I knew because I had told them. Then I made a threat. If the bodies were not uncovered immediately by the FBI, I would personally escort the press to the burial site and we would do a little "spade" work together!

I flew to Honolulu for an engagement at a club called Forbidden City. By the time I arrived, the FBI had found the bodies—exactly where I had said they were buried. The FBI hinted that they had been led to the burial site by an informer. I've always suspected that the same person who contacted me also got in touch with the FBI in an attempt to hustle both rewards. I don't know what price the FBI had to pay, but my reward was never claimed.

My distrust of the FBI deepened as a result of that experience. It was so clear that politics were being played. What other excuse could be given for the long delay? The bodies were found on the same day President Johnson ordered retaliation for the attacks upon United States destroyers by North Vietnamese torpedo boats. The Gulf of Tonkin resolution followed. The Vietnam war occupied the national headlines, muting the impact of the finding of the bodies. I refuse to believe it was all accident or coincidence.

When it came to protecting my civil rights, I honestly felt the initials FBI had a kindred relationship to those other familiar initials—KKK!

11

Nonconventional Conventioneering

I was glad to be working the Hungry i during the Republican Party National Convention of 1964. There's no place like San Francisco in the summertime, and the Hungry i was *the* spot in town. It was everybody's favorite watering hole—tourists, locals, delegates, politicians, newspaper and television reporters, and civil rights activists.

Presidential politics provided a wealth of material—Goldwater, Rockefeller, LBJ and, of course, Governor George Wallace of Alabama. I'd sit up on stage and have a ball:

"We had to fly over the state of Indiana to get here. I figured, with Governor Wallace makin' such a strong showing in the Indiana primaries, the only way I'd fly over that state is in a U-2 plane! I figured Governor Wallace might get a couple of votes in Indiana, but I didn't think he'd get that many. How does that song go? 'I used to be glad to be out of the land of cotton, but Wallace proved Indiana's just as rotten, look away, look away—'? A lot of people in Indiana and Wisconsin are pretty embarrassed about Wallace's strong showing. It's probably the first time the white tornado ever hit a place and left it dirty. In Wisconsin and Indiana, I thought at one time they had voting machines with curtains on them. Now I see it must be sheets.

"I was in a plane when I read about Wallace getting so many

votes in Indiana. But on the same day, in the same paper, on about page fourteen, there was an article that said three Negroes won elections in Alabama for the first time. So while Wallace was up North raisin' Cain, we're takin' over his state! When Wallace made such a strong showing in Indiana and Wisconsin, it was really a reflection on the North. You see, people in Alabama wouldn't vote for Wallace for anything but governor. Northerners voted for him to be president. People in Alabama know Wallace is uninformed about anything else but bigotry. Wallace was being interviewed not too long ago, and one of them newsmen asked him, 'Governor, if you were elected president, what would you do about Vietnam?' Wallace said, 'Viet who?' Wallace is so uninformed, if he was elected president, he'd probably make Bobby Baker secretary of the treasury.

"I understand the pope was planning on coming over to talk with Wallace to see if he could kind of cool him down a little bit. But some of the pope's top advisers killed the idea. They were afraid that when Wallace first saw that cross around the pope's neck, he might try to light it!

"I really think President Johnson made a serious mistake when he said he was going to share secret intelligence with any other candidates who are serious contenders. I understand Khrushchev tried to enter the Maryland primaries.

"I feel kinda sorry for Nelson Rockefeller. When you stop and think about it, Rockefeller was the front runner, until he got a divorce. And a lot of top Republicans put him down for it. I don't go along with that. I feel if a man's gonna run for the number one office in the land, and if he's havin' problems at home, straighten them out first. It coulda been a heck of a thing. Rocky could have kept that quiet, moved into the White House, got a divorce, and she might have got custody of this country."

There was a lot of press coverage and publicity surrounding my appearance at the Hungry i. My reward offer, coupled with the drama and excitement of the Republican convention, made the Hungry i the place to be. I began getting calls from various Black activists around the country, telling me they were coming to San Francisco. One of the calls was from Stanley Branch in Chester, Pennsylvania.

As soon as he hit town, Stanley came by to consult with me about demonstration strategies. I was staying in a room at the Hyde Park Suites overlooking Fisherman's Wharf with a beautiful view of the bay. Stanley was just as "country" as he was committed. He looked out the window and said, "There's a nice view of the river out there." I said, "Stanley, that river stretches all the way to Tokyo."

Stanley was having a problem. His luggage had been lost by the airline and he wanted it back. He kept calling the airline office every half hour asking about his luggage. Finally, the woman who had been receiving Stanley's calls realized she needed to take a maternal approach. She told him, "Mr. Branch, I want you to go to the drugstore, buy yourself some toothpaste and a toothbrush, a razor, and some shaving cream and lotion. Be sure to keep the receipts for your purchases. Then you go to bed. When you get up in the morning, brush your teeth and shave, come to the airline office, and your luggage will be here waiting for you. And we will reimburse you for your purchases." Stanley got the message.

Later in the evening, I went by Stanley's room to pick him up to go to the club. Stanley was already in bed. I said, "Stanley, what you doing in bed so early? San Francisco's just startin' to jump." Stanley replied, "The lady at the airline told me to go to bed so I could get my luggage tomorrow."

After retrieving his luggage, Stanley got involved with the others who were making picket signs and planning demonstrations against the Goldwater-right-wing takeover of the Republican party. I had mixed emotions and stayed out of it. I have never trusted Nelson Rockefeller. It always bothered me to see so many Black folks being gratefully sentimental toward Rockefeller because of his financial contributions to Black colleges, Black churches, and Black causes. As governor of New York State, Rockefeller would later justify my instinctive distrust by giving the orders that led to the massacre at Attica State Prison.

I also felt that Goldwater represented a clear choice if the Republican party wanted to go in that direction. He was out in the open for everyone to see. Nobody had any doubts about what he believed and what he stood for. But Goldwater did not represent the hidden money power held by Nelson Rockefeller. Goldwater had to persuade the country. Rockefeller already owned it.

In keeping with my "Elect a Rat for President" campaign button, I compared the election of Goldwater to plugging up a rathole. I felt that a Goldwater victory could only help Black folks because it would automatically bring 22 million Blacks together.

With Goldwater in the Oval Office, the back door through which Blacks have been slipping in and out making deals would be closed. Once that door is closed so that no Black could make a deal for another Black, it would be like plugging up a rathole. With that in mind, I really couldn't get too upset about the so-called Goldwater threat.

The real convention excitement for me was at the Hungry i each night. It was unbelievable how many people came by. Between shows and after the last show, I had an opportunity to sit and rap with news analysts like David Brinkley. I've always been addicted to reading newspapers and watching news broadcasts, and it was like a dream come true.

During the day my convention participation was limited to watching the proceedings on television. I'll never forget watching John Chancellor of NBC getting arrested and removed from the convention floor, earphones, sound equipment, and all. As Chancellor was dragged from the floor for simply doing what he had to do, I'm sure he gained a better understanding of the plight of civil rights demonstrators.

From the perspective of a Black television viewer, it looked like a convention which was called against us. I thought to myself, "It would take 22 million heart transplants for us to ever know in our hearts that Goldwater is right."

I'll always remember another scene from the convention floor. I turned on the television set one morning, and it was obvious that somebody's name had just been placed in nomination. The band was playing, folks were yelling, clapping, and chanting slogans, and marching around the convention floor. I looked a little closer and to my surprise I saw Stanley Branch in the middle of the march carrying a sign which read "Scranton for President." I couldn't believe my eyes.

After I went to the Cow Palace myself, I soon realized how Stanley could catch convention fever. A political convention is pure show business. It's a combination of a Broadway production, a Fourth of July parade, a country fair, and a circus. On the surface it really looks like the democratic process at work. You don't see the wheeling and dealing going on in the back rooms. The same charade of democracy carries over into every day of real life between conventions. We never see the real decision-making process nor do we know the real decision makers. I made up my mind then and there to try to make the scene at every presidential nominating convention.

It took a bit of doing to be at the Democratic Party National Convention in Atlantic City the following month. I asked my agent, Ralph Mann, to try to book me into a club during convention week. He booked me at a place called Basin Street. I paid a heavy price for my desire to be in Atlantic City. I did three or four shows a night. The first show didn't start until 11:30 P.M., so I never left the club before five or six o'clock in the morning.

I have an especially fond memory of opening night at Basin Street. I was running late for the first show. Jim Sanders and Jim McGraw were with me, and as I was racing toward the dressing room, I heard McGraw calling me back. Jim said, "I think you might want to stop by that table way over in the corner before you go on." It was very dark, and I couldn't see who was at the table. I walked a little closer and there sat Dr. Martin Luther King, Jr.

It was obvious that Dr. King wanted to remain inconspicuous. So I didn't introduce him from the stage, but I included him in my act: "Those riots in Harlem were somethin' else. The Negroes were standing on one side with coke bottles, and the cops were on the other side with bazookas, and Martin Luther King was in the middle saying, 'Cool it, baby. We're winnin'.' We found out later he was talking to the cops."

My motel became the headquarters for nondelegate activity. A cadre of Black activists operated from that base—Lawrence Landry from Chicago, Jesse Gray from New York City, Julius Hobson from Washington, D.C., and Stanley Branch. We planned strategy together on how to make our voices heard outside the convention hall. Aaron Henry, Fannie Lou Hamer, and others were making their voices heard inside. The Mississippi Freedom Democratic party had issued a challenge to convention leadership by requesting that its delegates be seated in place of the regular Mississippi Democratic delegation. The issue was to be resolved in the credentials committee.

Also, supporters of the MFDP were conducting an around-the-clock, day and night vigil on the boardwalk. Almost every morning, after finishing my last show at Basin Street, I stopped by on the boardwalk to address the demonstrators and encourage their effort. I seldom got to bed before nine o'clock in the morning.

Although they supported the MFDP effort, my activist cadre was more interested in focusing attention upon *all* the problems and injustices confronting Black folks in America. Remembering

the New York World's Fair stall-in, a strategy was suggested to tie
up all the traffic leading in and out of the convention hall. One
night, we held a meeting in the motel room to discuss details.

After fantasizing about the chaos which might be created, I
went around the room and asked each person how many
demonstrators they could get into Atlantic City to participate in
our protest. Everyone gave an estimate, until I got to Stanley
Branch.

"How many folks can you get, Stanley?"

"I can bring a whole town!" Stanley replied. I had visions of
the whole town of Chester, Pennsylvania, buildings and all,
moving down the turnpike toward Atlantic City.

I also happened to mention in passing that it would be wild if
we could bring in some donkeys to get stubborn in the streets and
help us tie up traffic. I thought it would be an appropriate use of
the Democratic Party symbol. The next morning I was awakened
by a funny noise outside my motel room door. I peeked out. There
stood one of Stanley Branch's people—leading a donkey! I wonder
what would have happened if that cat had been at the Republican
convention? He'd probably have had Dumbo the elephant flying
over the Cow Palace.

Any doubts I might have had about the reality of wire-tapping
and government surveillance were dispelled that week in Atlantic
City. We didn't need to issue press releases about our demonstration plans. Both the FBI and the press were as fully informed as
we were. We would hold a meeting and agree to meet at a certain
place at a certain time. When we arrived for the appointed
gathering, the police and the Secret Service were already there
waiting.

The wire-tapping and information-gathering about our demonstration plans placed an added burden on us. Since our wildest
ideas would be reported in the newspapers and on television, we
felt obligated to make good on our threats so as not to disappoint
the press! We felt an obligation to make our extemporaneous
prophecies self-fulfilling.

The threat to close down the convention was a good example.
The action was supposed to take place in the evening, as delegates
were returning from dinner for the evening session. During the
afternoon I had gone to bed for a long nap. When I woke up Jim
McGraw was sitting in my room watching television. I asked
sleepily, "What's happening out there? Is everything all set to

go?" McGraw laughed. "I really don't think so, Greg. I just looked in on Landry and Stanley and they're sound asleep."

Just then Walter Cronkite came on the screen with the evening news. We heard Walter talking about the imminent threat to close down the convention by tying up traffic and blocking entrances. We had only a few minutes to set the record straight and get ourselves and Walter off the hook.

A compromise had been reached in the seating of the Mississippi Freedom Democratic Party delegation. It gave only token recognition to the MFDP, but it produced an important rules change which specified that future convention credentials would be given only to those state parties whose membership was open to both Black and white. There was disagreement among Black leaders about whether or not to go along with the compromise. Some national Black leaders were also upset about our demonstration plans. They felt that any violence that might erupt spontaneously or by provocation by some undercover agents would only help Barry Goldwater.

I told Art Steuer to call CBS and get a message to Walter Cronkite. "Tell him we're cancelling the demonstration because we don't want to see any violence, and we don't want to create dissension among Black leaders." Art went to his room to make the call. In a few minutes I saw a note being passed to Walter Cronkite on national television. The next words I heard him speaking were an echo of my own.

Walter must have been smiling inside as he read the report, because I was sure he knew what had really happened. A couple of nights before I had been talking with Walter at a popular little spot where news people gathered. The conversation was a real education for me. I was amazed at what news reporters really know compared to what they report. They know everything! They get feedback and information from an underground system of sources and stringers which makes the CIA look like child's play. But when the camera starts to roll, they play it straight down the middle. As I talked with Walter Cronkite, I was overwhelmed by the extent of his knowledge on every issue, foreign and domestic. I realized that when Walter closes his show with, "That's the way it was," he really means, "That's all I'm going to tell you tonight."

I left Atlantic City with a strong premonition of things to come. The Mississippi Freedom Democratic Party challenge was the first nationally visible sign of that growing Black political strength in the South. The attempt of regular party politicians to silence and compromise that strength was a mistake. I knew they would be faced with greater challenges in 1968.

Lyndon Johnson won the election by a 15-million-vote landslide. On stage, I played it straight like Walter Cronkite. I didn't tell all I knew either.

"Hey, don't pay off your election bets. Barry just asked for a recount! Poor Barry! I think he was running on an unlisted ballot. The Democrats are singing to Lyndon Johnson: "Happy Days Are Here Again." And the Republicans are singing to Barry Goldwater: "We'll Get Along Without You Very Well." Some of them are singing: "We're Just Mild About Barry." I won't say where those 15 million Johnson votes came from, but they're celebrating with chitlin' dinners right now. And Johnson knows how much he owes us for our votes. I called the White House this morning, and LBJ answered, 'Yeah, baby?' Of course, everybody's wondering what Barry Goldwater will do now. All I can say is Barry made his concession speech on Wednesday morning—and Wednesday afternoon they fired that rocket to Mars!"

I'll say another thing for Barry Goldwater. He gave us a good slogan for the ongoing struggle for human rights and human dignity. In his acceptance speech, Goldwater said, "I would remind you that extremism in the defense of liberty is no vice. And let me remind you also that moderation in the pursuit of justice is no virtue."

12

Arlington Revisited

I saw those Arlington leaves rustling again in the wind, this time in New York City at the Jan Hus theater. Attorney Mark Lane was conducting a nightly lecture on the unanswered questions surrounding John F. Kennedy's assassination. Mark had been on the scene in Dallas shortly after the assassination and the subsequent killing of Lee Harvey Oswald by Jack Ruby. Oswald's mother, Mrs. Marguerite Oswald, asked Mark to represent her son before the Warren Commission.

Although the Warren Commission was supposedly conducting a thorough investigation of the assassination, it did not accept the legal services of Mark Lane. Instead, the commission designated the president of the American Bar Association as the protector of Oswald's interests. But Mark is not the kind of person who can be silenced so easily. He took his case to the people in the form of a best-selling book, *Rush to Judgment*, and his New York City lectures.

Mark's one-man show was fantastic. It consisted of cold, hard, legal facts, presented with Mark's real flair for show business. He exposed the shortcomings and coverups of the Warren Commission report, using both research and humor. Mark's "magic bullet" monologue, tracing the path of the bullet that was supposed to have gone through the president and into Governor John Connally, stands as one of the classic comedy routines of all time.

Mark Lane was not the only person raising serious questions about the assassination, but what he was doing in New York City was very important. Journalists, newspaper reporters, and other influential people came to his off-Broadway show and were thereby exposed to the lingering doubts and unanswered questions. Mark's influence was attested to by the number of government agents attending each performance. You could always tell who the agents were during the question and answer period. Only government agents could have come up with such technical questions.

While Mark was doing the original assassination show off Broadway, I carried the road show in my briefcase. It consisted basically of a copy of *Life* magazine, which showed still shots of the assassination taken from Abraham Zapruder's home movie of the motorcade, along with some other useful and revealing photos. I presented my assassination road show in nightclub and concert hall dressing rooms, press conferences, and personal conversations all across the country.

One night in my dressing room at the Village Gate in New York City, I showed my road show material to Walter Cronkite. I pointed out that the Zapruder film shows that Governor Connally was not hit until seconds after the president was struck. They couldn't have been hit by the same bullet (unless, as Mark Lane's magic bullet routine says, the bullet hung in midair for a few seconds before deciding to change direction and go after the governor)! I pointed out the picture of a man standing in the Dallas Book Depository entrance at the time the shots were fired. The man looks like Lee Harvey Oswald and is dressed exactly the way Oswald was dressed when he was arrested. The Warren Commission identified the man in the doorway as an Oswald look-alike named Billy Lovelady. But Lovelady swore those were not the clothes he was wearing that day. I also pointed out a curiosity in the picture of Lee Harvey Oswald standing in his backyard holding the gun he supposedly used to kill the president. By looking closely at the shadows on the ground and the shadows on the face and chin, serious suspicions are raised that the head of Lee Harvey Oswald was superimposed upon the picture of another person.

Walter listened to my assassination rap with interest and patience. My stuff never made it on the CBS evening news. But I also remembered Atlantic City. It wasn't out of character for Walter to know a whole lot more than he reports on the evening news!

13

Merry Christmas from the Colonel!

A couple of days before Thanksgiving, I'm getting ready to board a plane in Jackson, Mississippi, when one of the SNCC kids asks pleadingly, "When we gonna see you again, Greg?" I automatically answer, "I'll be back for Christmas."

I had in mind spending Christmas in Mississippi with my wife and kids. On the plane to New York, I got to thinking, "Maybe we could bring Christmas dinner down with us and eat it with some needy family." My thoughts kept rolling. "Why just one dinner and one family? Why not bring a turkey dinner to as many needy Mississippi families as possible?" By the time my plane landed, I had made a private promise to take 20,000 turkeys to Mississippi on Christmas Day.

I've always had a thing about food and hunger. If I have a hobby other than track, I suppose it's feeding hungry folks. My earliest involvement in the civil rights movement in the South reflected that concern. In retaliation against Black voter registration in Leflore County, Mississippi, white officials had stopped passing out free federal surplus food to poor folks, claiming they could no longer afford the $37,000 a year for storage and distribution. I hit the streets of Chicago and collected donations totaling 14,000 pounds of food and personally delivered it to Greenwood, the county seat.

I also felt that Mississippi was the key to the civil rights struggle, especially in the North. Mississippi was a symbol in the Black community. Northern Blacks made Blacks from Mississippi the butt of all kinds of jokes and put-downs. Mississippi had a stranglehold on the minds of all Blacks, just as it was strangling resident Blacks with poverty and oppression. Whenever there was a lynching, for example, everybody thought immediately of Mississippi, even though there were lynchings in other states. Focusing attention upon Mississippi, feeding hungry Mississippians at Christmas, would go a long way toward removing the lingering fears and racial stigma in the Black community.

I was faced with the problem of going public with my private promise. I had to find a way to get those turkeys to Mississippi. The highly touted return match between Sonny Liston and Muhammed Ali (then still called "Cassius Clay" by most fans and sportswriters) was coming up in Boston. I figured if I could get each of the two fighters to buy 10,000 turkeys, I'd be home free. I phoned Sonny Liston, and he was both surprised and confused by my call. I explained such things as tax deduction and publicity value, and I came off the phone with a tentative okay. I then called Ali and laid the idea on him, telling him Sonny was in agreement. Ali thought the idea sounded great.

My next call was to columnist Drew Pearson. Now that I had the financing, I thought, I needed an organization to give the project stability and respectability. Drew had recently gone through a conversion experience. Earlier in the year, after he had written a column criticizing me, Adam Clayton Powell, and the whole crowd from ACT—an open letter inviting me to stay out of Mississippi—Drew made the mistake of going to Mississippi himself. All of a sudden, new thoughts, new attitudes, and new opinions started appearing in his column. One beautiful column related his experience of sharing sweet potato pie with a Mississippi sharecropper family. I figured the time was ripe to get Drew involved—while he could still taste that pie.

I got him on an airport phone in Kansas City. Drew's first words were, "Dick, I must tell you that you were right and I was so wrong!" What an opener! I hit him with the idea of 20,000 turkeys for Mississippi. When I hung up the phone, Drew Pearson was co-chairman of a committee called "Christmas for Mississippi." Immediately the project became tax-exempt—taken under the wing of America's Conscience Fund, an established organization under the leadership of Drew Pearson and Harry Truman.

In his next column, Drew began plugging the idea. He had received a letter from a wealthy oil man named Emmett Thornhill of McComb, Mississippi. Drew had identified him as a Ku Klux Klan member, and Thornhill was writing to set the record straight. He said he had broken with the Klan after they dropped the first three bombs in churches. Thornhill insisted that he had always enjoyed good business relationships with "coloreds" and complained, "This publicity you've given me has hurt me with 'em."

Drew offered a suggestion in his column, "Probably there is no man in America, even Adam Clayton Powell, who is more hated by the Ku Klux Klan than Dick Gregory. He has given up performance fees of more than $6,000 a week to raise money for the Freedom Movement in Mississippi and elsewhere.

"Likewise, there is no organization more hated by Dick Gregory than the Ku Klux Klan.

"However, if a man who has now renounced the Klan, like Emmett Thornhill, would join in Dick Gregory's drive to give turkeys to the less privileged people of Mississippi—both white and black—it would prove beyond any possible doubt that he means what he says about a fair break for Negroes.

"Furthermore, and even more important, it would prove that Americans can rise above personal prejudice."

Art Steuer and I flew to Boston to tighten up details with

Sonny and Ali. I found management on both sides locked in what looked like an unbreakable clinch. I returned to New York discouraged, knowing that something was going to happen to call off the fight. The next day's sports page told the story. The World's Heavyweight Champion had discovered a hernia "the size of a small lemon," which the examiners just happened to miss a couple of days earlier. The fight had to be postponed.

Sonny Liston summed up the tragedy in these words: "It could have been worse—it could have been me." I thought to myself, "How do you identify with another cat's hernia?" I figured he was saying that this time, at least, he didn't have to twist a knee or dislocate a shoulder. Whatever the truth was about the fight cancellation, my 20,000 turkeys flew the coop—along with countless bookies.

Once again I decided the idea was too big to let go. I had an organization and a co-chairman. So I decided to do it myself—with a little help from my friends! I figured we could raise the money in Chicago through street donations and a big benefit show. With the latter idea in mind, I paid a visit to the New York City townhouse residence of Sammy Davis, Jr.

Sammy was starring on Broadway in *Golden Boy*. I was ushered into the living room and told that Sammy would be right down. Pretty soon he descended the center spiral staircase. Sammy seemed a bit nervous, and I could understand his reaction. He didn't know if this was a social call or if I was going to ask him to integrate a lunch counter in Alabama.

Sammy showed his nervousness when he said, "Dick, we all know that you are on the front line more than any of us in show business. We feel it, but we don't know what we can do. A group of us in New York got together the other night to try to think of ways we could be in the struggle more."

It was a perfect opening, but I played it cool. "Well, Sammy, I'm in a better position to be at the front line than you. I'm not an artist in the same sense you are. Don't have to perfect an act. Just look at my lines five minutes before my show, and if the line doesn't stick in my mind, it wasn't any good anyway."

Time was beginning to compete with apprehension for Sammy's attention. He was already forty-five minutes overdue at the "Tonight Show," where he was guest host for the evening. It was now or never, so I laid my turkeys-for-Mississippi idea on him. Before I could say "We Shall Overcome," Sammy agreed to appear at the Arie Crown Theatre, McCormick Place, Chicago, on Sunday evening, December 20. I had locked up America's greatest one-man show. Those turkeys came flying back to the roost!

Art Steuer and I flew to Chicago to start the ball rolling. I met with Lawrence Landry, Nahaz Rogers and other local grass-roots community leaders and they gave the idea their full support. It was all I needed to release "Christmas for Mississippi" to the press. Chicago's leading radio, television, and newspaper personalities picked up the turkey banner, particularly Irv Kupcinet, Marty Faye, Studs Terkel, Wesley South, Tony Weitzel, and Maggie Daley. That was in addition to almost daily coverage by the *Chicago Defender,* the city's leading Black newspaper.

We were given office space by Leo Rugendorf, a supermarket owner in Chicago's South Side Black community. Right away, I began to get criticism. People were saying that Leo was involved with the Mafia and I shouldn't allow myself to be tainted by his associations. But I had other personal reactions and needs which overruled any objections. Leo's store was located in the heart of the Black community, the legitimate side of his operation was making money from Black people, and I desperately needed office space. I was sure I could use the facilities without getting mixed up in organized crime.

My personal priorities were tested one Sunday afternoon when Leo invited me to attend a recital on Michigan Avenue. I dressed up for the occasion, and the recital was in progress when I arrived. There were only a few people in the dark recital hall and a magnificent tenor was singing a cappella onstage. It was really weird! I found out later that he was one of Italy's most famous singers and the "family" brought him over each year for a private recital.

After the recital we went upstairs for a little party. I was taken to meet somebody special. It was Anthony J. Accado. I knew the name, of course, from his Mafia reputation. In his book *Boss*, Mike Royko called him "the godfather" of the Chicago Mafia. Tony was reminded of my Christmas for Mississippi project. He said, "Oh, yeah. I heard about that. I like it. Good program. Help your people. Help your people."

Knowing who Tony Accado was and what he stood for, I really didn't want to talk to him about anything. So I walked away. A priest came over to me, and he was obviously drunk. Filled with the spirits, the father said, thickly, "Dick Gregory, I want to tell you something. You're a very likeable guy, but you're moving too fast."

I was outraged. I said, "Wait a minute. You're a priest. And you're in the same room with Tony Accado and Dick Gregory. Whatever you think about my activities, don't say nothing to me until you go over there and tell Tony Accado and his Mafia henchmen about their ways."

The priest sputtered, "That's what I mean. That's the attitude that's going to get you killed."

A "family" spokesman came over and told me, "You're really doing a good job. We like what you're doing. You don't have to worry about getting those turkeys. We'll take care of that for you."

I played ignorant. "Well, how? Christmas is only a few weeks away."

"We have our ways."

"Well, I suppose you're talkin' about hijackin' the turkeys like ya'll do whiskey. I'm taking those turkeys down to poor, honest folks in Mississippi. It would leave a bad taste in *my* mouth to feed them with stolen turkeys." I left the party.

I called in Jim McGraw to work with Jim Sanders in overseeing the collection of street donations. McGraw had a unique quality. He could walk into a new situation and throw a neutrality through his entire body. Whenever it was a situation dealing with the underdog, he could sit down and listen and observe and empathize, and when you talked to him fifteen minutes later, you'd swear McGraw had been part of that situation all his life.

McGraw was one of the special people I pulled upon for advice and personal support, along with Jim Sanders, Art Steuer, and Bob Johnson of *Jet* magazine. It gave me a blend of perspectives which made up for any educational deficiencies in my segregated school education. McGraw was white Irish, Art was New York Jewish, Jim Sanders was midwest rural Black, and Bob Johnson, the other Black member of the team, was a polished journalist with the amazing capacity to penetrate to the nitty gritty core of any situation or event. They were quite a backup team.

Jim Sanders and Jim McGraw were out on the street corners of Chicago every morning at six o'clock, in zero and sub-zero weather. They had a big barrel with chicken wire across the top, and McGraw was dressed as Santa Claus. It was so funny to see McGraw on those ghetto street corners playing Santa.

And it was so beautiful to see Black folks in Chicago reaching into their pockets and purses to help their brothers and sisters in Mississippi. I saw a girl in her late teens excitedly drop a dollar into the barrel and giggle, "I've never helped Mississippi before." I also saw a wino reach into his pocket and give four pennies. I thought of the New Testament story of the widow and her mite—giving all that she had. You have to understand what four cents means to a wino to appreciate the beauty of self-sacrifice. That puts him four cents further away from that half pint. Who knows how long it will take him to hustle up the needed change for that bottle? And it's cold outside. But he's helping his brother in Mississippi. Sheer beauty!

In the midst of our fund-raising activities, word came from Meridian, Mississippi. Twenty men indicted in the killing of the three civil rights workers had been released by a U.S. commissioner. Now we *had* to get those turkeys to Mississippi! I knew the government trick involved in dismissing those indictments. The tape I had sent to Bobby Kennedy identified *nineteen* killers. Indictments were handed down for *twenty*. The first man brought before the grand jury really wasn't involved. He had a very legitimate alibi. He was in jail in New Orleans at the time of the crime. As a result, Commissioner Carter dismissed all the remaining indictments. The guilty went free along with the innocent. Our turkey mission became a memorial.

The day of the big show at McCormick Place arrived almost before we realized it. Charles Evers and Drew Pearson flew into town. Charles, brother of slain civil rights leader Medgar Evers and then the state field secretary for the NAACP in Mississippi, had been in charge of setting up distribution of the turkeys when they got to their final destination. Drew had been busy collecting donations from his many contacts in high places. We all got together at the turkey office.

Drew truly looked like the ambassador of goodwill that he was. He looked so distinguished with his moustache, his black coat, and his black Russian-style hat. Drew sat down and started pulling checks worth thousands of dollars out of his pocket as casually as if they were telephone messages. He further pledged to make up whatever money we could not raise through benefits and street donations. My Christmas dream was now a full-fledged reality.

Back in New York City, United Airlines had a limousine at the stage door of the Majestic Theatre waiting to pick up Sammy, who rushed out the door after his Saturday night performance and raced to Kennedy Airport, where the last flight from New York to Chicago was being delayed until his arrival. It was red carpet all the way. Special matchbooks had been made with the inscription "Welcome, Golden Boy."

Other performers rallied to the cause. Eartha Kitt was playing the Palmer House and agreed to perform. George Kirby, a neighbor of mine, was in town and let it be known he would be proud to be on the bill. Red Saunders' band provided the music. And at the afternoon rehearsal, the Four Step Brothers showed up to volunteer their talent.

The show was slated to start at 8 P.M. At 7:30 Lil, McGraw, and I stood in the lobby waiting. We were all nervous. We needed ticket sales at the door to be successful. Then the good people of Chicago started pouring in. Our nervous jitters disappeared. I couldn't wait to get on stage.

The Four Step Brothers opened the show. Drew Pearson brought me on, and it was my crowd all the way. "Hey, we got a great show for you tonight. You just saw the Step Brothers, and in addition to Sammy, Eartha, and George Kirby, we got George Wallace singing 'I'm Dreaming of a White Christmas.' We're sending 20,000 turkeys to Mississippi, which means there will be 20,000 wishbones down South. So if Governor Wallace is still around on December 26, you'll know those things don't work. People say it's foolish to send all those turkeys to Mississippi, when the people don't have anything to cook them on. When the Ku Klux Klan hears what we're up to, they'll burn enough crosses to roast an elephant! Anyway, if they can't cook 'em, they can always break off a frozen wing and have a turksicle."

Eartha was next and knocked the crowd out with her sultry songs. I quipped, "Eartha sounds like good chitlin's supposed to taste!" Then I introduced George Kirby, and he closed the first half of the show.

Then the stage was cleared, and the most versatile entertainer in the history of show business held the audience spellbound for the next two hours and fifteen minutes. He sang and he quipped. ("You know my biggest problem these days? Finding kosher pigs' feet." And "My mother was Puerto Rican, my father was colored, I converted to the Jewish faith, and married a white woman. There aren't too many neighborhoods I can move into.") He did impersonations and he played every instrument in the band. When it was all over, the audience seemed more exhausted than Sammy.

Wednesday, December 23, 1964, was T-Day. Two refrigerated trucks were already rolling toward Mississippi from Iowa and one from Chicago. We went out to Butler Field in the wee small hours of the morning. A heavy fog choked the atmosphere, and some people were worrying that we might be grounded. I wasn't worried. We had God on our side. When we arrived, a truck was being unloaded and its contents lifted by conveyor belt into a chartered cargo plane. Five hundred turkeys were being loaded along with hundreds of toys donated by Chicago manufacturers.

I rode down to Jackson, Mississippi, on the cargo plane. Lillian and my two oldest girls, Lynne and Michele, came down on Delta Airlines accompanied by Jim McGraw. As I bade good-bye to the excited little shivering huddle of well-wishers, I was tempted to say, "I shall return."

Our planes landed simultaneously at the Jackson Air Terminal. An integrated reception committee of about 300 people had been waiting two hours for our delayed arrival—benevolent Baptist preachers, COFO workers, bodyguards, and Charles Evers. I was dressed for the occasion. A lot of white folks in Mississippi used to refer to me as "that millionaire nigger," and I didn't want to spoil their image. I was munching a big black cigar, and I was described by Associated Press as looking "splendid in buckskin boots, a three-quarter length black leather jacket and a cowboy hat."

After an onslaught by the gentlepeople of the press, I waded through to the reception committee. Charles Evers was all smiles as he said, "Welcome to the Magnolia State, land of the brave niggers and the nervous white folks."

At the Pratt Memorial Methodist Church, about a thousand people were jammed into the sanctuary—standing room only, with more and more people arriving all the time. The officiating preachers crowded around the pulpit and began competing with one another for the privilege of reading off the names of those who would receive turkeys.

We had a real problem. We only had 500 turkeys, with another 3,000 coming in on the truck from Chicago. Heavy fog had delayed the arrival, and the driver had phoned to tell us he couldn't make it until the next morning. The distribution committee announced that everyone with four kids or less would have to come back on the following day. Only four people got up and left! So the committee decided to switch it around by asking people with fifteen or more kids to come forward and get a turkey. That approach didn't work either. It set off a stampede!

It may sound strange, but at least 90 percent of those people had never had a turkey before in their lives. Fannie Lou Hamer had told us, "I'm forty-seven years old, and I've only had a turkey once in my life, and I had to buy that on the installment plan." Now we saw firsthand the truth behind Fannie Lou's words. We saw it in the faces of those who received the first 500 turkeys. We saw it in the tears of pure joy and gratitude streaming down worn and weary cheeks. We saw it in the hope, almost pride, which accepted a turkey not as a handout, but as a gift. We heard it in the hundreds of "God bless you's" and in the testimony of a woman who sobbed, "I got fifteen kids and I make fifteen dollars a week. I don't have to say no more—thanks." Another woman took a turkey from me and testified, "Mawnin', Lawd." In the most pious voice I could muster up, I answered, "Yes?"

It was such a beautiful sight. These beautiful people had only one thing to give on Christmas—honest and sincere gratitude. And now they were completing the joy of the act of giving, begun by their brothers and sisters in Chicago, by their act of pure and heartfelt gratitude.

That night I spoke at a rally at the Masonic Hall on Lynch Street in Jackson. The White Citizens Council of Rueville, Mississippi, had announced that they were sending two 'possums and a sack of sweet potatoes to me in Chicago. I opened my remarks by acknowledging their gift. "Sending me food—that's like sending a relief check to Rockefeller. They don't know my background! I'd jump over a whole carload of sirloin to get to a good 'possum. Why, I could sell those 'possums on the black market in Chicago and get enough money to send down 200 more turkeys."

I also had some more serious words for that wonderful crowd. "*We* didn't raise this money and send these turkeys. *You* did. It's *your* fault. You have completely purged this state of negative thinking. It's easy to raise money for Mississippi, because of you. Everybody who eats anything this Christmas will think of you.

"We brought turkeys for the champs. You earned that. What

you're doing in this state has put a lot of people off our backs. For a long time, Mississippi was the garbage can of race relations. Anything that happened up North was dumped in the Mississippi garbage can—'Look how much worse it is in Mississippi.' Now you folks have put a lid on that can, and there is no place to dump that northern garbage but in their own backyards. And the smell is beginning to spread.

"When you integrated that golf course down here, the Black cat in New York began to wonder, 'Where's mine?' Same thing with schools and libraries. The opening day of school, you integrated school after school without any kind of incident in Jackson, Mississippi. But in Jackson Heights, Queens, sixty-five white mothers were arrested for opposing the school integration plan in New York City.

"Some people up North said that Sammy Davis would do a benefit in Chicago, but he was scared to come to Mississippi. Well, he probably is! If the president of the United States hasn't been to Mississippi in fifty years, why should Sammy come? Well, if the president won't come to Mississippi, take it to him! Take your kids to the White House on Easter when they have the big egg roll on the lawn. Just dump your little ol' kids on the lawn and say, 'We want to play too.'

"White folks praise Bob Hope for going to Vietnam and criticize me for coming to Mississippi. Well, it's safer in Vietnam. At least there you know the government is on your side. Other white folks and Black folks say, 'It's wonderful the way you have sacrificed to help your people.' I'm more selfish than that. I'm trying to free *myself*. When a white wino gets rights that a Black millionaire can't have, it's the rich man that's in trouble. I just want to free my Blackness, before I free my bank account.

"I just want to say God bless you. And don't ever give up on freedom. Eat freedom, sleep freedom, breathe freedom, and drink freedom. Get drunk on freedom, and you'll find yourself stumbling on it when you don't even know it."

I received a standing ovation from those whom I had been applauding in my speech.

The next morning that truck from Chicago still hadn't arrived. The driver called about 9:30 A.M. and said he was in Columbus, Mississippi and still on his way. More tired, a bit more weary, but no less patient, the second-nighters waited patiently in front of the candy store next to the NAACP offices on Lynch Street. Finally, at about 2:30 P.M., the truck pulled in.

David Brinkley's camera crew was set up on Lynch Street. David had told them not to bother to come back to work if they didn't get exclusive pictures. Charles Evers, Jim McGraw, and I jumped on the back of the truck and began handing out turkeys. A lone white man was standing far behind the large crowd of Blacks. Evers called to him, wishing to show clearly on national television that this was, indeed, an integrated project. (In fact, 1500 turkeys went to whites, 300 to a Choctaw Indian reservation, and a number to Chinese families.)

The white man protested violently, indicating that he had a "bad back." McGraw realized that the poor guy thought we were going to make him help unload the truck, and he shouted, "We just want to give you a turkey!" Full of white assurance, the guy ran to receive, forgetting, evidently, about his bad back! Thus did David Brinkley get his exclusive, "The First Man to Receive a Turkey in Mississippi Was a White Man."

All kinds of motor vehicles were on hand to load up with turkeys and take them to the out-of-the-way districts. Farmers with their dilapidated flatbed trucks, and city dwellers with their station wagons. One woman suffered a heart attack, she was so excited. But when the ambulance arrived to take her away, she told the driver, "Don't take me to no hospital. I'm gonna cook this bird in the mawnin'." And she drove home in a car with friends. Another woman betrayed her unfamiliarity with cooking turkey when she said, "Oh, thank you, Mr. Gregory. And I sure am gonna ask God to bless you tomorrow when I'm fryin' this turkey."

I looked again at those faces, and it was like a breadline anywhere in the world. These were not just the hungry people of Mississippi. They had the same look of people you see in newsreels—of people who are waiting to be fed in China, in the Congo, in Europe, in America during the Great Depression. These faces had a universal expression. As I watched them, it dawned on me more strongly than ever that the number one job facing humankind, before landing on the moon or on Mars, before curing any more diseases, before inventing another invention, is feeding human beings all over the world.

That night we drove to Gulfport to check on the distribution of turkeys in that area. We stayed at the $20 million Broadview

Motel, guests of the white lady owner. Charles Evers and his crowd of faithful followers had desegregated this particular public accommodation a few months before. Now the owner insisted that we turkey-watchers stay there. We were given a luxurious three-room suite, two spacious double bedrooms, and a huge parlor. Southern hospitality dripped all over us.

It was Christmas Eve, and we had dinner in the main dining room, again as guests of the owner. The guys in the band and the maitre d' recognized me coming in the door. The band immediately swung into a chorus of "Chicago." When the emcee introduced me later in the evening, I got a standing ovation from the white diners in the room. At the close of their set, the band members came by the table one by one to wish us a Merry Christmas and a Happy New Year. It was beautiful.

On Christmas Day we had dinner at Charles Evers' home. As we sat around the table, I looked at Lil and thought of the Christmas before. She was away from home again on Christmas, but this time at least the two older kids were with her. But that humanitarian impulse had brought her to Mississippi. I realized that Lil was a year-round incarnation of what Christmas is all about!

I summed it up in a quote in *Jet* magazine. "We can't handle those problems that God has inflicted upon man, like the Northwest disaster; we're trying to solve some of those problems that *man* has inflicted upon man."

One decade and one year later, the sovereign State of Mississippi elected a new Governor, Cliff Finch. An old friend from Mississippi, James Allen, arranged for me to participate in the inaugural proceedings. What a difference the years had made! I was met at the airport by the governor's chauffeured limousine, and we were escorted by Mississippi state police.

I spoke at the governor's dinner. Later I was told that all of Mississippi's living governors were in the room. After my speech Governor Finch made me an honorary Mississippi colonel, along with Charles Evers and Aaron Henry! The old faithful turkey-watchers are now members of the governor's official staff. Since I was at the top of the awards list, I became the first Black colonel in the State of Mississippi.

Harlan Sanders may be the colonel of Kentucky Fried Chicken, but I'm the undisputed colonel of Mississippi turkey!

14

One Crazy Nigger

After the Christmas recess in Mississippi, we returned to the hard realities of the civil rights struggle. Drew Pearson got a letter from E. L. McDaniel, grand dragon of the Mississippi Ku Klux Klan, stating that Drew now outranked Congressman Adam Clayton Powell and Dick Gregory on the Klan enemies list. Dragon McDaniel sent carbon copies to all Mississippi editors. I guess he was trying to prove that the pen is mightier than the hood.

J. Edgar Hoover captured headlines by calling Martin Luther King, Jr., "the most notorious liar in the country." Dr. King had dared to tell the critical truth about the FBI and civil rights demonstrations. Hoover also lashed out at the Warren Commission report, claiming it was unfairly critical of the FBI.

Onstage, I had a lot of fun with Hoover, the FBI, and the Klan:

"J. Edgar Hoover called Martin Luther King 'the most notorious liar in the country.' Now you know why if we're caught in a dark alley, and there's the Ku Klux Klan at one end—and the FBI at the other, we flip a coin. I won't say Hoover's getting power hungry but he's now calling it the Federal Bureau of I. The way Hoover's been actin', you begin to wonder if he's appointed or anointed! But there's one thing Hoover never will call Dr. King—a little white liar.

"But you know what really shakes me up? The news that the FBI has infiltrated the Ku Klux Klan. I mean, it's bad enough my tax money's going for missiles, but I'll be durned if it's gonna go for sheets. I knew an FBI agent who got so confused—a G-man one week, a Ku Klux Klanner the next—they hadda let him go. He said 'Sir!' to Martin Luther King and called J. Edgar Hoover 'Boy!'

"The Ku Klux Klan always tries to give the appearance of respectability. But to me a Klanner is nothin' but a hood under a hood. In case you're interested in finding out more about the Klan, they're easy to find. Just look them up in the Yellow Pages—under 'yellow!' "

Offstage my encounters with both the Klan and the FBI were a bit more serious. The dangerous and horrible reality confronting civil rights demonstrators in the South was that local police could not be trusted to give protection. Many local police officers were members of White Citizens Councils, and those who did not hold official membership cards usually sympathized with council goals and sentiments. The only real protection to civil rights demonstrators was provided by the watchful eyes and persistent pens of the press.

Whenever I participated in a demonstration, I got good press coverage because I was a celebrity. Consequently I was constantly in demand to add my presence to all kinds of demonstrations. I was a sort of built-in security measure. Local police and white officials were more cautious when the press was around. And that special bond among press people made a difference. Local press would share information, provide leads, identify sources, and otherwise assist national reporters in their coverage.

I had also established a reputation among southern sheriffs and local police of being the wrong person to arrest. I was really more trouble than I was worth. I knew my constitutional rights, and law enforcement officials knew I would pick up the phone and call the Justice Department in a second if my rights were not granted. If *any* demonstrators got arrested, I made sure I got busted too. Local police had to think twice before making an arrest. They had to decide whether or not they wanted the hassle of dealing with Dick Gregory. Every time I was busted, I would insist that each and every one of my personal effects had to be itemized. Sometimes it would take hours to itemize the hundreds of notes, letters, cards, clippings, reports, contracts, checks, bills, loose change, folding money, honorary citations, and invitations I had in my possession.

And I would always stay in jail as long as I could afford the time. I would refuse bond for two reasons. I wanted to call attention to the plight of those who couldn't afford bail and are held for days, weeks, months, and longer, even though they may be innocent. And I also looked upon incarceration as rest and relaxation from a hectic daily schedule.

There were no phones, no deadlines, no planes to catch. And jailhouse food was *haute cuisine* to me. It was a soul food paradise!

Biscuits and fatback floating in a tin plate of syrup for breakfast. Collard greens, neckbones, and cornbread for dinner. Whatever other indignities a prisoner may have to endure, those Southern jailers didn't mess around with dinner. I remember a line I used after spending some time behind bars in Selma, Alabama: "That jail in Selma is on the American Plan even if the rest of the town isn't!"

I received several phone calls from the Reverend T.Y. Rogers, pastor of the First African Baptist Church in Tuscaloosa, Alabama. He was spearheading a drive to integrate restaurants as executive secretary of the Tuscaloosa Citizens-for-Action Committee. I went into Tuscaloosa to join a three-day series of crash demonstrations to integrate a dozen or more restaurants and lunch counters.

I met with Rogers and some of his associates before speaking at a rally in his church. Some FBI agents came into the meeting and told us that the son of the owner whose restaurant we planned to integrate that evening had escaped from a mental institution. The crazy boy was in the restaurant waiting for us, and he was promising to kill Dick Gregory. It made me mad. It seemed to me that the FBI agents were talking to the wrong folks!

I went into the sanctuary and spoke to the assembled crowd. "I've just been told that the restaurant owner's crazy son is waiting to kill me. I don't know if he's crazy or not. But I do know one thing. Crazy folks are not going to dictate our movement. If one insane individual can stop a restaurant from being integrated, then all the sane people of the world don't count."

Rogers announced a decision which had been agreed on in the meeting. Twelve men would go with me to the restaurant, and the women and children would be left behind at the church. A woman came down the aisle to the front of the church to speak on behalf of her sisters. "Mr. Gregory, whenever you're in town, all the men show up for demonstrations. But when you're not here, it's just Reverend Rogers and a whole lot of women and children. This is our town. We've got to live here and raise our kids here. If you're gonna die tonight, we demand the right to die with you."

I called Lillian before we left the church. I told her about the FBI report, that we were on our way to the restaurant, and that there might be some trouble. I bought a big, long, expensive cigar. I figured if I was going to die, I might as well go out in style. As we made our way toward the restaurant, I thought I was walking as fast as I could. But everyone else seemed to be passing me by.

Unconsciously, the horror of the knowledge that some crazy white boy was waiting to kill me slowed down my pace. I kept thinking of my kids and Lillian, of Chicago and show business, wondering if I would ever see any of them again.

As we approached the restaurant door, I had to run to get up front. The owner met us at the door. "There are no seats available. We're full up. You got reservations?" I said, "No." He drawled, "Well, it's not that we won't serve you. But you got to have reservations." I made reservations for the following morning for breakfast.

I was relieved to have a reprieve. But now I had a whole night to worry about dying. I began to understand how condemned convicts on death row must feel. The next morning we returned to the restaurant with a large crowd. By this time, I was ready for whatever was going to happen. The owner met us again at the door.

"We have your reservations, but we didn't expect this many people. We'll have to take some now and some later. Just take any empty tables you see."

There were very few tables. The restaurant was filled nearly to the brim with white kids. I was really disappointed. I couldn't believe that these young kids would be involved in this trick. I started to voice my disappointment to Rogers, but I noticed he had a big smile on his face. All of a sudden the white kids got up and left. They were Rogers' kids from the University of Alabama! They were just holding our places.

As soon as I sat down, I saw the crazy white boy. And he was crazy! He had a wild-eyed stare and a pistol stuffed in his shirt. He came over to our table.

"You Dick Gregory?"

"That's me."

"Then you're that crazy nigger!"

"Yep. I'm crazier than you, boy."

I reached up and grabbed him by his collar and pulled him close to my face. I had taken him completely by surprise. I looked him squarely in the eye and blew some smoke in his face.

"You got your daddy and all these police thinkin' you're crazy. But you better understand one thing. I'm not Martin Luther King. You might be crazy around him. But if you make one move for that pistol, boy, you'll find out who the crazy nigger is in town."

I blew some more smoke in his face. "So best you get away

from me and get back over there with your daddy where it's safe."

He did a weird thing. He just started banging on the table with his fists. His father rushed over and pulled him away.

The waitress took our order and served us. When she brought dessert, my piece of pie had a hair on it. Rogers was all upset. But I really didn't think it was intentional. I told him, "Wait 'til she comes back. We'll have some fun."

When the waitress got within earshot, I said, "Hey, Rogers. See this hair on my piece of pie? I got a witch doctor back in Chicago I can take this hair to, and she'll wipe out this whole block!"

The waitress came running over, offering to bring me another piece of pie. I declined the offer. I was going to let them worry about my witch doctor like they had me worrying about their crazy white boy!

Back at the nightclub microphone, it was fun and games once again. Nobody would have known my narrow brush with death.

"Tuscaloosa! Ain't that a wild name? Sounds like an Italian elephant with tooth trouble. We integrated fourteen restaurants in three days. Think of it, fourteen dinners in three days! When we got finished, we didn't sing 'We Shall Overcome.' We burped it! After three days of eating in those Southern restaurants, I didn't know if I was a freedom fighter or a test pilot for Alka Seltzer. In Tuscaloosa, an Uncle Tom was anyone on a diet!

"The newspapers said we had a lot of guts integrating those southern restaurants, and they were right. But it ain't because of the cops, it's because of the food! We ate in one restaurant that was so bad, even the roaches ate out. Some restaurants are on Diners Club. This one was on Blue Cross!

"I went into one restaurant and said, 'I'll have a table for one, please.' The owner said, 'There's none left.' I said, 'None left? All the tables are empty!' He said, 'They're reserved.' I said, 'Is that so? Well, if Governor Wallace called up and said he was coming in fifteen minutes, do you think you'd be able to find a table for him?' The owner said, 'Of course.' So I said, 'Well, he ain't coming. Gimme his!'

"Actually, the whole thing went real smooth. The only trouble we had was in one restaurant where the Grand Dragon of the Ku Klux Klan was eating. We had fried chicken, and he didn't like the way I wiped my hands on his sheet."

15

Our Shining Black Prince

Sunday afternoon, February 21, 1965, Malcolm X was shot and killed as he was addressing a rally of the Organization of Afro-American Unity at the Audubon Ballroom in Harlem. I wasn't really surprised. I had seen clues all around pointing to his impending murder.

The Sunday before Malcolm's murder, his home in Queens was fire-bombed. The police report said that someone had thrown a Molotov cocktail from a speeding car. I couldn't accept the official explanation. It's hard enough to throw something from a moving car, to say nothing of a speeding car. Besides, Malcolm's house was so far back from the street that such accuracy and precision would have been impossible. I figured the police must know more than they were telling.

That same Sunday Malcolm announced his rally at the Audubon Ballroom. Jim McGraw asked if I was planning to attend and if I wanted him to make arrangements with Malcolm. I told him, "No way, baby. I'm afraid that's going to be the shot that doesn't miss!"

I really felt that Malcolm was being set up for the kill, probably by agents of the government. He had just returned from Africa and was talking about human rights and Pan-Africanism, strengthening the cooperative ties between Black people in Africa and Black people in America. Whenever Black leaders begin talking seriously about the universal and international bond of Blackness, whenever they start dealing with Black Africa on terms other than those specified by the State Department, strange things begin to happen. Malcolm X was shot down in public. Six years later, Whitney Young was in Africa voicing some of the same sentiments and opinions. Whitney suffered a surprise fatal heart attack while he was swimming.

Malcolm had visited Ghana, Nigeria, Sierra Leone, the Congo,

Mali, and a number of other African states. He had asked the heads of independent African nations to submit the question of the treatment of Blacks in the United States to the United Nations for debate. And Malcolm had also recently been in Selma, Alabama, demonstrating his solidarity with the civil rights struggle. He was beginning to emerge as a Black man with the potential for linking up the North and the South as well as the international scene.

I was in an airplane when Malcolm was shot. When the plane landed I was surrounded by news people who asked if I had heard that Malcolm X had been shot and killed. I asked, "Who shot him?" They said, "The Black Muslims." I answered, "I'll never believe that. I think it is a lot more involved than that."

Malcolm had made people listen who didn't want to hear— Black and white. Malcolm had a listening audience far greater than his visible numerical band of followers indicated. He spoke for all Black folks, articulating our felt oppression and frustration, by insisting, "No more!" And he wasn't speaking as a Muslim or as a representative of Islam. Rather, his rejection of the oppressive status quo was shared equally in the hearts and minds of Black Baptists, Black Catholics, Black Methodists, or Black folks who didn't go to church.

I remembered the first time I met Malcolm. I was appearing in a New York City club, and Malcolm sent word asking me to speak at the Temple. Malcolm's religious convictions prohibited his coming to a nightclub, and I remember telling him, "I'm ahead of you. I can come to your gig, but you can't come to mine!"

I never will forget how Malcolm tried to protect my image. He was worried about the effect it would have on my career as a Black entertainer if my picture appeared in association with Muslim activities. So he issued instructions that no pictures should be taken.

I heard him warning the photographers. I told Malcolm, "Look, the only way I'm going to walk into this temple is if you *guarantee* my picture will be in *Muhammed Speaks.*" I'll never forget that beautiful, surprised look on his face as he asked, "Really?" He was so pleased, and he really wanted a picture of my appearance, but his marvelous human sensitivity had caused him to think first of me and my career.

I attended Malcolm's funeral. He was laid to rest amid the same kind of controversy, misunderstanding, and turmoil that plagued the days of his life. Rumors were running rampant that there would be violence at the funeral. Since the blame for Malcolm's murder had been laid upon the Muslims, further acts of revenge and retaliation were anticipated. Police were everywhere. Ironically, the funeral services were carried on national television, not out of respect for Malcolm, but because, I believe, the network didn't want to miss out on live coverage of the violence. Such thinking illustrated the sickness Malcolm had tried to expose and eradicate. There was no violence. Malcolm's funeral was for family viewing.

Ossie Davis was so magnificent and so beautiful that day. He delivered the eulogy and put into words those feelings which were groping to find expression. Ossie read from a letter Malcolm had written from Africa to a friend: "My journey is almost ended, and I have a much broader scope than when I started out, which I believe will add new life and dimension to our struggle for freedom and honor and dignity in the States. I'm writing these things so that you will know for a fact the tremendous sympathy and support we have among the African States for our Human Rights struggle. The main thing is that we keep a United Front wherein our most valuable time and energy will not be wasted fighting each other."

Then Ossie rose to the full stature of his genius and uttered those words which were to capture the imagination and challenge the vision of a whole generation of young Black kids: "However much we may have differed with him, or with each other about him and his value as a man, let his going from us serve only to bring us together now. Consigning these mortal remains to earth, the common mother of all, secure in the knowledge that what we place in the ground is no more now a man—but a seed—which, after the winter of our discontent, will come forth again to meet us. And we will know him then for what he was and is—a Prince!—our own black shining Prince!—who didn't hesitate to die, because he loved us so."

Malcolm was, indeed, both prince and prophet. As I listened to Ossie, I thought of those words Malcolm spoke when asked his opinion of the assassination of John F. Kennedy. Malcolm said, "It's an example of chickens coming home to roost." Everyone was outraged, white folks and Black folks. The statement was cited as one of the reasons for his expulsion from the Muslims.

But Malcolm knew what he was saying. It would be another decade before his fellow Americans would begin to understand. I am sure Malcolm was telling us that a sick nation cannot go around the world with its CIA killing off some heads of state and plotting against others, without one day witnessing the same forces and the same techniques coming to roost at home.

Like Jesus of Nazareth, Malcolm X grew in wisdom and stature during his brief years on this earth. But his most profound influence was to come after his death. His words were resurrected in the hearts and minds of young Blacks, and his truth goes marching on.

16

From the Big Apple to the Bloodbath

The action was getting really heavy in Selma, Alabama. Martin Luther King and some 260 other demonstrators were arrested while marching to the courthouse to protest discrimination against Black voter registration applicants. Another 500 school kids were arrested for picketing the courthouse. Dr. King refused the $200 bail and stayed in jail for five days. Arrests continued in the hundreds on a daily basis, and finally members of the United States House of Representatives went into Selma as observers.

I had been getting phone calls asking me to come down. One night I was sitting in my Village Gate dressing room talking to Art Steuer and another friend, Berk Costello. Berk is a nice guy and fun to be around, but he was always somewhat of a mystery. I knew he must be up to something, but I didn't know just what. All I knew was that he always had a pocketful of money, lived in a luxury apartment, drove a Rolls Royce, and had no visible means of support, except a camera! Berk was a good photographer, but hardly in a class to support such a life style.

I was putting Berk on about the New York image: "Man, you Black cats sit around here in New York City and talk your game.

Ya'll act like you're God's gift to Black folks! Always talkin' about the Big Apple and how hip you are, just because you know about Miles Davis and Thelonius Monk and have seen some Broadway shows.

"Why don't you come down to Selma with me so I can show you some real culture? I want to show you what it's like when your pocketful of money's no good, your contacts can't help you, and your Rolls Royce is back up North, and your pretty suit and your alligator shoes work against you."

Art and Berk agreed to accompany me to Selma. Neither of them had ever been arrested in civil rights demonstrations. Berk had had many brushes with the law, but never for civil rights! We caught a flight to Selma the following day.

We were met at the airport by a white woman who was with the movement. She said there was a bloodbath going on in Anniston. We decided to go directly to the scene. I had made motel reservations at the Holiday Inn.

Berk was shook up. He couldn't conceive of riding in the same car with a white woman in Alabama! I said, "Berk, I've never seen a Black woman in your Rolls Royce! But if it will make you feel any better, just make believe you're driving down Madison Avenue instead of an Alabama highway. Make believe we're going to the Stock Exchange, and then to the Chase Manhattan Bank, then on up to Broadway to catch a show, and then up to Smalls Paradise to hang out!"

We were in a hurry to get to Anniston. We were speeding along, narrowly missing cows crossing the road, and the drive alone was frightening. When we hit Anniston, it was obvious there had been a bloody conflict between demonstrators and the police. Blood was literally flowing in the gutters. But by the time we arrived, the streets were deserted. It was like a ghost town.

We talked to some of the folks sitting on their porches and waited around to see if there was going to be any more action. About midnight, we headed back to Selma and the Holiday Inn outside of town. The desk clerk said they had my reservations but policy dictated that reservations would not be held past 8 P.M. I was told I was too late and the motel was full. As I waited around in the lobby trying to decide what I was going to do, I saw other people come up to the desk and get room assignments. I asked a couple of them if they had paid for their reservations in advance.

They said they had not. So I announced to the desk clerk that I wasn't going to leave until my reservations were honored.

Pretty soon Sheriff Jim Clark arrived. He greeted me and said, "Who're your friends?" I said, "Just folks with the movement." He pointed at Berk, "How about that New York City slicker over there?" I asked the Sheriff for clarification. He said, "We ran a check on ya'll. The rest of you are clean. But you leave him home next time!"

Sheriff Clark asked if I was going to find another room or stay at his place that night. I told him we were going to jail. He obliged. I went through my usual ritual, making the arresting officer record the serial numbers on all the money in my pocket. I didn't want them to get cute and run a counterfeit rap on me.

Art and Berk got out on bail the next morning. I stayed for the week. I didn't have any obligations until my weekend engagement at the Village Gate, and I needed a few days of rest, soul food, and Kool Aid.

Back in New York City, Jim McGraw ran across Bill Cosby at the opening of Oscar Brown, Jr.'s one-man show. Bill said, "I read about Dick being in jail. Tell him, if he's not out by this weekend, I'll fill in for him at the Village Gate." McGraw smiled knowingly and said, "Thanks anyway, Bill. But you know Greg's not going to miss his gig."

Jim was right. I was onstage right on schedule Friday night. And I had a lot to talk about.

"I've got a suggestion for you if you're making out your income tax this year and you're short on medical deductions. Come on down to Selma with me and demonstrate. Can you imagine why the police shoot tear gas at us? In Selma, we got enough to cry about already! I understand there's an entire Marine Division standing by with two maps in their pockets—one of Saigon and the other of Selma. But one thing you have to say for those Selma cops. They're still southern gentlemen. Every time they wade into a crowd with those billy clubs and cattle prods, they always say: 'Women and children first!' And Selma, Alabama, is the only town I know where the traffic lights in the Black neighborhoods don't say WALK and DON'T WALK. They say RUN and RUN LIKE HELL."

17

The Month of (the) March

In 1965, my career took a sudden new turn which posed a threat to my freedom to be involved in civil rights demonstrations. I was asked to do a movie based on John A. Williams's novel *Night Song*. It was a story based on the life and struggles of the famous jazz saxophonist, Charlie "Bird" Parker, although the hero of the novel was called Richie "Eagle" Stokes. I was to play Eagle. The movie was entitled *Sweet Love, Bitter* (later re-released under the title *It Won't Rub Off, Baby*).

Ralph Mann, my agent, was quite excited about the movie. He felt it represented a whole new career potential and that I could tap a large movie-going audience I would never reach through nightclubs or even television. I was both excited and fearful. I had never done any film acting, and I was also apprehensive about the time commitment involved. Once I was locked into filming, it would be very difficult to respond to the call of civil rights demonstrations.

My fear was compounded by the fact that the other stars were all seasoned pros. Don Murray had scored triumphs in films like *Bus Stop, Advise and Consent,* and *The Hoodlum Priest.* Robert Hooks was an experienced stage actor and one of the founders of the Negro Ensemble Company in New York City. He was also slated to do a key role in Otto Preminger's *Hurry Sundown.* Diane Varsi was making her return to the screen in this film. She had fled Hollywood in 1958 after scoring successes in *Peyton Place* and *Compulsion.*

Everybody bent over backward to help out the beginner. Director Herb Danska and my acting coach, Woodie King, Jr., were both patient and brilliant. The other stars did everything they possibly could to make things easier for me. In the presence of all that wonderful support, my fears melted away. I was soon enjoying my new career.

We were filming in the City of Brotherly Love, Philadelphia, when all hell broke loose on the Edmund Pettus Bridge in Selma. Two hundred state troopers and sheriff's deputies attacked 525 civil rights demonstrators who were attempting to march from Selma to Montgomery. John Lewis, chairman of SNCC, suffered a concussion. The Alabama "peace" officers said they were simply enforcing Governor Wallace's ban against marching. George Wallace himself defended the attacks against the marchers as "absolutely necessary," insisting that public safety had been protected and that Negro lives had been saved by forcible prevention of the march. It was the old "cripple a few to save the many" argument!

I told Herb Danska I was going to have to find a way to get to Selma. As always, he was cooperative and understanding. He began filming my scenes so that filming could continue uninterrupted with the other actors if I had to leave for the South.

Martin Luther King issued a call to "all persons of goodwill" to join him in Selma in another attempt to cross the Edmund Pettus Bridge and march to Montgomery. I stayed in Philadelphia because it was not at all clear whether or not the march would come off. United States District Court Judge Frank M. Johnson, Jr., had issued a temporary restraining order against the march, and President Johnson had made a public plea urging both civil rights demonstrators and Alabama officials to respect the law. LBJ also deplored the earlier brutality against demonstrators trying to cross the bridge.

Jim McGraw was in Selma, and I was packed and ready to split at a moment's notice if Jim sent the word. He kept phoning every hour with a progress report. Martin Luther King was on the scene, huddling with his advisers at Brown Chapel Methodist Episcopal Church. The uncertainty remained until the very last moment. Jim called and said, "We still don't know if we're going to march. Dr. King's still inside. I'd stay put if I were you, Greg. You might just be wasting your time."

It was another couple of hours before Jim called again. "Well, you're not going to believe it, Greg. King came out and announced, 'We're going to march.' And it was a crowd. Bill Jones (the Reverend William A. Jones of Brooklyn) looked at the line and said 'It's a number no man can number!' We got across the bridge, and Jim Clark and his guys were standing behind barricades a few yards up ahead. Jim and Dr. King had a few words. Then everybody knelt down and sang 'We Shall Overcome.' Dr. King said a prayer.

"Now here's the wild bit. We got up, turned around, and followed King back to Brown Chapel. And you know what they were singing, Greg? 'Ain't Goin' To Let Nobody Turn Me 'Round'! We shoulda sung 'He's Got the Whole World in His Hands,' and dedicated it to Jim Clark!"

Two weeks later, the march was on. A new district court order upheld the right of demonstrators to march to Montgomery. Appeals by the State of Alabama against the order were rejected. LBJ got into the act by signing a proclamation citing the danger of "domestic violence" in Alabama and an executive order federalizing the Alabama National Guard and authorizing use of whatever federal troops the secretary of defense "may deem necessary." I flew into Selma.

The night before the march, a mass meeting was held at Brown Chapel. The sanctuary was filled with visiting clergy—nuns, priests, ministers, and rabbis—who had come to march in an act of conscience. I used my turn at the microphone to preach to the preachers.

"They blow up our churches. That's all right, too. It just puts religion out in the street, where it ought to be in the first place. When they blow up a church, then you know it's been *saying* and *doing* something. If the minister up North would get into his pulpit and start reading off the names of the syndicate leaders and the top racketeers, don't you know his church would be blown up the next day?

"What touched LBJ the other night? You did. You religious leaders. I just hope it doesn't end here. When you realize that 99.9 percent of Black America that goes to church on Sunday never sees a white face, and 99.9 percent of white America that goes to church on Sunday never sees a Black face, then you realize that the church is the most segregated form of American life in the country today.

Martin Luther King heard my "sermon." He asked if he could speak to me about something—alone! I wondered what was up. I knew the FBI had been giving him a hard time, and I thought maybe he had something personal on his mind. We went into a room in Brown Chapel, and Martin said, "I heard you make a reference while you were speaking. I've heard it before, but I've never felt I could ask anybody about it. If I ask you something, promise you won't laugh at me?"

"Of course, Doc. What is it?"

"Well, I just wanted to know, what's the syndicate?"

I didn't dare laugh, but it was so beautiful. It was Martin at his most humble, honest, sweet, innocent self. I explained to him about the Mafia and organized crime. When I came out of the room, I just had to tell somebody I could trust not to repeat it. I told Jim McGraw what had just happened. He said, "Greg, you probably wasted your breath. Somebody probably just asked Martin to write a syndicated column."

The next morning, Sunday, it was Martin's turn to preach, just before setting out on the big march. It was an open air sermon delivered from the steps of Brown Chapel.

"We are a group determined to march on, and 'we ain't goin' to let nobody turn us around.' Like men of old, we are in Egypt. There are three groups here in Egypt, like the days of old. One group even includes some Negroes who want to go back to Egypt. They are so used to segregation that they accept it. Another group doesn't like segregation, but they are not willing to stand up and challenge it. But there is a third group. And this morning by your presence you show that you represent this third group: a group determined to face all of the self-inflicted suffering necessary.

"We come today with marching shoes on. Most of us who are Negroes don't have much—but we do have bodies and souls. We represent the power to transform the heart of the president of the Universe (Martin quickly changed it to 'President of the nation' although LBJ probably preferred the former title). President Johnson spoke out of his heart the other night. Never has a president spoken more eloquently and more passionately. Things are happening here in Alabama. And now we have come to transform the heart of Dixie into Dixie with a heart."

We moved out from Brown Chapel, a phalanx for freedom, numbering in the thousands. At the head of the line, along with Dr. King and others, were Dr. Ralph Bunche, undersecretary at the United Nations; John Lewis, now recovered from his concussion; Rabbi Abraham Heschel; and Cager Lee, grandfather of Jimmie Lee Jackson, who had been slain by a state trooper in Marion, Alabama, the month before.

The Dixie Dandies, the Alabama National Guardsmen, were

right alongside us, in body if not in spirit, with their Confederate flags sewn above the names on their uniforms. And the United States Army, under direct orders from its commander-in-chief, was keeping a watchful eye on us too.

We marched across the Edmund Pettus Bridge, unimpeded, with two whole lanes of Highway 80 to ourselves. We stopped and knelt in prayer at the spot where people were beaten in the infamous Sunday massacre of two weeks before.

Our line of march really looked like an army on the move. Food and supply trucks followed behind, and latrine trucks moved alongside with their commodes in motion. Across the way traffic was backed up for blocks in the remaining two lanes available for vehicles traveling between Selma and Montgomery. Drivers and passengers looked out of their car windows, bewildered.

Some passing cars had messages for us. A green Oldsmobile passed announcing, "The White Citizens Council welcomes you. Help maintain segregation." Another car bore a sign demanding, "Go Home, Scum. We Are Rebels. Peace in Selma." On the rear fender was scrawled, "Rent your priest's uniform here."

About three miles out, we stopped for sandwiches, cookies, and relief. The secret was out: Even Martin Luther King has to stop on occasion to urinate. I wondered aloud to Jim McGraw, "How'd you like to have 10,000 people watch you go in to piss? After seein' that line file in and out, I don't want nobody to hand me any more food."

We walked and laughed and sang. Folks began to complain about their aching feet, their corns and bunions. As we finally limped into the first campsite about ten or twelve miles outside of Selma, I suggested to the complainers that Dr. Scholl must have underwritten the march! I drove back to Selma and caught a plane to Philadelphia.

I was back four days later. It was the eve of the final day of the march. The last campsite was set up at City of St. Jude, a predominantly Black Roman Catholic hospital and school located about two miles inside the Montgomery city limits. A big outdoor show was planned for that evening.

And how the show-business community rallied to the cause! It was beautiful. No amount of money or production genius could have put together so many stars on the same stage at the same time. Only the appeal of Martin Luther King and the power of nonviolence could have done it. Most of the entertainers who showed up never made any pretense of being nonviolent. And they knew that their lives were in danger. Some entertainers travel with bodyguards, but that was no comfort in the heart of a hostile South. Anyone who had decided to do some killing could have wiped out the star *and* the bodyguards. But the courage and commitment emanating from the spirit of nonviolence pulled the show folk to Alabama.

Some entertainers had been with the march all along. Gary Merrill headed up the crew that took down the tents each morning and set them up again at the next campsite. Pernell Roberts, one of the stars of "Bonanza," had left the Ponderosa to join the march.

The night of the show, star after star paraded across the makeshift stage, improvised under a tent from coffin crates lent by a local undertaker. There was no hassle about billing, time, or anything. Just show folks gathered to show their support—Ossie Davis, Harry Belafonte, Sammy Davis, Jr., Alan King, Tony Bennett, Nipsy Russell, the Chad Mitchell Trio, Peter, Paul and Mary, George Kirby, Shelley Winters, Tony Perkins, James Baldwin, Leonard Bernstein, Odetta, Leon Bibb, Mike Nichols and Elaine May, Billy Eckstine, Floyd Patterson.

The march was almost over, and the marchers were ready for a good laugh. I tried to give it to them. "I read in the paper a week ago where Sheriff Jim Clark said, 'They'll make that march to Montgomery over my dead body!' And I thought that wouldn't be a bad route.

"But a lot of folks were surprised you made it this far. Like George Wallace. I understand the first day he said, 'Those rabble-rousers have just left Selma.' The second day he said, 'Those trouble-making outside agitators have marched twenty miles.' The third day he said, 'Those civil rights marchers are more than halfway here.' The fourth day he said, 'The freedom walkers are on the outskirts of Montgomery.' And tomorrow, when he looks out the window and sees 30,000 folks marching toward him, Governor Wallace'll probably be waiting on the steps of the Capitol saying, 'Hey, baby, what took ya'll so long?' "

The next morning we lined up for the last leg of the march. Martin Luther King was up front with that courageous little remnant of marchers who had walked every step of the way. Alongside was Mrs. Rosa Parks, the courageous lady who had refused to give up her seat on the bus one day, thus sparking the

Montgomery bus boycott. The celebrities followed close behind. All kinds of folks were trying to push their way as close to the front as possible.

The march began, through the muddy streets of the Black section of town, past an all-Black elementary school. It was a beautiful sight to see the kids hanging out the windows, smiling and waving at Harry Belafonte. Harry joined in the fun, waving back to his little fans and saying, "Come on down and join us." Others in the line picked up the spirit and repeated Harry's words, including Urban League Director Whitney Young, Jr. Jim McGraw said to me, "If we could get him to do that in New York City, our school boycotts would be 100 percent more successful." Whitney heard him and realized the implication of his words. He changed his tune quickly, "We'll fight the battle out here; let them stay in school."

We were downtown by now, on Dexter Avenue, and heading straight for the Alabama State Capitol Building. There was a reception committee halfway up the capitol steps—a solid wall of state troopers standing at ease. The Confederate flag flew above the American flag atop the capitol building.

But none of it mattered. The army of truth, justice, and the real American way was on the move. This was our America, and we had claimed our citizenship and demonstrated our patriotism with our marching feet. Even the most hostile bystanders had to concede our victory. When you are confronted with so much truth, you can cuss it, you can spit at it, you can despise it, but you can't *deny* it.

Within an hour of Martin Luther King's final "Glory Hallelujah" shouted from the platform in front of the capitol steps, the marchers began to scatter toward their various destinations and the haters began to gather in little clusters all over the downtown area. I could feel the resentment and heard it expressed as Jim McGraw, Art Steuer, Jim Sanders, and I—two whites and two Blacks—walked past a group of white teenagers who mumbled, "Like to beat the shit out of all of 'em—the white niggers especially." I sensed that something horrible was going to happen that night.

By the time I got to the airport, the rumor was out. Someone had been shot. I was so glad to see Dr. King at the airport, so I knew it wasn't him. But who? Roy Wilkins? Whitney Young? One of the entertainers?

Before my plane took off, the answer was official. It was a white woman from Detroit named Viola Liuzzo. I thought to myself, "Well, the Ku Klux Klan's in trouble now. They've outsported themselves. They've killed a white lady. They will be crushed."

18

My Kind of Town— Chicago Is?

During the summer, we changed the focus of our demonstrations in Chicago. We shifted the summer heat from School Superintendent Benjamin C. Willis to Mayor Richard J. Daley. The rationale was a simple formula: Nothing happens in Chicago without direct approval from Mayor Daley. If Mayor Daley wanted Ben Willis to go, he would be out of work the next morning. So if we wanted Ben Willis fired, we had to get to Richard Daley. Our battle cry became, "Crush the head of the snake, and the tail will surely die!"

At first, demonstrations against Mayor Daley took place outside City Hall. Ben Willis was a symbol of our broader protest against *de jure* public school segregation (in violation of the 1964 Civil Rights Act), which had resulted in overcrowded classrooms and a lack of quality education in predominantly Black grade schools and high schools. For example, between 1963 and 1965, the percentage of segregated grade schools (either all white or all Black) rose from 81.6 percent to 82.3. Segregated high schools rose from 73.2 percent to 74.4. Twelve percent of the teachers in the average white school were noncertified, whereas the figure was 27 percent for Black schools. White grade schools averaged 29.7 kids in a class, but the Black classroom average was 34.4. Black schools also had fewer facilities, such as libraries and auditoriums.

The demonstrations had the support of all the community groups in Chicago, under the banner of the Coordinating Council of Community Organizations (CCCO). It was the first time an all-out, communitywide protest had been lodged personally and directly against Mayor Daley, and hizzoner didn't like it one bit!

Al Raby, convener of CCCO, and I were arrested one day during a vigil outside City Hall. We knelt on the sidewalk and prayed and refused to interrupt our personal devotions when the police asked us to move on. I also refused to pay the twenty-five-dollar fine, choosing instead to remain in jail. It was widely publicized in the press that I had $2,000 in my possession but had still refused to pay the fine. The $2,000 was in checks, without my signature. Of course they couldn't cash them.

But the publicity led to a nasty confrontation with the police a few days later. A huge march was in progress which had brought together the combined forces of the NAACP, the Urban League, and all the lesser-known groups. We had been promised free access to a portion of the street along a specified march route. But when we got downtown, the police insisted that we move out of the street and onto the sidewalk. After conferring with the police, Al Raby came back and announced, "We're in an arrest situation. The police have ordered us out of the street, but we're not going to move. Everybody sit down."

Lillian, Lynne, and Michele were marching along with me. We sat down in the street. I had Lynne on my lap, and Lil was holding Michele. All of a sudden the cops descended upon us. One of the cops pulled Lynne from my arms, and I saw another one do the same to Michele. Then a couple of cops grabbed me. Somewhere in the background, I could hear little Lynne saying, "Daddy, we're in trouble, aren't we?"

As I was being pushed toward a waiting paddy wagon, I felt the hand of one of the cops going into my pocket. He had evidently remembered the earlier news reports and was checking out my personal finances for himself. Instinctively I reached for the cop's hand and tried to wrestle it from my pocket. The other cops thought I was trying to resist arrest, and I'm sure that's how it looked. But I was really trying to prevent an unauthorized withdrawal from my pocket money. A flurry of billy clubs started whipping me from all sides. One cop grabbed my thumb and began pushing it back, trying to break it. I looked up and saw two things: the look of hatred in his face and a chain with a cross hanging from his neck.

My mind flashed back to every moment I'd ever spent in church. In that cop's face, I saw the face of Judas and the Roman soldier who nailed Christ to the cross. I thought of all the atrocities throughout history which had been committed in the name of the cross. I reached up with my free hand, grabbed that cross, and clung to Jesus. A strange thing happened. I began twisting the chain, and the harder I twisted, the stronger it seemed to get. The cop began to choke, his eyes bugged out, and he let go of my thumb. Then both the chain and all hell broke loose!

Some cops were beating me while others were carrying me into the paddy wagon. In the process, my wallet and my credit cards fell onto the street. After I was inside the wagon, I looked out and saw my wallet. I'll never know how I did it, but I pushed the paddy-wagon doors open, and the cops went flying away from the doors like tin soldiers. I got out, reached down and got my wallet, with the cops whipping me all the while. Then I walked back into the waiting wagon.

At the police station, I reported that some forty dollars in cash and a couple of credit cards were missing. As a result, I was charged with assault and resisting arrest. The cop who had been picking my pocket charged that I had kicked him and bit him.

Then I made an honest and innocent mistake. I offered to make a deal with the police. I said I was really more interested in changing the public school system than in a fight with the Chicago police. So I offered to forget about the missing money and credit cards if they would drop charges. The next day the press reported my offer as a bribe attempt. It was the first time I realized the collusion between some members of the press and the police.

I checked into Provident Hospital with a badly swollen thumb and ankle and severe back pains just above the kidney. I also filed charges against the arresting officers for theft, assault, and battery. I had to postpone a trip to London to do some television shows and a meeting I had scheduled with Lord Bertrand Russell. Instead, I did the BBC interview via live telephone hookup from my hospital bed. And Lord Russell sent a telegram to the hospital: "Deeply shocked to learn of your beating. Issuing press statement wishing you quickest recovery and hope our meeting will soon take place. Warmest wishes. Bertrand Russell."

While I was recuperating in the hospital, the city of Chicago held the largest tickertape welcome in its history in honor of astronauts Edward H. White and James A. McDivitt, who had just returned from their Gemini-Titan 4 flight and White's twenty-minute walk in space. Three days before their scheduled arrival in Chicago, I sent the two space heroes a telegram inviting them to join our demonstration while they were in town.

On June 16, two days after the astronauts had received their tickertape welcome, I received the following reply:

"We are in receipt of your invitation to astronauts White and McDivitt to lead the demonstration march on June 14 in Chicago. We regret that we did not receive your message in time to send a reply to you prior to the planned event, although the prearranged schedule of the astronauts would have precluded their participation. I am sure you are familiar with the position of NASA in the areas of fair employment of persons regardless of race, creed, or color. As stated frequently by President Johnson, and so often reiterated by Administrator Webb, NASA seeks to secure equal treatment and equal opportunity for all Americans. Your congratulations on the success of GT-4 are sincerely appreciated. Alan B. Shepard, Jr., Chief Astronaut, Office NASA Manned Spacecraft Center."

As soon as I got out of the hospital, I was determined to set the record straight about whether or not I had kicked or bitten any cops. Once again I made an honest, innocent mistake. I offered to take a lie detector test. I had sent a telegram to the Policemen's Benevolent Association in Chicago saying, "If the lie box confirms your charge that I bit a Chicago policeman—or any policeman—I will give you a check in the amount of $10,000 for the association's fund and pack my bags and leave Chicago forever."

I should have been suspicious of the immediate response to my offer. It came the same day as the NASA reply. "Dear Mr. Gregory. I was pleased to receive your telegram today and am happy to hear that you have agreed to take a lie detector test. Pursuant to your request, an appointment has been made for you at Mr. John E. Reid and Associates, 600 South Michigan Avenue, Room 614, Wednesday, June 16, 1965, at 1:00 P.M. I am sure that you will agree that John E. Reid and Associates are considered by many as the foremost polygraph experts in the country. Signed:

Joseph J. Lefevour, President, Fraternal Order of Police, 360 North Clark, Chicago, Illinois."

I was confident that the truth would be brought out into the open once and for all. I really trusted lie detector tests. All my life I had always believed that there were two things a person couldn't trick—fingerprints and a lie detector. I honestly believed that a lie detector test couldn't be used to trick me and I couldn't trick it. And I knew I had nothing to hide. My lawyer, Dick Shelton, begged me not to go through with it. But I insisted that I had to do it. If I backed out, it would be the same as a confession of guilt.

I took the test. Everybody in the room was congenial and in good spirits. After the test was over, I waited for the results. Pretty soon a guy came back into the room with a message that left me stunned and bewildered. I had flunked the test! I simply couldn't believe it. What I had always believed was a sacred safeguard was now obviously a fraud. I literally broke down and cried.

Of course I have to admit I was naive to have put so much trust in a lie detector test. After all, why couldn't a lie detector be rigged? And why couldn't the people administering the test simply lie about the results? I should have demanded that the lie detector be rigged up to the testers themselves, John E. Reid and Associates! But those questions came too late. I had allowed myself to be tricked. Evidently the Policemen's Benevolent Association knew what had happened because they did not accept my money nor did they demand that I pack up and leave Chicago. Their purpose had been accomplished.

We kept the pressure on Mayor Daley all summer long. And we kept the Chicago police busy escorting us all over town on our daily marches. When Mayor Daley left town to attend a mayors' conference in Detroit, we followed him. The mayor spent his time scurrying in and out of side doors to Cobo Hall, sneaking up and down back escalators, trying to avoid the pickets. Reporting to his fellow mayors, Mayor Daley insisted, "We're improving our housing. We're improving our education. We have one of the finest Head Start programs in the country." But his words were mocked by the presence of pickets outside, and Richard J. Daley had to devise secret routes to get to his hotel right across the street from Cobo Hall.

The pressure of daily protests began to take its toll. The mayor began to lose his cool in press conferences, "Many of the people who are marching are Communists. That's been printed. And the Police Department files show this is true." Every time the press asked the mayor to comment about Dick Gregory, the mayor would answer, "Who's Dick Gregory?"

It was a feeble attempt to avoid the issues unless, of course, the mayor's memory was slipping in his old age. I remembered how Mayor Daley and the entire Chicago City Council had given me an official "welcome home" citation back in May, 1961, after I had first made it big in show business. The mayor and the city council cited me for "exposing much of the hypocrisy of social injustice." I remember telling the city council, "I voted six times in the last election, but I never thought I'd meet all of you face to face." Mayor Daley seemed to think it was funny at the time, but now he had lost his sense of humor.

Now, for the first time, Mayor Daley was the butt of jokes spoken out in the open. The newspapers began saying sassy things they hadn't said before. Even little old ladies in the streets began talking back to the machine. Black cops and Black politicians began to adopt a more independent attitude. The stranglehold of fear that had always kept Black folks under the thumb of the Daley political machine began to lose its grip.

And the credit belongs to that brave, determined little band of marchers who came out every day, seven days a week. They were Black and white, young and old, rich and poor, educated and lacking in formal education. People like Ma Hueston, a Bible-believing senior citizen with faith, who started us out on our march each day with prayer and who personally marched every step of the way. What an inspiration she was to the younger marchers! And a lawyer named Ann Langford, who later became a member of the city council. And, of course, the real heroine was attorney Jean Williams. She was on hand all the time to handle legal problems and arrests. Folks marched a lot more confidently knowing that Jean was there and would represent us in court. The marathon street lawyer, Jean Williams, has now become a sitting judge in Tucson, Arizona.

I was convinced that the marches had to continue nonstop every day. In the South, where the problem was the fear of physical violence, large numbers of demonstrators were impor-tant. In Chicago, where the problem was the fear of a political machine, persistence was more important than the body count; numbing the system was more important than numbers of demonstrators. During the month of July, I had an engagement at the Hungry i in San Francisco. I couldn't cancel out because the owner, Enrico Banducci, had done so many personal favors for me. But I also had to continue the marches in Chicago.

I ended up commuting every day for a month between San Francisco and Chicago. I'd take an early morning flight from San Francisco, participate in the marches, catch a late afternoon flight back, and be on stage each night. I ended up spending $6,240 in airline fares. But the reaction to my daily commuting was unbelievable. People who had never marched before would join the demonstrations just to see this guy who was rich enough to fly back and forth between Chicago and California every day! Even the cops were impressed.

On stage at the Hungry i, I talked about Chicago:

"You know, if the cops ever went on strike in Chicago, our crime rate would drop 50 percent! One thing you gotta say about Chicago, we got the best cops money can buy—and some judges too! And we got some cops that'll steal anything. A cop approached me the other day who was sellin' hot tombstones. He came up to me and said, 'I got a good buy for you, if your name is Smith!'

"But right now I got two cops in Chicago suing me for kickin' and bitin' them, while they were tryin' to throw me in front of a train! I called one of them the other day. I said, 'Hey, baby, this is Dick Gregory. I just called to say you're darn right. I bit you.' Man, he started cussin' and carryin' on. I told him, 'Cool it, baby, until you've heard it all. I also wanted to tell you that the day before I bit you, I was bitten by a dog that had whoopin' rabies!' Oh, that upset him. He said, 'Is anything going to happen to me?' I said, 'Not this week. But if you wake up next week with a strange taste for dog food—and watermelon—!' "

One day I was marching in Chicago, and I got the shock of my life. I thought my marriage was going to break up on the spot. Lillian handed me a newspaper and challenged, "What have you got to say about that?" It was a copy of the *National Enquirer*. I looked at the headline: I WAS DICK GREGORY'S WHITE MISTRESS. I couldn't believe my eyes! My first reaction was that the FBI or the CIA had planted a story to try to discredit me. But I would still have to convince Lillian that I was an innocent victim of governmental intrigue. I told my wife, "We'll deal with this later."

The first chance I got, I sneaked a look at the story. Then I realized Lil had been putting me on. The story was simply an interview with Jeri Archer, who had played the role of my white mistress in *Sweet Love, Bitter.* She was talking about Herb Danska's film rather than FBI footage.

A strange thing happened that month which suggested possible CIA involvement. One night between shows at the Hungry i, I was told I had a visitor waiting in my dressing room. I went back and there sat Adlai Stevenson, United States Ambassador to the United Nations, who was in town for a special UN anniversary ceremony. He needed a shave and appeared to be both disheveled and somewhat incoherent. I could tell something was bothering him.

Ambassador Stevenson told me how much he admired me and appreciated the stand I had taken against the war in Vietnam. He also spoke of how he personally had to do something to save this nation because we were headed in the wrong direction. I really couldn't talk to him. I was embarrassed by the praise this great statesman was heaping upon me. And I was also embarrassed to see him in his rather disoriented condition.

I told him, "I have another show to do. When can we get together again?" He suggested New York City. "I really want to talk to you about the war," said the ambassador. "Just call me at the Waldorf when you get to town. But don't come within the next ten days. I'm leaving for Europe in a couple of days." I said, "I'll see you when you get back."

After Ambassador Stevenson had left the dressing room, I said to Jim Sanders, "I guess I'll find out what that's all about when I get to New York." Then I added nonchalantly, not really knowing what I meant, "If there is a New York!"

A few days later Adlai E. Stevenson dropped dead on the street in front of the American Embassy in London, apparently the victim of a heart attack. A photographer jumped in front of him, snapped his picture, and he dropped dead. Stevenson had no previous history of heart ailment nor was an autopsy performed. But evidently Ambassador Stevenson had been voicing his concern to others about American policy in Vietnam. David Schoenbrun, senior CBS correspondent in Europe, reported having dinner with Ambassadors Stevenson and Averell Harriman in Paris a few evenings before Ambassador Stevenson's death. At one point in the dinner conversation, Ambassador Stevenson is supposed to have said that he was finding it increasingly difficult in the United Nations to defend United States policy in Vietnam and the Dominican Republic.

A few days later in London, the night before his death, Ambassador Stevenson had dinner with Eric Sevareid. According to Mr. Sevareid, Ambassador Stevenson said, "I am going to quit. I can't take it any more. I have stayed only because everyone would take my resignation as an indication of my disagreement with our policy. I owe my country that much—to stay until some of this blows over and I can get out with a few of my ideals still left intact. But I tell you this, I can't take it more than two or three weeks."

It was only a matter of hours until Adlai Stevenson's opposition to United States foreign policy fell silent. In Chicago our march to City Hall became a silent vigil in his memory. Before the march we gathered in front of Buckingham Fountain in Grant Park, and I spoke to the marchers. I recalled the famous incident in 1962 when Adlai Stevenson had confronted Russian Ambassador Valerian Zorin on the floor of the United Nations. Ambassador Stevenson asked, "Do you deny that the USSR has placed missiles and sites in Cuba? Yes or no?" Ambassador Zorin replied, "In due course you will have your answer." Knowing that the Russian ambassador understood English, Adlai Stevenson said, "I am prepared to wait for my answer until hell freezes over."

I used Ambassador Stevenson's remark as my text. "Here in Chicago, we've been asking plain, simple questions of Mayor Daley for a long time now. Like Governor Stevenson, we're prepared to wait 'til hell freezes over for some answers. We're living in hell here in Chicago. And if we don't get some answers soon, it's not going to *freeze* over, it's going to *boil* over.

"Adlai Stevenson is dead. He was a man too big to play politics. A great and good soul is gone, but the evil that men do to one another lives after him. We march to protest against it."

On August 1 we made a dramatic and significant change in our parade route. We started marching to Mayor Daley's home in the Bridgeport section of Chicago. Bridgeport is a two mile square, lower middle class, almost exclusively white neighborhood, where Mayor Daley and his wife were born, and where the two mayors before Daley were also raised. It is a neighborhood of tiny bungalows, freshly painted iron fences, tidy lawns, and flower boxes. Bridgeport was the symbol of the Daley machine. About 900 political patronage civil servants lived in Bridgeport.

When we marched into Bridgeport the first night, Mayor Daley's neighbors were waiting for us. Some were gathered on the front porches in black face and minstrel garb, strumming banjos and singing,

> I'd like to be an Alabama trooper,
> That's what I would truly like to be,
> 'Cause if I were an Alabama trooper,
> I could kill the niggers legally.

Some turned on the sprinklers on their lawns in an attempt to dampen our spirits as we marched by. Others held Ku Klux Klan signs and hurled eggs and tomatoes, as well as insults, "Get back to the zoo."

On the second night, August 2, Mayor Daley's neighbors got so nasty that the police had to act. And they acted as the Chicago police so frequently acted—wrongly. We were marching around the square block in which Mayor Daley's house was located, singing "We Shall Overcome." The longer we marched, the more Mayor Daley's neighbors massed across the street to yell at us and harass us.

The police captain informed me that the crowd was getting very hostile and unruly and that he didn't think he could continue to guarantee police protection. He asked us to leave. I told him that it was the job of the police to protect us. We had gathered to exercise our constitutional right of peaceful protest and peaceful assembly. If we had to leave, we might just as well tear up the United States Constitution.

We continued to march. The mob grew more hostile, and the police grew more edgy. Again the police captain told me, "If you march around that block one more time, I really think all hell is going to break loose." I told him, "Let me handle it." I went down the line of march and told everybody to keep a watchful eye on the person in front, in back, and on either side of them. "If anybody looks like they're getting ready to throw a brick," I warned, "take it from them." I knew our line of march had been heavily infiltrated by police and government agents, and I didn't want one of them to create a situation.

It was beginning to get dark, so we quit singing. We didn't want to be charged with disturbing the peace. I was leading the line of march, with Lillian, Lynne, and Michele marching alongside. Little Lynne in her innocence couldn't understand the problem of protection. "Daddy, why doesn't Mayor Daley just ask us to come inside?" I wish Mayor Daley could have heard her innocent, trusting question. I would have liked to have heard his answer.

When we got to the corner, I changed strategy. Instead of turning and continuing around the block, I told the police captain, "All right, open 'em up. We're marching across the street." When he realized that I intended to march right through the angry white mob, the police captain was horrified. "You've got to be out of your mind," he exclaimed. I answered, "Well, you don't seem to be able to control the crowd. You've got to handle them with kid gloves because they're Mayor Daley's neighbors. If you can't control them, we will!"

I had noticed a difference in the mob reaction. When we had stopped singing, the mob had also become quieter. The cops moved ahead of us and started pushing people aside. We followed right behind. Our action had a strange effect upon the mob. When they saw that we were not afraid, they seemed to fade back in fear themselves. The mob was afraid of what it did not understand. As I walked through that mob, I saw the faces of a confused white America. I could read the questions in those bewildered eyes. How do they dare to come into the mayor's own neighborhood? How do the cops dare to protect them? Is nothing sacred anymore?

The cops were happy because they thought we were finally leaving the neighborhood. I marched straight ahead for about a block. Then I turned and started marching back. The cops were furious. We marched around Mayor Daley's house a few more times as the white mob began to reassemble across the street. I saw the cops huddling and conferring, and I knew we were about to be arrested.

Pretty soon the police captain stopped the march and said, "We can't control that mob any longer. We're going to arrest you for your own protection." I informed him once more of our constitutional guarantees.

He said, "I'm in charge here. I've always made it a practice to arrest the cause of a problem."

"Do you mean to tell me if we were at a baseball game, and

the crowd started rioting because they didn't like a decision the umpire had made, you would arrest the umpire for his own protection?"

"Yes, that's just what I would do."

"It won't hold up in court, you know."

"I think it will."

"Well, it won't hold up in the Supreme Court."

"We'll face that later."

The paddy wagons were brought in, and I was arrested along with sixty-five fellow demonstrators. None of the screaming white mob were arrested. The police captain was right. We were convicted in municipal court, and the conviction was upheld by the Illinois Supreme Court.

Four years later, my United States Constitution provided the final word. A brief was filed before the United States Supreme Court in the name of Dick Gregory, *et al.*, which concluded, "Defendants were convicted under an ordinance that is unconstitutional, charged with annoyance by their mere presence, with violence they did not provoke, and burdened with a baseless instruction that made the jury believe that they had violated some legal obligation. This Court should note the prejudice by the instruction, but should reverse outright and hold that the defendants, in the exercise of free speech, cannot be charged with the violence and disorder of their hecklers, and that the Chicago disorderly conduct ordinance is void for vagueness and unenforceable."

The United States Supreme Court agreed. Our conviction was reversed. As I had done many times before on the nightclub stage, I had the last word over the hecklers!

amily

Courtesy Johnson Publishing Company, Inc.

Dick Gregory, with Stephanie and Paula.

From the ground floor: the Gregorys, left to right, Paula, Stephanie, Pamela, Dick and Lillian with Gregory, Lynn, Michele.

Courtesy Johnson Publishing Company, Inc.

Courtesy Johnson Publishing Company, I

Whetting my son's appetite and satisfying mine: young Greg with his father; and cooking soy bean cutlets, Chicago (1972).

Courtesy Johnson Publishing Company,

ht: Taking the measure of
an: Big Mike Watley, who
ps the Gregory boat house
rder, Plymouth, Mass.

ow: The Gregorys on their
n near the boat house (1974).

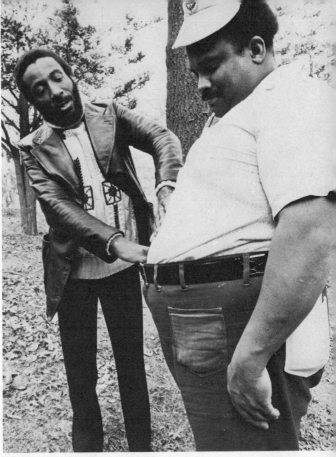

Courtesy Johnson Publishing Company, Inc.

Staff photo by G. Marshall Wilson, courtesy Johnson Publishing Company, Inc.

Family portrait: top row, left to right, Lynn, Michele;
second row, Stephanie, Pamela; third row, Dick Gregory,
Missy, Lillian with Yohance, Gregory; front, Christian,
Ayanna, Paula (1974).

19

Watts Happening, Baby?

I was playing a club called the Royal Tahitian in Ontario, California, about forty miles outside of Los Angeles, when all hell broke loose in Watts. Watts was the twenty-square-mile Black ghetto, a daily reminder that the mansions of Beverly Hills and the tinsel of Hollywood do not tell all of the Los Angeles story. The one- and two-story frame and stucco houses of Watts often contained four and five Black families, two-thirds of whom had less than a high school education, one-eighth of whom were technically illiterate. Only 13 percent of those houses had been built since 1939. Some 13 percent of the children in Watts were from broken homes, and the school dropout rate was 2.2 times the city's average.

I shared the bill at the Royal Tahitian with Sarah Vaughan. We were staying at the same motel. After the show on the third night, Sarah was driving back to the motel and I switched on the car radio. We heard the news. A riot had erupted in Watts after two white California state troopers had arrested a Black man for drunken driving. A scuffle occurred, and the troopers beat their prisoner while a crowd of Blacks stood by watching.

The crowd soon numbered more than a thousand. Rocks, bricks, bottles, slabs of asphalt and concrete were thrown at store windows and passing motorists. More than a hundred helmeted police, most of them white, rushed to the scene. A battle ensued. Some fifty vehicles were overturned, damaged, or burned, including two fire trucks. When the crowd dispersed at dawn, nineteen cops and sixteen civilians were officially reported as injured and thirty-four persons were arrested.

Later that morning I called Don Smith, chairman of the Los Angeles chapter of the Congress of Racial Equality (CORE), and arranged to visit the riot area. When I arrived on the scene, I saw something which told me the riot was far from over, even though the police were saying things were under control. I saw a different pattern from other riot areas I had been in. Windows of Black-owned businesses had been broken on a large scale. Black businesses had been looted and burned along with white businesses. I knew that this riot was not Black against white, but rather some angry, frustrated Black folks lashing out against a whole system of oppression.

It was hard to be funny that night. I joked about the riot, of course, but deep down I knew it was no laughing matter.

"I just want to say, this show is being taped tonight for our fighting forces in Watts. Coca Cola may be a soft drink manufacturer to you, but it's a prime defense contractor to us. I went over to Watts today. I saw a cat walk into a store and say, 'Give me six bottles of Coke, please.' The storekeeper said, 'To take with you?' The cat said, 'No, I'll throw 'em right here.' I won't say how many bottles are being thrown, but Imperial Highway is knee deep in deposits. The new status symbol in Watts is getting arrested for throwing a bottle—of Chivas Regal!

"Let me tell you how bad it was in Watts. I saw Clark Kent go into a phone booth, and he never came out! I saw the wildest things. I saw one cat running down the street with a couch on his back. I said, 'Hey, baby, you're not one of them looters, are you?' He said, 'Hell, no, man. I'm a psychiatrist on my way to a house call.'

"But I tell you what takes guts. Guts is a Watts storekeeper with a big front window—running an August White Sale! Everybody expected the rioting to spread to San Francisco, but I knew it wouldn't. Did you ever hear of anybody rioting uphill? And the sad part is, the cops still don't understand how it all happened. I heard one of them being interviewed today, and he told the reporter, 'I don't know why they're rioting. We've always treated our niggers with respect.'

"But I'll tell you who I feel sorry for. The folks from Hawaii. Can you imagine how it must feel being halfway between Vietnam and Watts?"

My instincts proved to be correct, and my worst fears were fulfilled. Thousands of Watts residents hit the streets that night, and at least 900 cops swarmed the area. Immediately after the last show, I went to Watts to see what I could do to help.

It was all-out war, a stark and horrible expression of raw

violence. The carnage bore a sickening similarity to the television news footage from Vietnam. I saw a man lying on the street, his head completely severed from his body. And I saw a little child tearfully approach that headless body that had been his father.

As in any war, the curious bystanders became accidental participants and innocent victims. I found myself in the area the police had designated as no-man's-land, between Central and Imperial Highway. A lull had momentarily descended, but a couple of hundred cops and state troopers had reassembled and were ready for action. There was a housing project across the street, and women and children were milling around in front of it.

The cops and state troopers were crouched behind parked cars facing the housing project. I was in the street with my back to the police, urging folks to get back inside. All of a sudden, a volley of about twenty shots came from the direction of the project. I heard the police behind me screaming, "Get back, Mr. Gregory!" But I kept walking toward the crowd. I decided that if the cops were going to shoot, they would have to shoot through my back.

I continued to plead with the people to get back inside. "There's a hundred cops across the street fixin' to wipe you all out. We can avoid a bloodbath. Get back inside!" Then, for the first time, I felt something warm trickling down my leg. I knew I was scared, but I didn't think I'd lost bladder control! Then I felt the burning sensation, and I realized I had been shot. I walked right up to one of the cats who had been doing the shooting and said, "All right, goddamit, brother. You had your fun. I been shot. Now get the hell out of here!"

The shock value worked. The crowd began to disperse, and, on that corner at least, we avoided a potential bloodbath.

But now I had another problem. I knew I should get to the hospital for treatment, but I also knew how rumors spread like wildfire. I didn't want the rumor to spread that I had been shot by the police. So I stayed on the street long enough for questions and answers until I was convinced people had the story straight.

"Hey, brother Greg, did those jive cops shoot you, man?"

"No, not this time, baby. Not this time."

"Oh, man. You know we weren't shootin' at you. We love you, baby."

"Good, now why don't you love yourself and each other enough to get back inside?"

A white cop came up to me after it was all over and said, "I've got a wife and kids at home too. I want to thank you for what you did tonight. As long as I live, I'll never forget it. I'll never forget you turning your back on our guns." It was like being eulogized while you're still alive.

I went to the emergency room and was treated for a flesh wound. But the next day front pages of newspapers all over the country blazoned the headline: DICK GREGORY SHOT. It was an eerie feeling.

I was a hero to many folks and a villain to some others. Some of the so-called Black militants said, "Nigger, you shoulda been killed out there tellin' Black folks not to riot!" But I knew the true story. And I knew what could have happened. Any armchair militant who talks about the ends justifying the means probably hasn't seen the horrible consequences of uncontrolled violence on the loose.

I knew I had saved many lives that night: Black lives and white lives, the lives of cops and the lives of civilians. But I also knew that I had to be willing to die to save those lives. I thought once again of the words to the "Battle Hymn of the Republic": "As he died to make men holy, let us *die* to make men free." Freedom is worth dying for, but nothing justifies killing.

20

Denting the Machine

I'd been hearing a lot about John Lindsay and his campaign for mayor of New York City. And I liked what I saw and heard. He was putting together a fusion ticket that cut across party lines and reminded everybody of the reform spirit of former New York City Mayor Fiorello LaGuardia. I felt that a John Lindsay victory in New York City could strike a blow against machine politics in cities all across the nation—especially Chicago.

I felt that John Lindsay had at least three things going for him. He was a Republican, which made him a good symbol to oppose

Democratic machine politics, which had dominated big cities since the days of the New Deal. He had the glamor, charm, and charisma to be a national figure and a personal favorite of the press. And, if he was elected mayor, John Lindsay would have to stay honest in office because ousted machine politicians would be watching him closely for evidence of corruption so they could expose him and get their power back.

Whitney Young, Jr., invited me to speak at a National Urban League luncheon at the Waldorf Astoria. When I took my place among the dais guests, I found myself in the company of none other than John Lindsay. I asked him if we could huddle for a few moments before he left the luncheon. John Lindsay was everything I had expected him to be. I remember telling him, "You're beautiful, baby. Just beautiful. But you're the dumbest cat I ever saw." Not that John Lindsay lacked intelligence. Far from it! But I looked upon him simply as an antimachine candidate. John Lindsay was so sweet, so innocent, and so dedicated, he really thought he could make some basic changes. And it was obvious that people sensed his personal warmth and compassion. He was one of the few political figures who could walk into a riot area and people would put down their bricks to shake hands with the mayor.

I told John I would give him all the help I could. I set aside three or four days, came into New York and hit the street corners in all the Black ghettos—Harlem, Bedford-Stuyvesant, the South Bronx, Jamaica. My message to my Black brothers and sisters was the same on every corner, "I've just come to say that you here in New York can help us in Chicago. And you can do yourselves a favor at the same time. If you break this political machine in New York by electing John Lindsay, it will make it easier for us to put a dent in that vicious Mayor Daley machine in Chicago." And the brothers and sisters understood what I was saying. When the votes were counted on election night, John Lindsay was the new mayor of New York City.

A few days after John Lindsay's victory, all the lights went out in New York City for a few hours. The blackout was caused by a failure in an east coast power plant. A couple of nights later I was performing at the Village Gate. I had fun with both Lindsay's victory and the blackout:

"Look, I know John Lindsay is charming, handsome, honest and dedicated. But the big question is, can he see in the dark? But

I want to say, even though John Lindsay got a lot of votes in the Black community, there were absolutely no deals made. And if you don't believe me, just ask the new police commissioner—Sonny Liston!"

A couple of weeks after John Lindsay's inauguration, I launched my new and short-lived career as a movie star. The world premiere of *Sweet Love, Bitter* was held at the Carnegie Hall Cinema, Monday evening, January 30, 1966. The magic spell of the event was enhanced by the attendance of the new mayor of New York City.

Mayor Lindsay came into office faced with a desk-load of problems. The subway workers were on strike as he took the oath of office. Then Mayor Lindsay cracked down on illegal parking in midtown, strictly enforcing tow-away regulations and fines. The tow-away crackdown brought all kinds of protest, including a demonstration outside city hall by handicapped individuals.

So, as Mayor Lindsay and I were smiling for photographers in the lobby of the Carnegie Hall Cinema, Art Steuer couldn't resist his little joke. Art came rushing up to John Lindsay and said, "Mr. Mayor, I just wanted to tell you that two paraplegics just hooked their braces to your limousine and they're towing it away!"

I really appreciated John Lindsay's presence at my world premiere. He added that special touch of glamor and excitement. And my artist friend Brahim Ben Benu had arranged a magnificent display of his works in the lobby, giving the premiere a unique Black cultural flavor.

It was a great evening. I was seeing the movie for the first time. As I sat watching myself on the screen, I went back in memory to my childhood. I remembered the excitement of the movie changing at the theater each week and seeing my favorite actors and actresses on the big screen—Ava Gardner, Alan Ladd, Humphrey Bogart, Clark Gable. Now I was seeing myself on that screen, bigger than life, and it was a funny, beautiful, exciting feeling. I wondered if Ava, Alan, Humphrey, and Clark had the same feelings when they saw themselves in movies!

It brought tears to my eyes to remember the movie fantasy world I had lived in as a kid. I didn't separate the script from reality, the actors and actresses from the roles they played. Movies were an escape, a brief respite from poverty and pain. But, of course, movies didn't solve any problems. Whatever problems I had when I came into the theater were always out there waiting for me after the movie was over.

Now I could differentiate between performance and reality. I was up there on the screen, playing a role, but it wasn't me. I was sitting in the theater. At the end of the movie, I died on the screen. But I was very much alive sitting in the theater. No matter how much I enjoyed my own performance, it had no effect upon my real life problems and responsibilities. I thought to myself, "Gee, maybe in real life, Clark Gable really *did* give a damn!"

When I read the movie reviews, the tears welled up again. Judith Crist wrote in the New York *World Journal Tribune:* "*Sweet Love, Bitter* is probably one of the most realistic and trenchant explorations we have had to date of the mystique of the Negro jazz musician, monkey on his back, music in his soul, agony in his heart, and society at his heels . . . brought to complex life by Dick Gregory, who displays in this film an impressive dramatic potential. . . . He is convincing every step of the way, whether . . . in an agony of clowning away anguish or in the throes of making music. He does a brilliant and touching job."

Hollis Alpert wrote in the *Saturday Review:* "Dick Gregory plays with surprising conviction and considerable realism and now adds movie stardom to his other attainments." And Archer Winston wrote in the *New York Post:* "One has the impression that Dick Gregory, the stand-up comedian and serious civil rights fighter, has carved a new career for himself. His acting shows deep conviction and fine camera presence."

I never made another movie. There were a few other "careers" waiting in my future.

21

Who's Who???

It's a standing joke with my wife and my closest friends about how I never recognize or remember the names of famous folks—

especially people in show business. I suppose the classic example of my nonrecognition occurred during one of the trips my wife and I made to London.

Folks in London are just the opposite of me. They recognize everybody who is anybody at all. I had appeared many times on British television with David Frost, Eammon Andrews, and others. So I was a recognizable celebrity in London. Everywhere Lillian and I went we attracted a crowd. Folks would stand outside our hotel waiting for us to come out. When we emerged, they would follow us wherever we went.

One day we were walking down the street, accompanied by our little following, when I suddenly realized I had to make a phone call. London is not like New York City, where there's a phone booth on almost every corner. You have to hunt for a phone in London. I saw a building that looked like a hospital, and I was sure there must be a public phone inside. We went in and our entourage waited outside.

When we came back out, we noticed strange looks on people's faces. They were whispering, some were giggling, and we wondered what it was all about. I happened to mention the incident to a friend who lived in London. He asked, "Where did you say you made that phone call?"

I repeated the location.

"No wonder! That's the V.D. clinic."

We happened to be in London on the night of an annual charity benefit given by the Queen Mother at the London Palladium. The show was loaded with American stars—Sammy Davis, Jr., Jerry Lewis, Wayne Newton. I got the most expensive tickets, assuming I would be way down front where I could see Sammy real good. I didn't realize that choice seats for folks in London are further up, where you can look into the royal box and see what the Queen or the Queen Mother is wearing.

Lil and I were a conspicuous isle of Blackness in the sea of white folks surrounding us. I doubt that very many Blacks, if any, ever sat in such choice seats at a royal affair. It also happened to be at the time of the Rhodesian crisis, and there was a lot of tension and uptightness in London. Our presence and our seat location must have looked suspicious. I began to notice out of the corner of my eye that there was a lot of activity going on around us. People would get up and leave their seats, and others would come and take their places—always men in formal attire.

The Queen Mother arrived. Everybody stood up—except Lil! We all began singing "God Save the Queen," but Lil remained firmly and stubbornly planted in her seat. A guy behind me leaned over and whispered, "Pardon me, old chap. But it is customary to stand when 'God Save the Queen' is being played." I said, "Well, man, why don't you tell that to that colored woman sittin' next to me. I'm standin' and I'm singin'. Why you got to assume we're together?" He apologized and admitted that he had made that assumption. By the time we finished our little dialogue on Black independent action, the song was over.

I sat down and said to Lil, "Wow, baby, why didn't you tell me? I'm all for you protesting any time you want to. But at least let me know."

Lil answered, "Oh Greg, I'm so sorry and so embarrassed. My gown was caught in the seat and I *couldn't* stand up." I had thought Lil was protesting, but she was really trying to keep from streaking.

After the show we went to the Playboy Club. We spent some time talking with Victor Lownes, manager of the London club whom I knew very well from his days in Chicago, and then we went upstairs to the penthouse. A man left his table across the room and came over to where Lil and I were sitting. He was humble and apologetic for intruding into our conversation, literally kneeling down in front of me as he said, "I really admire you. I can't tell you how much I admire you."

I thought I recognized him as a Puerto Rican guy who used to work at the Chicago Playboy Club. I assumed he was now working in the London club and that he was enjoying a night off as a patron rather than an employee. I was embarrassed by the open display of adulation, and I really didn't know what to say. I introduced him to my wife and invited him to join us for a drink. He declined, saying he was with another party, and he left our table.

I noticed that Lil had an attitude. "What's wrong with you?"

"You didn't have to be so cold and abrupt toward him."

"What you talking about?"

"You could have been more friendly. You know who he was."

"Sure I know. He's a Puerto Rican guy who used to wash dishes at the Playboy Club in Chicago. I invited him to have a drink with us."

Lil just shook her head. "Greg, that was Omar Sharif."

One night Jim McGraw and I went to the Elysée Theatre in New York City for a benefit telethon for Channel 13, New York's Public Broadcasting Station. The show was called "Thirteen Stars for Channel 13." Garry Moore was the host and I was one of the stars. As we entered the stage door, I noticed a white lady relaxing on a couch. She was obviously known by the other people backstage. As she spotted me walking in she said, "Oh Richard, dah-ling! It's so good to see you. We're so proud of what you are doing." I smiled, embraced her, thanked her, and otherwise exchanged pleasantries.

As Jim and I went out into the audience to watch the first half, before my own spot, McGraw said, "Gee, Dick, I didn't know you knew Tallulah Bankhead."

I said, "Who?"

"Tallulah Bankhead. The lady you were just hugging and talking to backstage."

"Is that who that was? I thought it was a rich white lady who had given some money to Channel 13. I was just bein' nice to her."

My recognition problems most frequently take place on airplanes. One afternoon I was seated on a plane waiting for takeoff. A guy walked down the aisle, recognized me, and asked if the seat next to me was taken. It wasn't and he sat down. He had reddish hair and looked very familiar. It was obvious that he assumed I knew him. I figured it was an agent or a producer I had met some time before.

We got into a heavy conversation about everything—the economy, the food crisis, all the things going on in the country and in the world. He seemed fascinated, which was all the encouragement I needed. I really enjoyed talking to him. I was embarrassed to ask his name so I asked him to write down his name and address so I could send him a copy of a book we had been talking about when I got home. He did. It was Red Buttons.

Another time on a plane, a couple of Black brothers came over to me, introduced themselves, and I understood them to say, "We're the pimps." It really took me by surprise. Then they started telling me how much they admired me, praising me for the sacrifices I had made, and so on. I thought to myself, "I wonder when pimps got so bold? And I wonder what makes me so popular with pimps?"

One of the guys pointed to a Black lady seated further back. "There's Gladys sitting back there." Since they were pimps, you can imagine who I thought Gladys was. I wondered if I was as popular with Gladys's crowd as I was with them pimps.

When I arrived at my destination, I picked up a newspaper and read the advertisement for a concert that night, starring Gladys Knight and the Pips!

22

Sole Power

At the end of January I was playing a club called the Edgewater Inn in Seattle, when I suddenly found myself involved in a whole new kind of demonstration. Some Black folks who were familiar with Indians' problems in the state of Washington came to see my show, and they heard me include some lines about Indians.

"I saw on television the other night where your state troopers had a battle with the Indians over whether or not they could fish. So I called the state trooper office and told them they better leave those Indians alone. 'Cause those Indians don't sing 'We Shall Overcome.' They do the 'Tomahawk Concerto!'

"But one of these days, the Indians are really going to raise hell in this state. I can see it coming. Of course, I'm not worried about 'us.' 'Cause I ain't never heard of a colored cat being scalped.

"But really, some of my best friends are Indians. And every Brotherhood Week I take an Indian out to lunch. We have a good time, sitting around talking about what a hell of a fighter Geronimo was. A real credit to his race!"

After the show some of the Black folks from the audience came to my dressing room. They asked if I'd be interested in hearing about the problems Indians were having in Thurston County firsthand. I said, "By all means." So the next day they took me to a powwow.

I learned that the Nisqually Indians were fighting with the state of Washington over treaty rights. The Nisqually tribe has had a treaty with the United States government for over a hundred years, which gives them the right to fish in any water, using any means. But the state of Washington did not see fit to honor the treaty obligation. The state allowed the Indians to fish, but prohibited their fishing with a net. The state insisted that Indians must fish with a hook. As a result, out of all the steelhead fish being caught by the state's three types of fishers—commercial, sports, and Indian—Indians ended up catching less than 2 percent of the total.

The prohibition against fishing with a net ensured a pitifully small catch, due to the peculiar habits of the fish. Wherever a steelhead is born, it will return to that same area at spawning time. The fish may travel all the way to Tokyo, but they are sure to be back home to lay their eggs and die. Also, at spawning time the fish don't have an appetite. So fishing with a hook is an exercise in futility. But sports fishers come out with their hooks and lines anyway and spend a great deal of money trying to break the fish's fast. And, of course, the whole game helps the economy of the state of Washington.

The powwow was sponsored by an organization called The Survival of the American Indians. I told representatives that I would participate in a fish-in with them as soon as my engagement was over at the Edgewater Inn. I wanted to use whatever publicity value my celebrity status provided to focus attention upon treaty rights and other Indian problems. I had remembered the publicity surrounding Marlon Brando's arrest a couple of years before, when he joined the Indians in a fish-in on Washington's Puyallup River. I also remembered the prosecutor's dropping charges against Marlon and saying, "I don't see any purpose in allowing Brando to sit in jail and make a martyr of himself."

So, the morning after my closing night at the club, I went fishing with the Indians. But I had a problem. A few months before I had become a vegetarian. It happened all of a sudden one night as I was sitting in a San Francisco hotel room in the wee small hours of the morning talking with Jim Sanders. I told Jim that I had become convinced that killing animals for food was immoral and unnatural. I just couldn't accept any longer that it was right or necessary for human beings to kill something to get their dinner. And I also felt that for the commandment "Thou shalt not kill" to mean anything, it had to be applied across the boards, with *no* exceptions. Right then and there, I decided it was wrong to eat meat.

So I told my fellow fishers that I didn't want to kill any fish.

They said that was no problem. They had a couple of fish that were already dead. All I had to do was pull in a net with the dead fish already in it.

We went to a place called Frank's Landing and went out on the Nisqually River. And it was cold. I couldn't swim and I had always been afraid of water. And here I was trying to demonstrate in a canoe! I told my companions, "If this canoe tips over, you all grab me. We'll worry about the fish later!"

Of course, our every move was being carefully watched by game wardens. We threw our net overboard, with the dead fish in it, and pulled the net back in the canoe. When we got back to shore, we were arrested. I went to jail, got out, and went fishing again. Again, I went back to jail. This time it was harder to get out. I had established a reputation as a repeating offender.

Before long, telegrams started coming to the jail, such as:

Dear Dick: You are to be congratulated on the forthright stand which you have taken in the cause of human justice on behalf of another oppressed minority, the Nisqually Indians. Feel assured that my prayers and best wishes are with you in this matter, and any support I can render is yours. Sincerely, Martin Luther King, Jr.

Dear Greg: At last! An American Negro has made common cause with Indian brothers. I applaud your action and have demanded immediate federal investigation. Jim Farmer

Dick Gregory, Thurston County Jail: Fully support stand on fishing rights. Stop. Have cabled [President] Johnson for your release. Stop. Kind regards. Bertrand Russell.

I also received telegrams of support from the United Federation of Teachers and the United Federation of College Teachers in New York City. I called Lillian and asked her to come out and join the fish-in. She had never fished before in her life, but she came to Washington to fish with the Indians. She fished twice and was arrested twice. I got out of jail and went fishing one more time.

The fish-in got a great deal of newspaper coverage. Radio and television talk shows began taking a hard look at the problem. College students began demonstrating on behalf of Indian rights. And so many Black folks came to me and expressed their admiration for what I was doing for the Indians. The fish-in seemed to help them recognize that oppression and racism were bigger than just the Black struggle; that civil rights was only a part of the larger issue of human rights.

On the Monday afternoon after Thanksgiving, Lillian and I were back in the Thurston County Superior Court for our trial on five counts of illegal fishing. A five-man, seven-woman jury was selected. My lawyer, Jack Tanner, moved to have the list of prospective jurors thrown out because it included no Indians. Judge Hewitt A. Henry denied the motion, saying that Tanner had failed to show a specific instance where an Indian was denied the right to serve.

While the jury was being selected inside, the real show was in the halls of the courthouse. I had some of the most colorful sympathizers ever assembled in the history of trials. There was Mad Bear Anderson, who represented the Six Nation Iroquois Confederation; Semu, the last of the Chumash medicine men, accompanied by one of his followers, Messenger Boy; and Jay Silverheels, the Lone Ranger's sidekick "Tonto" on television. The press was fascinated by the full Indian regalia, and perhaps also a little frightened. Messenger Boy claimed that Semu had been responsible for the Thanksgiving Eve power failure, which left downtown Seattle in darkness. Semu modestly disclaimed all responsibility, professing only the power to heal the sick.

County prosecutor Harold Koch paraded a number of game wardens onto the witness stand to testify. The first game warden, Bill Streeter, said he had been maintaining a vigil on the banks of the Nisqually River, across from Frank's Landing, on February 6. "About 80 people were gathered on the bank," Streeter testified. "A dugout containing Gregory and two Indians left the shore and headed for midstream where all three handled the net. They caught two steelhead." Brother Streeter had caught me in the act of reclaiming our dead fish!

Jack Tanner made my purpose clear in his opening statement to the jury: "He agreed to lend his name to anything that would help them [the Indians] obtain their rights. It was never a matter of catching a fish. Anything he participated in was to publicize the plight of the Indians and their treaty rights. His whole purpose was to draw public attention to the Indian situation here."

When I got on the stand, prosecutor Koch accused me of not

caring at all about the plight of the Indians, but merely seeking publicity for myself.

"Isn't it a fact," the prosecutor asked, "that you personally called the press before each fish-in?"

I answered, "I would have had to be out of my mind not to place the right phone calls before going out to fish." The prosecutor pointed out that these right phone calls went to two national wire services and a major television network.

I also told the jury about the two dead fish. "When we went to the net," I testified, "we wanted a guarantee that some fish would be there. If we didn't catch anything, we wouldn't get any publicity, and that's why I'm here."

When the jury returned, Lillian and I were found guilty. I was guilty on three counts of illegal fishing, and Lillian was guilty on two. In handing down the sentence, Judge Henry suspended the sentence against Lillian, citing our large family and the need of the children to have their mother's care. But he gave me ninety days in jail on each charge, to run concurrently.

I asked, "What about the kids' need for their father's care? Who's going to earn the money for rent and food while I'm in jail?" But the judge held firm, and Jack Tanner began the long process of appealing the conviction.

23

Al Lingo Revisited

May 3, 1966. It's seven o'clock in the evening, one year after the Selma-to-Montgomery March. Nearly a quarter of a million Blacks are now registered voters in Alabama, and here I am, on the eve of the Democratic primary election, sitting behind the pulpit in a Black church in Huntsville, Alabama, waiting my turn to speak at a rally.

Hosea Williams of the Southern Christian Leadership Con-

ference had asked me to come down. All the candidates, white and
Black, were on hand to court the new Black vote. In talking with
Hosea, I learned that Al Lingo had some kind of falling out with
George Wallace, and Al was not running for his old job as head of
the Alabama state police. Instead, he was running for sheriff. Jim
Clark was also running for reelection. George Wallace couldn't
run for reelection, so his wife, Lurleen, was running instead. I also
learned from Hosea that the Southern Christian Leadership
Conference was supporting Al Lingo's candidacy. It seems Al had
promised to appoint a Black deputy if he was elected.

Just as the rally was about to begin, Al Lingo entered the
church. He saw me sitting on the platform. His smile and greeting
reflected an attitude of friendly apprehension. Al Lingo knew that
I was both uncontrollable and unpredictable. I smiled back and
said, "Come on up and sit down, Brother Al!"

I was really turned on that night in the presence of that new
southern Black voting strength. It was a beautiful sight, and when
my turn came to speak, I tried to tell those new Black voters how
important they were to Black folks up North.

"I was in Birmingham last night, and honest to God, it was the
first time I ever closed my eyes in Alabama. I'm more afraid now
in Chicago than I am in this state, believe me. This state has
changed. I ain't talking about thirty or forty years. This state has
changed in a few months, and it will change some more.

"Do you know you all have embarrassed Negroes and white
folks so bad up North? You remember Watts? Them niggers got so
mad at seeing you all getting all those goodies down here! And the
white folks is scared 'cause they been tricking us for so long by
telling us that we was better off than you. And we believed it!

"Now all of a sudden, we look around, and here you are talking
about a colored sheriff! Have you ever heard of a Northern town
with a colored sheriff? You all got kinfolks up there that write you.
Did any of them ever mention a colored sheriff?

"You see, up North we've had the right to *elect*, but we never
had the right to *select*. And I'll tell you something else. Up North,
we ain't never made that white man scared enough to make him
run home and get his wife to do anything. And if George Wallace
had been a bachelor, he'd have run home and got his momma!

"The whole world's gonna be watching your election tomorrow, 'cause the whole world knows it ain't been treatin' Black

folks right. The world will be watchin' your elections as previews of coming attractions of what's about to happen to them.

"Election day is a time to live up to the white folks' image of us. All our lives we've heard white folks say, 'All colored folks want to do is have fun—they're irresponsible.'

"Well, tomorrow, live up to that image! Don't dress up. Be yourself. Take your wig off and let folks see your nappy hair. Eat biscuits for breakfast and leave the syrup on your hands. Wear your work clothes and leave the mud on your overalls. Voting is your real right, so do it as your real self!

"My only regret is that I'm not a registered voter in Alabama. I'd be at the polls tomorrow *before* early. I'd be there fightin' everybody who was ahead of me, just so I could be the first one to shoot that juice through the machine. And I'd bring a crowd with me. I'd bring a gang. Because tomorrow, the Negro vote is the only vote that really counts. 'Cause it's the *new* one."

Then I turned my attention to the endorsement of individual candidates. I said, "Before I close, let me say a word about Al Lingo, because Brother Al and I go way back together." Al Lingo smiled, figuring I was going to emphasize the SCLC endorsement. "I know Al Lingo so well," I continued, "that I'd not only endorse him, I'd take a stick and make you all vote for him." Al was really beaming now, not realizing what was coming next.

"That is, if he were running for any other office than one which requires him to carry a gun! If he wanted to run for tax collector, if he wanted to run for genius, I'd back him up on anything, if only he didn't get a gun in his hand. I know how this fella acts with a gun in his hand. This is the one cat I wouldn't trust with no gun. No guns, no bullets, no clubs."

Al had stopped smiling, and I remembered his phone call to me in Chicago. I remembered his saying that a sheriff was not a sheriff until he's tangled with me. And I thought to myself, "That goes for candidates, too, boy!"

The next day, more than 80 percent of Alabama's registered Black voters showed up at the polls. Lurleen Wallace received the Democratic nomination for Governor. But both Al Lingo and Jim Clark lost their bids for reelection.

24

Marching against Fear

A month later, I had just returned home to Chicago from California when I heard the news on the radio: James Meredith had been shot! He was walking along Highway 51, just outside Hernando, Mississippi, when the shotgun blast came.

Like so many others who heard the shocking news, I didn't know if he was dead or wounded. But I was determined to get to the scene of the crime as quickly as possible. I felt there was a lot at stake for the civil rights movement. James Meredith had begun his solitary walk as a "march against fear." If his being shot down was permitted to create a resurgence of fear among Black folks in the South, I was afraid there was a possibility of our losing all the advances we had made so far.

I told Lil, "Call Delta Airlines and get me a reservation. I'm going down there. I'd like for you to go with me, but I want you to think about it first. You have to consider there's a real possibility we might be killed." As always, Lil wanted to go in spite of the danger.

I sent a telegram to President Johnson, with a copy to Attorney General Nicholas Katzenbach, and released it to the press. I said that Lillian and I would take up James Meredith's walk from the point where he was shot and march for eight hours, a full working day. I included our flight number, departure time from Chicago, and scheduled arrival time in Memphis. I also added these lines: "James Meredith could have walked anywhere in the world without being shot because America would not stand for that. He could not walk in the South and he was shot in Mississippi because America does stand for it."

Word gets around Chicago very quickly, and by the time Lillian and I arrived at the Delta terminal at O'Hare Airport, a huge crowd of well-wishers had assembled. It was unreal! It looked like everybody we'd ever met in Chicago was there to see us off. And they were all scared. Folks tried to cover their fear by saying, "Hey, good luck, baby." But I could see in their eyes and hear in their voices that they really thought they were saying, "Good-bye, baby."

On the way down on the plane, I thought about James Meredith. I had known him for quite some time, since those hectic days in the summer of 1962 when Mississippi Governor Ross Barnett literally blocked his entrance into the University of Mississippi. It took action by President Kennedy to open the Ole Miss doors to James Meredith. The president federalized the Mississippi National Guard and had a detachment of U.S. Army troops on stand-by alert in Memphis. James Meredith later indicated that he might drop out of school. That's when President Kennedy and Bobby Kennedy and I had become the closest. JFK and Bobby felt it would be a political disaster if James decided to quit, and they put pressure on me to exert whatever influence I could to get him to stay in school.

I always had a lot of respect for James Meredith. I knew what he had to go through to integrate the University of Mississippi. I respected his strength and courage and singularity of purpose. And I developed a close relationship with James Meredith and his good friend James Allen.

James Meredith had a lot of folks worrying about his status in the University of Mississippi. The president and the attorney general were worried that he would drop out. And Black folks all over the country were worried that he would flunk out! But I knew that would never happen legitimately. Because I knew what kind of mind James Meredith had. Once, when he was visiting my apartment in Chicago, I had given him a book to read. A little bit later in conversation, I referred to the material in the book, and I was amazed that James could recite it word for word. He had a photographic memory.

James Meredith stayed in school and graduated. But he continued to keep folks holding their breath. At the end of the first semester, he held a press conference and announced that he had concluded that "the 'Negro' should not return," but he went on to say, "However, I have decided that I, J. H. Meredith, will register for the second semester."

When we got to Memphis, we visited James Meredith at the William F. Bowld Hospital. I was his first outside visitor. His other visitors had been with him on the march. He told me that he had awakened after his first fitful night's sleep to see a huge bouquet on a shelf across the room. Lillian and I had sent it to him.

I was surprised to see James in such good condition. But since I had first thought he was dead, I guess anything short of a corpse looked good to me. James thanked me for coming down and said he would some day complete the march. He emphasized that nobody should let fear keep them from marching.

My original intention had been to pick up James Meredith's route from the point where he was shot down and continue the march. But I decided instead to go to the place where he fell and retrace his steps back to Memphis. James had passed many Black folks in the fields and along the side of the road. They had waved at him and been inspired and uplifted by his courage. I felt it was very important for these same Black folks to see someone else marching along the same path, in spite of what had happened to James Meredith. I did not want fear to become the victor.

We rented cars and drove along Highway 51. Lillian and I had been joined by a few others including Frank Ditto from Chicago and Stanley Branch. I suddenly realized we might not be able to determine the exact spot where James Meredith had fallen. I needn't have worried. The blood was still on the highway. Across the road a Mississippi state patrol car was parked. I went over to talk to the troopers and heard the following conversation on the car radio:

"Dick Gregory's party just arrived."

"How you goin' to handle it?"

"The same way we did before!"

I was determined to march against fear, but that conversation scared me to death! But the trooper put out his hand to shake mine and said, "It's a pleasure to meet you. A lot of people are upset because you're down here. But I'm one who's glad you're here and I appreciate your being here. You're doing what has to be done." My fear dissolved, and I realized I'd misinterpreted the radio conversation. I was also comforted by the large number of federal marshals, and I knew the attorney general had received my telegram.

We started walking toward Memphis, and for the first time, I had second thoughts about what I was doing out there on the highway. I wondered if I had acted hastily, or if this action really made sense. Any doubts I had were erased by the reactions of the folks along the way. Black field hands, standing with their white employers, waved from a distance. And, now and then, a wave would turn into a clenched fist, and I knew fear had lost the battle. Other folks ran down to the fence, smiling and waving and shouting encouragement.

As we walked along, more and more FBI agents and Justice Department officials appeared on the scene. And my fear started playing games with me again. I kept wondering where a shot would hit me if it came. In the head? In the shoulder? Would I have any warning? Would I have a chance of surviving?

And then I looked at Lil and the others, and I saw true civil rights soldiers! They couldn't have cared less about any violent haters who might be lurking in the bushes. And the farther we walked, the more people came up and asked if they could march along. Before I realized it, our line of march had grown to nearly three hundred people.

Then my fear disappeared completely. I realized it had not really been caused by the potential hate of white folks. My fear was really an anxiety about the fear other Black folks might have. But when I saw my beautiful southern Black brothers and sisters, clamoring to be on that line of march, with tears in their eyes and carrying their kids on their shoulders, thanking me over and over again for being there, I knew a new day of fearless pride had dawned in Mississippi. I realized also that my picking up James Meredith's March against Fear had really been a march against my own fears and apprehensions. And those fears have never returned.

I had another realization as I walked along that Mississippi highway. I suddenly recognized that individual reactions are determined largely by a person's economic conditions. When I heard that James Meredith had been shot, and possibly killed, I was angry. And I expressed that anger by reaching in my pocket and pulling out my credit card and making an airline reservation.

Other Black folks didn't have the luxury of that reaction. When they heard that James Meredith had been shot, they were angry too. And they had to react. So they reached down and picked up a brick and broke some windows. I'm sure they would much rather have been with me, putting their bodies on the line where the real action was. But they couldn't afford to make the trip, so they grabbed the closest thing at hand. I realized that my credit card was my brick and my pistol.

While I was marching back to Memphis, James Meredith was being visited off and on in his hospital room by a galaxy of civil rights stars: Dr. Martin Luther King, Jr.; Floyd McKissick, national director of CORE; Stokely Carmichael, chairman of SNCC; Charles Evers; Whitney Young, executive director of the Urban League; and Roy Wilkins, executive secretary of the NAACP. Plans were afoot to resume the 250-mile march originally planned by James Meredith. Over the next twenty days, the Meredith March against Fear was continued by an assortment of civil rights groups. I returned to Chicago, and James Meredith went back to New York.

I kept in touch with James over the next couple of weeks. He had vowed to return to the march, but he hadn't set a date. We both decided to go back to Mississippi on Friday of the last weekend of the march. The march was to end at the state capitol in Jackson on Sunday, so we figured on two days of marching if James felt up to it. Then we held a few press conferences to announce the return of James Meredith to Mississippi.

When we got to Mississippi, we discovered that the Saturday leg of the march had been canceled. All the members and the leaders were in Tougaloo, staying at the university. A big outdoor rally was planned for Saturday night.

But James Meredith had promised to walk from Canton to Jackson, and he was determined to live up to his promise, in spite of the decisions made by those who had taken over his march. Early Saturday morning James and I and a tiny group of loyalists gathered outside the Madison County courthouse in Canton. Claude Brown, author of the bestseller *Manchild in the Promised Land*, was with us, since he was on assignment from *Life* magazine.

The Mississippi Highway Patrol had refused to give any protection whatsoever. So James went inside the courthouse to take the matter up with Sheriff Jack Cauthen. The sheriff agreed to provide police protection to the city limits. Beyond that point, he could make no guarantee.

We began walking toward the city limits, our numbers growing as word began to spread that James Meredith was back and was on the move. Before we got out of town, Charles Sims and some of the members of his Louisiana-based Deacons for Defense joined our ranks. Other Deacons drove alongside in automobiles.

At the city limits police jurisdiction changed. James Meredith was stopped by a Mississippi state trooper. James made it clear that he intended to continue walking, with or without police protection. But James had also been quoted earlier to the effect that he might be armed when he returned to Mississippi again. So the state trooper drawled, "I have to ask, are you armed?"

James had come dressed for the occasion. He was wearing a pith helmet and carrying an ebony-and-ivory cane which had been given to him by a village chief on the banks of the Nile River in the Sudan. He looked like a parody of the white safari leader in all those old Tarzan movies. James answered the trooper by dramatically raising his arms above his head, cane and all, and offering to be searched. Of course, he was unarmed. But I had to chuckle to myself. The Deacons for Defense had carbines in the back seat of every one of those automobiles!

The march continued, swelling by more and more hundreds as the hot afternoon wore on. By midday, all the other march leaders came running out to meet us. And we all marched back to Tougaloo to the step of James Meredith. The March against Fear was back in his hands.

That night, we had a great show at Tougaloo. The civil rights stalwarts from show business were in the march. Marlon Brando was there, as were Burt Lancaster and Tony Franciosa. James Brown had a concert that night in Cincinnati, but he flew down in his private jet to entertain the Tougaloo folks first. Sammy Davis, Jr., also came down between engagements to be on the show. I was master of ceremonies, and I did a comedy bit. As always with an audience of my fellow civil rights soldiers, I really had a ball.

"You all sure have got folks shook up with these two words 'Black Power.' I get on a crowded bus the other day, and there were no seats. I just shouted, 'Black Power!' and two little old ladies got up to give me their seats. And they were colored ladies!

"But I don't know why the words 'Black Power' should upset folks. Hell, we've always had Black Power. Joe Louis had the fastest right hand in the history of boxing. That's Black Power. Jackie Robinson had a lifetime batting average of over three hundred. That's Black Power. Sidney Poitier won an Academy Award. That's Black Power. And if my wife ever divorces me, she's going to get everything I own. That's 'sho-nuff' Black Power!

"Black Power's cool, but sometimes you gotta use other techniques. I was down here in Mississippi a couple of months ago, just before Easter. As soon as I got off the plane, the old redneck sheriff grabbed me and said, 'Boy, what'd you give up for Lent?' I told him, 'Nonviolence.'

"But then there are other times when you've got to do a little tommin'. If you don't like to be thought of as an Uncle Tom, think of it as your civil rights survival kit! I remember one time I was down here in Mississippi, and as I was leavin', the sheriff chased me all the way to the airport. I was just enough ahead of him to make it out of town. I went up to the airline counter and said, 'Reservations for Dick Gregory.' The white cat behind the counter said, 'We ain't got no reservations for no damn Dick Gregory!' I scratched my head, shuffled a little closer, and said, 'Mr. Gregory sure is gonna be mad!' "

The next day we marched into Jackson and to the state capitol. And there were beautiful sights along the way. It seemed as though white folks also had lost their fear. They came out with Kool Aid and soda pop for the marchers, and on some lawns were signs saying, "You can use the rest room here." Other signs were more universal, saying, "God Bless You."

The march to the state capitol was the beginning of a new mood of solidarity. Whereas "We Shall Overcome" had been the predominant slogan of previous marches, the words "Black Power" and "Black Is Beautiful" were the new phrases of freedom. The clenched-fist salute emerged as a means of communication. It became the body language of brotherhood and sisterhood, a sign of empathy and identity. To those who had reason to fear Black anger and frustration, the clenched fist was a threat. But to those in the know, it was a sign of affection and solidarity.

It meant "I love you, baby, and I identify with your suffering." And it soon spread beyond the Black community into the white youth culture. It became a handshake and a greeting, a symbol which transcended race and color. The clenched-fist salute and the soul-grip handshake became shared reminders that Blackness is not a color, but rather an attitude.

Stokely Carmichael and these young kids from SNCC deserve credit for moving the March against Fear on up to a higher level. Stokely recognized that a white racist system in America included Black folks as well as white folks. Black folks living under that system learned to both like and hate the same things white folks liked and hated. Consequently, there has always been a tremendous amount of hostility, envy, conniving and self-hate among

Blacks, focused upon each other. Before the clenched-fist salute and the soul handshake, Blacks didn't speak to one another, or greet one another in a way which recognized their common bond of Blackness.

Stokely changed all that. He was the first one to say "Black is beautiful" and sound like he really meant it. For the first time, all Blacks were lumped together in common solidarity; dark-skinned Black folks and light-complexioned Black folks. As Blacks began to internalize that phrase, "Black is beautiful," the fear of Blackness as a problem began to melt away. Resentment against lighter-skinned Black folks by darker-skinned Black folks began to disappear. White folks didn't look as glamorous as they once did. The false need to try to hide and cover up our Blackness was gone. We could just be ourselves, and proud of it. Black folks began to realize, "If it's true that Black *is* beautiful, then what I have felt all along is also true. I am somebody!"

Stokely made Black folks realize that our Blackness was not the problem. The problem was being Black *in a racist system.* In so doing, Stokely helped us all to grow "up from nigger." And things will never be the same again.

After the march, James Meredith and I did a couple of benefits together. We had announced them before returning to Mississippi. The benefits were to help defray some of the personal expenses James had incurred because of the march. The first benefit was a concert at the Kiel Auditorium in Saint Louis, featuring Mahalia Jackson.

And Mahalia was so beautiful that Sunday afternoon. She told me, "I don't want no money or no travel expenses. I'm just glad to be here. And I just thank God for people like you and James Meredith." As always, Mahalia sang from her heart and her deep soul. It was too bad there wasn't a larger crowd to hear her. But we had made a scheduling error. We were competing against those all-day services in the Black churches. And that's stiff competition.

The next day, the Fourth of July, we held a benefit in Chicago. This show featured the Jimmy Smith Trio and Roland Kirk. I also did a spot, and it gave me a chance to make some stage comments on the March against Fear.

"How about James Meredith? I mean, you've got to admit he's got guts. 'Cause walkin' through Mississippi is like trying to make out with a gorilla!

"There's a whole lot of Black folks who's scared to go down to Mississippi. I asked a couple of my friends to go down there with me. Man, them cats burned their NAACP cards! We don't call them 'draft dodgers.' We call them 'death dodgers.'

"But did you see on the news where that white cat was following behind the Mississippi marchers, carryin' a sign that said, 'Vote for Wallace in 1968'? One of the leaders of the march asked me if I thought he should try to get the FBI to arrest him. I said, 'Hell, no! 'Cause if somebody decides to shoot at the marchers again, he just might have bad aim!' "

25

Ho Ho Ho Hanoi

I got a wild idea during the fall of 1966. I was thinking about what I might do for Christmas. My opposition to the war in Vietnam was escalating as fast as the intensity of the fighting. One thing that had always bothered me was the annual Christmas truce, where both sides agreed to stop fighting to celebrate the birthday of the Prince of Peace. I felt it was a mockery since both sides intended to resume killing the next day.

I also got to thinking about Bob Hope's Christmas trips to entertain the troops. While I respected Bob's right to go and admired the personal sacrifice he made in giving up his holiday every year to entertain American soldiers, I couldn't help thinking about the other American soldiers, who had been captured and were going to spend their Christmas as prisoners of war.

So I got in touch with Ralph Schoenman in London. Ralph was Bertrand Russell's personal secretary. I asked Ralph to get word to Ho Chi Minh, seeking permission for me to come to North Vietnam at Christmas to entertain American prisoners. I realized I would not be able to take any fellow entertainers with me, even if they were willing to go. But I planned to take along other kinds of entertainment, like tapes of the Ed Sullivan Show, other variety shows, professional football games, and so on.

The first reply from the North Vietnamese government was a flat refusal. The message indicated that my compassion and concern were both understood and admired, but American prisoners of war were guilty of killing innocent North Vietnamese civilians.

I asked Ralph to send another cable. I wanted to make sure that my opposition to the Vietnam war—indeed to all war and killing—was completely understood. I asked Ralph to make it clear that I considered the bombing raids conducted by a huge world power against a tiny Asian country an atrocity. And I also asked Ralph to relay an offer, which I hoped would demonstrate the sincerity of my intentions. I offered to return to North Vietnam with my wife and children and to live in a North Vietnamese village for the duration of the war. I hoped that offer would show that I was willing to die for my convictions, but not willing to kill for them.

Ralph received a long cable in reply. My offer had completely changed the minds of the North Vietnamese officials. They gave me the green light to come at Christmas to entertain and visit American prisoners. But they also rejected my residence offer. They made it clear that they were not inhumane "beasts" nor would they require me to make such a sacrifice as the condition of entry into their country.

As soon as I got the word of clearance from Ralph Schoenman, I held a press conference in Chicago. I announced my Christmas plans, emphasizing that my trip had been cleared by the North Vietnamese government. I also mentioned that I was going to bring greetings to Ho Chi Minh from George Williams. I could tell that the press didn't know the name George Williams. So I explained that George Williams was a South Side (Chicago) janitor who remembered Ho Chi Minh when he was living in America. Ho Chi Minh had worked in the Black neighborhood, and he was a familiar open-air speaker in the park. Many Black folks remembered him as the man who was always talking about returning home to free his country.

When I finished my statement, a reporter asked, "Has your trip been cleared by the Americans?" I said, "Americans haven't got anything to say about who goes to Hanoi." He answered, "Yes,

I know. But I meant has the American government cleared you to go to Hanoi?" I insisted, "The American government can't clear me to *go* to Hanoi, because the American government doesn't run Hanoi."

About two days later I got firsthand word about American governmental clearance. Dean Rusk was visiting Chicago. I was watching the evening news on television, and the next thing I knew, there was Dean Rusk on the television screen answering a reporter's inquiry. The Secretary of State of the United States of America was saying, "Well, if Dick Gregory goes to Hanoi, we'll deal with him when he gets back."

I turned to rubber. My knees got weak and my stomach fell out. I was being threatened by the whole United States government! As I remember that feeling, I can begin to understand how Paul Robeson or Muhammed Ali must have felt. My threat was just a one-time shot on the evening news. But they had the American government after them day after day.

But Dean Rusk said something else that was very revealing. He said, "I don't think he will be invited to make such a tour." I didn't realize the implications at the time, and I thought it was strange. I had *already* been invited.

Of course, I could understand why my visit would be a touchy political situation from the point of view of the American government. I had met before with North Vietnamese representatives in Paris. And I had a feeling that eventually the release of American prisoners would be negotiated. The North Vietnamese told me that they had to feed American prisoners better than they fed their own soldiers, because of the greater food intake in the American diet as compared with the Vietnamese diet. And it was well known that North Vietnamese soldiers ate better than civilians. Feeding American prisoners would become a touchy domestic issue in North Vietnam. If American prisoners were going to be released eventually, I'm sure the American government would not want it to appear that I had a hand in initiating the negotiations.

On the advice of Attorney Leonard Boudin, I officially notified Dean Rusk by telegram: "I will depart from Kennedy Airport in New York City via TWA flight 702 on Monday, December 5, at 10 A.M., arriving in London at 9:40 P.M. I intend to travel from there by the most appropriate means to Hanoi, North Vietnam, to discuss with officials there the arrangements for entertainment of captured U.S. pilots at Christmas. I accept full responsibility for my personal safety."

Art Steuer and I flew first to London and then to Paris. In Paris I was given the route and travel plans for getting into Hanoi. Just as I was ready to leave, word arrived from Hanoi. Cancel the trip. American planes had resumed heavy bombing of the Hanoi airport. The North Vietnamese government felt it would be unsafe for me to come in under these conditions.

I remembered Dean Rusk's words on television that night, and I figured he knew what he was talking about. I felt that LBJ was bombing the airport to keep me out because he knew the North Vietnamese were too humane to allow me to take such a risk. I felt that LBJ just could not stand to have an American Black in Vietnam who wasn't fighting.

When I got back to Kennedy Airport, it looked like there were a thousand reporters waiting for me—and even more government agents. A couple of agents came up and asked for my passport. I said, "What law have I violated? Going to London or to Paris?"

So they said they wanted to search my bags for narcotics. I exploded. "You mean you're going to search *my* bags for narcotics and you're not going to search this white boy's bags? And he's with me? That just shows this racist mentality in America, and that's what that war in Vietnam is all about!"

But they confiscated my passport anyway. It took Leonard Boudin and the help of the American Civil Liberties Union to get it back.

Since LBJ had successfully kept me out of Hanoi, I decided to entertain American prisoners at home on Christmas Day. I did a show at the Cook County Jail in Chicago. And I didn't forget to include LBJ in my material:

"I was in London when I read about LBJ driving eighty-five miles an hour down the highway on his way to church. I don't mind saying it scared the hell out of me. I figured we might have a nuclear attack any minute if LBJ was in that big a hurry to get somewhere to pray.

"President Grant was an alcoholic. President Andy Jackson killed a man. But this is the only president we've ever had who qualifies for the Hell's Angels!

"But I'm really upset that LBJ dropped all those bombs to keep me from landing in Hanoi. You have to be a comedian, or in show business to understand why. I mean, for a comedian, those

are frightening headlines that could ruin your career: DICK
GREGORY BOMBED OUT!"

26

Taking on Massa Daley

Everything I had been doing was unconsciously leading to a big
decision. I finally made that decision. I announced that I was
running as an independent write-in candidate for mayor of
Chicago in 1967.

I'd been doing a lot of campaigning for other mayoral
candidates: John Lindsay in New York, Ohio State Representative
Carl Stokes in Cleveland, and Ken Gibson in Newark.

Campaigning for Ken was both sad and inspiring. I remember
so well those rainy mornings when Ken and I would be standing
on a street corner greeting folks on their way to work. Folks would
spot me and come running up to shake hands. And I'd have to
direct their attention to Ken Gibson and tell them not to forget
him on election day.

Many did forget him, and Ken lost that election. Just as Carl
Stokes lost his first election. But they had both ignited a spark and
held up the vision of an impossible dream. And both Ken and Carl
hung in there and set their eyes toward the next election. Carl had
less time to wait. Two years after his first defeat, Carl Stokes was
mayor of Cleveland.

Four years after his first try, Ken Gibson was elected mayor of
Newark. I'll never forget watching the victory celebration on
television that night. It brought tears to my eyes to see all the
hugging and shouting in Ken's campaign headquarters, and it
made all of those rainy mornings worthwhile.

I'd also been gathering a cadre of committed campaign
workers through the school desegregation marches, Christmas for
Mississippi, and other local grass-roots activities. They became my
own little group of untouchables, friends and comrades whom
Mayor Daley couldn't touch, couldn't intimidate, and certainly

couldn't control. Folks like Nahaz and Mary Rogers, Lawrence Landry, Robert Lucas, Thelma Isbell, and Bill Robinson. And they were ready when I needed the nucleus of a campaign organization.

Drew Pearson set the stage for my candidacy in February 1966, more than a year before the Chicago elections. Drew wrote in his syndicated column:

"Two knockdown, dragout poltiical battles in Illinois are scheduled to attract attention.

"One is between the Negro comedian—civil rights scrapper Dick Gregory and veteran Mayor Richard J. Daley to rule the second city in the United States: Chicago. Dick Gregory is almost certain to run for mayor.

"For years the bosses of the big cities have been Irish and, in latter years, Italian. . . . They were elected largely by Catholic voters. If now the huge Negro population of these cities, largely Protestant but also Democratic, can throw out Irish-Italian domination, it will mean social revolution."

Taking a cue from Drew, I adopted the revolutionary strategy of being a write-in candidate. Since I was fighting the Daley-controlled political machine, I felt it was important to operate totally outside the established political structure. I didn't work with elected political officials, nor did I enter the primary election. I started at the top and went directly to the people. I was their candidate for mayor of Chicago if they wanted to buck the corrupt political machine. All they had to do was write my name on the ballot. From the very beginning, the independent write-in strategy put me on equal footing with Mayor Daley and his Republican opponent, John L. Waner.

The reaction in the Black community was a mixture of joy and fear. Black folks were overjoyed that I was going the ultimate distance with Mayor Daley. I'd already done everything else. I'd marched around his house, bugging both him and his neighbors. I'd chased him to Detroit. I'd made him the target of both demonstrations and nightclub routines. Now I was taking him on at the polls. It was the final blow! Blacks folks couldn't believe it was really happening, and their enthusiasm for the effort was witnessed by the financial contributions which they gave to my campaign. Republican party politicos were equally amazed and enthused.

But the enthusiasm was mixed with fear and concern over my

personal safety. Black Chicagoans remembered that a Black alderman named Ben Lewis had also tried to buck the Daley machine. He was shot down in his campaign headquarters on election eve. Politically aware Black folks in Chicago were convinced that the murder of Ben Lewis was more than coincidence. So when they heard me talking about the corrupt Daley machine and its ties with the Mafia, Black folks couldn't help remembering Ben Lewis.

I set up my campaign headquarters in the heart of the Black community, at 1251 West Sixty-third Street. Ruby Burrows, a Black attorney from Washington D.C., resigned her job with the United States Equal Employment Opportunity Commission, and came to Chicago to be my campaign manager. Ruby had solid credentials and political experience, having earlier worked in the office of Senator Teddy Kennedy.

Mike Watley had also relocated in Chicago to work in the campaign. Big Mike is an absolute prince. He tips the scales at some 300 pounds and has a heart bigger than his body! I first met Mike when he was working as a skycap at the San Francisco airport. Mike is a living example of being his brother's keeper, and his sister's, too. His greatest joy in life is making other folks happy.

At my press conference to announce the opening of my campaign headquarters, I tried to make the purpose of my campaign "perfectly clear." I suggested that folks might be surprised at the number of white Chicagoans who would vote for me in the privacy of the voting booth and added, "If I do nothing more than reinspire the enormous number of citizens who are fed up with the elective system, with vote fraud, intimidation, and machine candidates, I will have served my purpose."

I campaigned all over Chicago, in white neighborhoods as well as Black. Everywhere I went I tried to deal with real issues so that my candidacy would be viewed as truly pro-people rather than simply anti-Daley. At every campaign stop I left a three-page filler entitled "Dick Gregory Speaks on the Issues," dealing with open occupancy, housing, police, the fire department, civil disturbances, civil service, welfare, and Vietnam.

"When a Russian spy can come to this country and move into a neighborhood where an American Negro cannot, we are sowing the seeds of our own destruction with prejudice. . . . Chicago must treat its people as well as cars and provide some 'expressways' for them to live in. . . . We need *better* police—not *more* of them. The policeman is underpaid, overworked, and uneducated for his complex role as a public servant. . . . Landlords must be made to correct housing violations, and roaming two-man emergency fire-fighting units should be immediately employed [in ghetto neighborhoods]. . . . As crime is the symptom of the disease of poverty, riot is the fever of the epidemic . . . Farmers, airlines, railroads, and oil companies receive federal subsidies. Yet, somehow, poor families must apoligize for receiving public aid. . . . I am not against the war in Vietnam—I am against war."

During the final month before the election, my campaign really began to pick up momentum. When the Chicago *Sun-Times* published the results of its straw poll, my name was in the headlines because of the surprising number of people who had indicated a preference for my candidacy. I was off and running, and it really began to look like I had a chance. Things were looking so good that I had a private breakfast meeting with my Republican opponent, John Waner. I thought I had better check him out, since he might be the next mayor if I pulled enough votes from Mayor Daley.

Then I got an idea for the greatest possible publicity boost my campaign could have. I didn't know if I could pull it off, but it was worth a try.

Congressman Adam Clayton Powell was living in self-imposed exile on the island of Bimini. He had been stripped of his chairmanship of the powerful House Committe on Education and Labor, and later he was barred from assuming his seat in the Ninetieth Congress.

When Adam's troubles in Congress first began, I had sent him a telegram of support. I suggested that Democratic leadership had begun to fear his independent stance on all human issues and his growing influence at the polls with Black voters and, therefore, I would "hold the Democratic Party responsible for any indignity you might suffer." I also urged him to consider announcing as an independent candidate for the presidency in 1968.

I had kept pressing Adam to take his case to the people. And I thought that now might just be the time to really bring it off. I envisioned Adam making a triumphant entry into Harlem on Palm Sunday. Art Steuer wanted to release thousands of doves and scatter palm branches in his path. I would accompany Adam to

New York City. Then we would return to Chicago together, and Adam would campaign with me in the streets. It would be the best possible publicity gimmick.

I flew to Bimini to see Adam. I spent a couple of days there just watching Adam. I saw him sunning himself, drinking Scotch and milk at the Small World Bar, laughing, and having the time of his life. It was as though a great burden had been lifted from his shoulders. He no longer had the responsibility for representing not only his constituency in Harlem, but 22 million Black folks all across the nation. I knew Adam was not yet ready to return home. But I had to. I had an election to win.

As the momentum of my campaign grew, I began to see evidence of the Daley machine at work intimidating Black folks. I could see the looks of hostility and hatred in the eyes of Black precinct captains. I could tell that they wished I would just disappear. My candidacy was challenging their political morality on the one hand and what they understood as their personal survival on the other. They lived off the patronage of the Daley machine and its representative in Congress, Black Congressman William Dawson, and for the first time they were feeling pangs of conscience over that unholy allegiance.

Some of them admitted it to me privately. They came to me and said, "Hey, baby, I really hate to do what I'll have to do on election day. But you know how it is." They were saying quite simply that they would have to intimidate Black folks on behalf of the Daley machine, just as they had done in past elections. Black folks on welfare or living in the projects would be reminded of their debt to Congressman Dawson and Mayor Daley. They would be told that a wrong vote might result in eviction from the projects or the shutting off of relief checks. In such an atmosphere of political intimidation, Massa Daley was able to keep the Black slaves under control on his plantation.

Quite naturally, I was suspicious of everyone and constantly on my guard. I was sure that the Daley machine had spies among my own campaign workers.

One day I returned to campaign headquarters and someone handed me a box of salads. A woman by the name of Alvenia Fulton, who ran a health-food store on Chicago's South Side, had stopped by and left the salads. I threw them out. I didn't know Alvenia Fulton. Those salads might have contained arsenic-coated lettuce. But I made a mental note to visit her health-food store one day and check her out.

I received a well-placed television plug during the campaign. World Heavyweight Champion Muhammed Ali fought and successfully defended his championship belt. As he stood in the ring after the fight and the microphones were shoved in his face, Ali's first words were, "I want to ask folks to vote for Dick Gregory as mayor of Chicago." But Ali was also fighting a social and political system that did not appreciate his personal convictions. A short time later the World Boxing Association stripped him of his title because he refused to enter military service and kill in Vietnam.

Election day arrived, and it was my day! I was a candidate for mayor of Chicago and treated as such. When Lillian and I arrived at the polls to vote, the newspaper photographers were there to snap our pictures. I realized that you have to be a candidate to fully appreciate the thrill of election day.

After I voted I went to my campaign headquarters. Complaints had already started rolling in. Precinct after precinct was reporting election law violations and voting frauds. The Daley machine had developed an innovative technique of intimidation. Since I was a write-in candidate, voters would use the pencil in the voting machine to vote for me. The pencil was hanging on a string, just long enough so that it extended under the curtain of the voting machine. Massa Daley's poll watchers could see who picked up the pencil, and they could be pretty sure those voters were voting for me. Their names were recorded for future reference. The technique was as clever as it was vicious.

That night I gathered with my supporters to watch the election returns on television. Of course we lost the election. And many of my most ardent supporters were disappointed. But I couldn't share their disappointment. I knew we had won a victory far more significant than the total number of votes. We had kicked the machine, and it would never work quite the same way again. Others would be encouraged to probe scandal and corruption in the city administration. Other candidates would emerge who were not handpicked by Massa Daley, and they would win.

27

Marching in Milwaukee

I've got ten kids, and I guess I'd have to credit Merv Griffin and Mike Douglas for that. Before you draw the wrong conclusions, I'd better explain. My wife's hospital expenses were paid by the American Federation of Television and Radio Artists. AFTRA has one of the best hospital and health plans in existence. But to qualify for the coverage, I had to do a certain number of television shows each year. I could always pick up a phone and call Merv Griffin, and I would be on his show. The same was true of Mike Douglas. Merv and Mike kept me a member in good standing in AFTRA, and Lillian always had the best hospital care.

But nightclub engagements were becoming more and more scarce because of my civil rights activities. Some nightclub owners ruled me out as an act because I couldn't commit my schedule far enough in advance. Others ruled me out, I'm sure, because they didn't approve of my civil rights activities. And I was really feeling the pinch financially.

Not that I was unemployed. I did a week's concert tour in England with Nina Simone. One of the highlights of my career was playing Albert Hall in London. I'd never seen a place more beautiful. It was the epitome of elegance. And the room was packed. Nina's performance added further beauty to the room. Her sensitivity and artistry on stage were overwhelming.

I also had an unexpected engagement at the Village Gate. I had come to New York City to participate in a benefit at the Village Theater for *Renewal* magazine, a publication of the Chicago Community Renewal Society, which Jim McGraw and Steve Rose edited. The show was held on the eve of Pentecost and was entitled "An Evening with God." I was "co-starred" along with Dr. Timothy Leary, Father Malcolm Boyd, Dr. Harvey Cox, folksinger Len Chandler, and Paul Krassner, editor of *The Realist* magazine, who was billed in the capacity of "speaking of the devil."

Just before the first performance, Art D'Lugoff, owner of the Village Gate, came by and told me Carmen MacRae had been taken ill. He wondered if I could fill in for the night. I was caught in the middle. I wanted to help Art, but I couldn't back out on Jim McGraw. So Jim rearranged the lineup of the show, and I shuttled back and forth between the Village Gate and the Village Theater all night. Two performances at the Village Theater and three at the Gate.

The "Evening with God" was a great night. I had known Malcolm Boyd, Len Chandler, and Paul Krassner before. Malcolm had been on the bill with me at the Hungry i. Len was a fellow civil rights marcher from way back. And Paul Krassner and I had been friends ever since I did one of his "Impolite Interviews" in *The Realist*. But I met Harvey Cox and Tim Leary for the first time.

After the show, I promised Tim Leary that I would come up to his farm in Millbrook the following weekend. Tim was performing his first wedding ceremony in his capacity as the high priest of the League of Spiritual Discovery (LSD). I'll never forget that weekend. I knew I was in for quite an experience when we were driving up to Tim's house and I saw a white kid sitting on the lawn eating a flower. He must have been saying to himself, "A rose is a rose is a rose is a popsicle."

I joined the wedding circle, and it was obvious that all of the participants had taken the LSD sacrament. After the wedding I remember Tim coming up and asking, "Dick, do you want to turn on?" I said, "Do I want to what?" He said, "Do you want to drop some acid?" I told him, "Man, my ancestors came over to this country on an illegal trip. I don't want to take another one!"

I was also doing more and more college lectures. I had met Bob Walker, head of the new American Program Bureau in Boston. Bob was young, energetic, and well-endowed with both ego and drive. He sensed the growing mood of political and social awareness on the college campuses, and he had the genius to put together packages of speakers who would fill the needs of these hungry young minds.

Bob Walker's agency and I sort of grew up on the college campuses together. I soon became very much in demand. I was also able to put Bob in contact with other friends of mine whom the kids on campus wanted to hear. Bob, in turn, got me more and more college dates. But I deliberately kept my lecture fee at a minimum so I could reach as many young college kids as possible.

My shift to the college lecture circuit was rather ironic. The very activites which had closed many nightclub doors were the reason for my popularity on the college campuses. And the college lecture circuit was more comfortable for me personally. It wasn't like being locked into a nightclub commitment. If I had to cancel a lecture date because I was in jail or participating in a demonstration, the college kids understood, and it was merely a matter of scheduling another date.

But the college lecture circuit closes down over the summer months. And the summer of 1967 was a "long hot summer" for me financially. While the ghettos were burning all over the country, in Newark, Detroit, and elsewhere, I was sweating out paying my bills in Chicago. I was flat broke. I didn't even have rent money. I was literally on the verge of eviction from my apartment. I started making phone calls, and, miraculously, I made it through the summer with the kind help of my friends. It was really a cash flow problem. I had hundreds of college dates scheduled, beginning at the end of September.

Toward the end of the summer, I was fascinated by the television news reports coming from Milwaukee. All summer long the television screen had been filled with the flames and smoke of ghetto rebellion. "Black Power" was the phrase of the hour, and I had just attended the Black Power Conference in Newark. But in Milwaukee something different was going on. Just when it looked like the old style civil rights marches might be over, a white Roman Catholic priest named James Groppi was leading daily marches to get a fair housing law passed in Milwaukee. Father Groppi was the pastor of St. Boniface Church in Milwaukee's predominantly Black North Side. He was constantly surrounded, supported and protected by the Commandos, a special task force of the Milwaukee NAACP Youth Council.

Every day, Father Groppi and the Commandos led marches across the Sixteenth Street viaduct into the predominantly white South Side of Milwaukee. They faced considerable resistance and hostility, and the hostility was sometimes returned by the marchers. The police were extremely heavy-handed in dealing with the marchers. As I watched Father Groppi being interviewed on television, I sensed a look of both fear and exhaustion. I figured he could use some help. So I went to Milwaukee to offer my assistance.

I fell in love with Father Groppi as soon as I met him. And I also fell in love with his church. Father Groppi used his church building completely. It was truly a people-oriented church. It wasn't just a place to hold rallies. It was the center of community life, on all levels.

St. Boniface Church was the Fort Dix of the civil rights movement. Folks ate at the church, many slept there, and it was a twenty-four-hour-a-day operation. It was the barracks, the chapel, and the military headquarters where the marchers assembled and to which they returned. From St. Boniface Church, Father Groppi developed a local army of civil rights soldiers, under the command of the Commandos.

Every day after the march was over, a meal would be served. Consequently, a lot of hungry folks participated in the march. They didn't march simply to get a free meal. But they were free in their minds to march because they knew they would be fed. They didn't have to worry about where that next meal was coming from.

Father Groppi had a tremendous influence upon Black and white relationships. At a time when the Black Power movement was being interpreted by some folks as the end of Black and white cooperation, Father Groppi came on the scene and called that interpretation into question. He talked about white folks in a way we had only heard white folks talk about us! Almost overnight Father Groppi's name became a household word in Black ghettos across the country. My first time in Milwaukee I spoke at a rally, and I told the audience, "Just when I was getting ready to dislike all white folks, along came Father Groppi and I had to postpone it for another month!"

Father Groppi was particularly disliked by the white bigots of Milwaukee. He was more hated than Dr. Martin Luther King. Even a bigot had to admit that Dr. King had a vested interest in leading demonstrations. But Father Groppi caught the bigots off guard. They couldn't advocate sending him back to Africa as they did Dr. King and other Blacks. And sending him back to Italy didn't have quite the same impact. The only recourse was to call him vicious and vile names and to question his credentials as a priest. And Father Groppi was subjected to such abuse every time he walked over the viaduct.

While I was participating in the Milwaukee demonstrations, a small band of outside militants tried to drum up support for unseating Father Groppi and replacing him with a Black leader. I nipped such thinking in the bud. At the next rally I said, "If I had a choice, I would rather have a white boy leading us. Since Whitey stole our freedom from us in the first place, he has the best chance of finding it."

I was really excited about the Milwaukee demonstrations. And I spent as much time there as I could. I saw the same kind of day-after-day determination that we had displayed in our school desegregation marches in Chicago. I felt such prolonged pressure was very important. One of the problems of other civil rights demonstrations had been too quick victories. Governmental stubbornness and resistance are sometimes necessary. They provide the atmosphere for the application of continuing pressure. And when the victory is finally won, it is a lasting victory, one which is accepted and fully implemented.

There was also a special sensitivity and spirit on those marches and in the North Side community. Folks opened their homes to outside marchers with no questions asked. In the bars, bowling alleys, and lunch counters, the spirit of true brotherhood and sisterhood overflowed.

I never will forget marching past a laundry one day in Milwaukee. An old Black sister ran to the door, grabbed my hand, and said, "Thank God for people like you, Mr. Gregory. And I know things ain't been goin' too good. So here, take this." And she pressed a bill in my hand.

When I opened my hand, I saw a ten-dollar bill. I didn't have any money in my pocket. But I wondered how that old Black lady knew I was broke, when everybody else talked about me being a millionaire.

Then I figured it out. She must have been the seer that made Milwaukee famous!

Civil Rights

With Congressman Adam Powell and Malcolm X, Brooklyn (1964).

With General William Gelston
Maryland National Guard (196

Photo by Maurice Sorrell, courtesy Johnson Publishing Company, Inc.

Photo by Gil Baker,
courtesy Johnson Publishing Compa

With a steelhead,
Washington State fish-in (1966).

Photo by Lawrence Henry, courtesy Johnson Publishing Company, Inc.

Courtesy Johnson Publishing Company, Inc.

James Meredith's March
t Fear: with Jim McGraw,
, Miss. (1966).

With Mayor Charles Evers
etteville, Miss.,
son (1972).

Rapping with Rap Brown, New York City (1971).

28

Farewell to Food

During the long marches in Milwaukee, I had time to do a lot of thinking. My thoughts kept returning to how I could personally help to bring an end to the Vietnam war. I decided not to get a haircut until the war was over, and I urged others to join my Samsonesque protest. I figured if enough people stopped getting haircuts, it would create a large lobby of barbers who would instantaneously join the anti-war effort. I also urged people not to shave until after the war, reasoning that even little old ladies who owned stock in Gillette Blue Blades would join the peace movement.

I also began thinking about going on a long fast. I had been hearing and reading about fasting, and I thought an extended fast would be the best possible personal witness I could make, considering the publicity it would inevitably attract. I kept thinking of Mahatma Gandhi and his nonviolent movement in India. It seemed to me that fasting was the ultimate weapon in the nonviolent arsenal.

So I held a press conference and announced that I would fast for thirty-two days, beginning on Thanksgiving and ending on Christmas Day. In my press conference opening statement, I said, "I am determined to set an example as an individual American, lawfully protesting against my government's policy in Vietnam. From Thanksgiving until Christmas, I will fast in sympathy with the millions of Americans who are also opposed to the war in Vietnam. I will not eat, drink juice, or take prepared vitamins or other food supplements.

"I suggest that true Christians and humanitarians celebrate Christmas this year in simplicity and sacrifice, and, in sympathy with the suffering on both sides of the war, avoid traditional decorations, Christmas trees, lights, ornaments, toys, and the exchange of gifts and presents, until peace on earth and goodwill to men become a reality."

I realized that there would be doubters and scoffers who would insist that I was sneaking food during the fast. So I asked Jimmy Smith, editor and publisher of the *Chicago Gazette*, and Irv Kupcinet, *Chicago Sun-Times* columnist and television personality, to hold a $1,000 bond against any challenge to my fasting fidelity. I said that I would willingly submit to a medical examination to see if any food had entered my digestive system, as long as a doctor of my own choice was allowed to be present during the exam. I was betting a thousand dollars that an honest medical exam would prove that I was living only on distilled water. I also asked any potential challengers to post a $100 contribution to SNCC against my $1,000.

Whether by accident or by Providence, I happened to be going through some papers and I came across a name and address: Dr. Alvenia Fulton, The Fultonia Health Food Center, 521 East Sixty-third Street. I said to Lillian, "Look, Lil, here's the name and address of that lady who sent those salads to the campaign headquarters. We really should go by and thank her."

We did, and that visit changed my life. I had no idea that Dr. Fulton knew anything about fasting. But it turned out that she is one of the world's leading authorities on the subject and had personally fasted many, many times before. She had read about my impending fast in the newspaper, and she asked if I had ever fasted before. I told her I hadn't. She began immediately to teach me the techniques of scientific fasting. She told me to begin cleaning out my body by drinking only freshly squeezed juices for seven days before Thanksgiving. She explained the condition of toxemia, the retention of poisonous toxins in the body as a result of bad eating habits and improper elimination. She told me how the poisons would be flushed out of my body during the period of fasting. She told me to cleanse my colon with enemas and to continue the enemas after my fast began. I couldn't help thinking about the irony of my original reaction to her salads. I had suspected her of possibly trying to poison me, and here she was telling me how to get the poisons out of my system!

Dr. Fulton was so excited about my fast that she promised to fast along with me. Under the tutelage of Dr. Fulton, my "hunger strike" became a "scientific fast." What began as a protest against the war was later to become a way of life, a whole new understanding of the functioning of the human body and the laws of Mother Nature.

On Thanksgiving Day, I began my fast. But I maintained my hectic schedule of college lectures, benefits, nightclub dates, and radio and television shows: the Wesley South show in Chicago, a benefit for Imamu Baraka (LeRoi Jones) in Newark, the Merv Griffin show in New York, a lecture at Brown University, a benefit in McKeesport, Pennsylvania, a benefit at New York's Town Hall with Sidney Poitier, the Senior Class Dinner at Yale University, college lectures in the South, the Midwest and on the West Coast—Iowa, Texas, California, West Virginia, Colorado, Wisconsin. In a forty-day period I visited fifty-seven cities and gave sixty-three lectures.

Every night I would call Dr. Fulton. Her knowledge of fasting was so complete, she knew in advance—each day of the fast—what feelings and sensations I would be experiencing. For example, she told me that I would experience a sudden burst of energy at the end of the third week. It was difficult for me to believe, especially at those times when I felt weak during the *first* three weeks. But she was absolutely right. At the end of three weeks, the body begins *consuming itself*, thoroughly ridding itself of stored-up poisons which have been accumulating for a lifetime. And there is an accompanying resurgence of energy.

She also warned me to beware of lifting anything heavy as the fast progressed, and also to avoid sudden movements, like getting up suddenly or changing positions suddenly. Again, since the body was going through such a thorough cleansing process, especially the cleansing of the bloodstream, any sudden movement would be a shock to the system in the process of renewing itself. Her words of advice were especially valuable to me, since I was a man on the move with loads and loads of luggage. During that fast I came to have a special appreciation for my skycap brothers!

Even with Dr. Fulton's wise counsel, I still went through some mental changes. Everywhere I went, I could tell people really thought I was going to die. Before long I began to share their concern. I would come back to the hotel room after a lecture, flop down on the bed, and pass out in slumber. Then I'd wake up in the middle of the night. The room would be dark and everything would be quiet and I'd wonder if I was dead or alive. Then I would get to thinking, maybe that's what death feels like. Since I'd never died before, I thought death might be "one eternal pinch!"

I also found that my hunger disappeared after the third or fourth day of the fast. But the temptations to *get hungry* were all around me. You don't realize how many food commercials there are on TV, how many food ads in magazines and newspapers, how many restaurants, lunch counters, and hot dog stands, until you go on a fast. Then they all seem to jump out at you.

I would go to sleep, and the "hot dog parade" would start marching through my dreams, even though I'd long since given up eating hot dogs. I came to realize the great extent to which hunger is a mental attitude rather than an actual physical need. And I realized why there are so many overweight folks in America. The temptations to eat are all around, appealing to people's minds, whether their bodies need the food or not.

For two successive weekends before Christmas, I played the Village Gate, sharing the stage with an old friend, jazzman Charles Lloyd. I did three shows a night, Friday and Saturday nights. The room was packed. I don't know if folks came to hear my funnies as a standup comedian, or if they came thinking it was funny that I could still stand up!

Of course I had to talk about the fast during my act:

"Everybody keeps asking me about my fast. A reporter asked me the other day if I had any unusual things happen to me as a result of the fast. I said, 'Yes. Yesterday I had a button drop off.' He said, 'What's so unusual about a button dropping off?' I told him, 'It was my belly button.'

"People ask if I have to take any special precautions. Well, after the third week of the fast, I started wearing a protective covering around my knees—my jockey shorts! I've lost so much weight, I look like Wilt 'The Stilt' Chamberlain, after taxes. My stomach is so shrunk, if I swallowed a marshmallow, I'd look pregnant.

"But I don't mind telling you, I'm hungry. I don't dare allow myself to be near anybody with food, even if it's meat. And I don't ordinarily eat meat. I'm so hungry, do you know what NAACP means to me these days? Never Associate with Anyone Carrying Porkchops!"

On the Friday before Christmas, I got into New York City early and held a press conference at the Village Gate. I announced that I was extending my fast until New Year's Day. "When I began this personal, nonviolent demonstration as an American citizen and a Christian," I told the press, "I chose to make it during the Thanksgiving and Christmas holidays because of their significance to me as days of peace and thankfulness and blessing. I have received an enormous number of communications from all over the world. I now realize that this time of year is also precious to many other people of different faiths and nationalities, and in respect to those throughout the world who celebrate Hannukah as Jews, Ramadan as Moslems, and Tet as Buddhists, I have resolved to extend my fast until the New Year."

Some of the reporters asked me again what I hoped to accomplish by my fasting. I answered, "This is the only country in the world where more people die each year from overeating than undereating. So I've deduced that America's conscience must lie in her stomach. I just hope my fast will locate that American conscience and cause people to think about the war in Vietnam. Everywhere I go people are worrying about the possibility of my dying. Perhaps they will also begin worrying about the *reality* of people dying every hour of every day in Vietnam."

Once again, *The New York Times* probed deeper than the press conference in covering the story. *Times* reporter J. Anthony Lukas checked with doctors at the Columbia Presbyterian Medical Center for expert medical opinion. The doctors said that my forty-nine-pound weight loss was "about right" for someone who was doing what I was doing. When asked if they thought I was really fasting, the doctors were noncommittal, but observed that it was "not at all impossible for a man as deeply committed as Mr. Gregory."

A medical opinion of a different sort came from my friend and physician, Dr. Charles Lee Williams, in Chicago. He was really worried about my health, and his concern was recorded in an article in the *Chicago Courier* written by Wesley South. Dr. Williams had examined me and found acetone in my blood, indicating that the remaining fats in my body were rapidly breaking down. He said the ingredient acts like alcohol in the blood and makes a person behave like he is drunk. Dr. Williams seemed to feel that my extension of the fast was the act of a drunken fool. He was quoted as saying:

"I warned him to stop this fast a long time ago. He is fast approaching the point of no return. He has made his point, and I can see no reason why he should continue it.

"Whenever a person survives a fast for thirty days, we write them up in the medical journals. Now Dick is planning to go even further. The prisoners in the Nazi concentration camps were better off than Dick. Those unfortunates were on a starvation diet. They were at least eating some food. They were partially starved. Dick is completely starved.

"If you don't put gasoline in an automobile, it will stop. If you don't put fuel in the human body, it will die. Dick is playing a game more dangerous than Russian roulette. Instead of using a revolver with five empty chambers and one bullet, by extending his fast, Dick is using a revolver with five bullets and one empty chamber."

At the time I was examined by Dr. Williams, a Cook County circuit court judge was also visiting the office. He suggested that it might be necessary for the courts to declare me incompetent in order to save my life. In other words, the judge seemed to feel, as the title of a record album by my friend and colleague-in-comedy Richard Pryor would declare, "That nigger's crazy!"

While I appreciated the love and concern about my health, I knew I wasn't crazy, nor was I playing Russian roulette. I had already learned from Dr. Fulton how Mother Nature would tell me when I was in real danger. During the period in which the body is cleansing itself of all impurities, a chalky coating, sometimes yellow and sometimes white, will appear on the surface of the tongue. As long as the coating is on the tongue, there is no danger of dying from starvation. When the coating disappears, the fast must be broken because starvation has set in. And at that point, true hunger returns.

My tongue was still coated. So even though my doctor thought I was foolish and the judge thought I was crazy, the true momma of us all, Mother Nature, was saying, "You're all right, son. I'll tell you when to quit."

I was losing weight from head to toe. And one night onstage at the Village Gate, I found out I was losing weight in my fingers too. Well into my performance, I got up from the stool I usually use in my act and was pacing back and forth across the stage, microphone in hand. At one point I made a dramatic gesture, swinging my arm away from my body. My wedding band went sailing across the room! My fingers had gotten so skinny that the ring no longer fit. Fortunately my wedding band was recovered by a customer, and I returned it to my finger after I had fattened up a bit.

I broke my fast on New Year's Day. Of course, I couldn't eat solid food. After a long fast, a person must gradually return to eating by remaining on a diet of juice one day for every ten days of fasting. During the fast, the villi in the stomach have gone to sleep, and they must be awakened gradually.

But that first sip of juice is a real trip! You can feel those stomach villi waking up. You can almost hear the stomach sending a message to the brain, "Hey, he's eating again. Get ready. Here it comes!" You close your eyes, and it seems like every star in the heavens comes down to introduce itself to you personally! It is Mother Nature's trip, a real mind-blowing experience, which does not need to be induced by unnatural and artificial substances.

I had a party to go to that night. It was inauguration day in Gary, Indiana, for the city's new mayor, Richard Hatcher. Lil and I attended the swearing-in ceremony and the inaugural ball. I knew I had gotten down to ninety-eight pounds during the fast, but I didn't fully realize how much weight I had lost until I was being fitted for a tuxedo. All my life I've been fighting against being called "boy," and here I was back in the boy's department!

It was like a double celebration for me. It seemed so appropriate to be at Dick Hatcher's inaugural on the same day that I had broken my fast. Both Dick Hatcher and I had been through a period of struggle and testing, and we had both emerged victorious. We had seen our respective ordeals through to the end.

Dick Hatcher had overcome all kinds of obstacles to become the mayor of Gary. The Indiana State Legislature had even passed new laws to try to stop him. But he brought together that growing northern Black political power that was beginning to say in Cleveland, in Newark, and now in Gary, "No longer will the office of mayor be viewed as a job for whites only!" Just as my fast had thoroughly cleansed my body, Black power was beginning to cleanse the American political system. Dick Hatcher's victory and my fast were symbolically related.

The next day I held a press conference at the Knickerbocker Hotel in Chicago to release a letter I had just sent to the White House. A copy was sent to John M. Bailey, chairman of the Democratic National Committee.

I told the president and the chairman that the selection of Chicago as the site of the 1968 DemocraticNational Convention was a "cruel insult" to all those progressive Democrats, both Black and white, who would see the choice as an endorsement of the repressive local Democratic administration headed by Mayor

Daley. I said further that if five steps were not taken immediately, the convention would be held in Chicago only over my dead body. The five conditions were: 1) enacting a fair housing bill for Chicago, with a guarantee that anyone could walk anywhere in Chicago without fear of racial attack; 2) appointing a Black to the top echelon of the police department; 3) guaranteeing the safety of the Reverend Jesse Jackson, founder of Operation Breadbasket, who had received many threats on his life; 4) lifting the injunction against Martin Luther King, Jr., and others on marching in the Chicago suburbs; and 5) making the Chicago police and fire fighters the highest paid in the nation.

I sent similar letters to Mayor Daley, to each of the fifty aldermen in the Chicago City Council, and to the police and fire commissioners. I personally delivered Mayor Daley's letter to his office, along with a copy of the book *Before the Mayflower* by *Ebony* magazine Senior Editor Lerone Bennett, Jr.

The next day some headlines read: DICK GREGORY VOWS CONVENTION HELD OVER HIS DEAD BODY. I thought of the line I'd used at the Selma march about Sheriff Jim Clark. I'm sure some Democrats felt that wouldn't be a bad route either!

29

Kicking the Computer

Shortly after my campaign for mayor of Chicago, I announced that I would be an independent write-in candidate for president of the United States in 1968. I'm not really sure when I first made the announcement. But by October the word about my candidacy had filtered down to Mississippi. On October 5, 1967, Jackson (Miss.) *Daily News* columnist Jimmy Ward wrote in his "Covering the Crossroads" column:

"Another guy from show biz is trying to get into politics. Dick Gregory, the former comedian who turned professional Negro, told a student audience in Kansas that he was going to run for president of the United States on an independent ticket. It would have been more appropriate if Gregory had made his announcement flat on his stomach during one of his lie-in events at the White House in Washington."

But I suppose I would have to credit Al Capp, creator of the Li'l Abner comic strip, with giving me presidential ambitions. Long before I had ever considered running for elective office, Al Capp was writing and telling interviewers that Dick Gregory should be president of the United States! Al first nominated me in his syndicated column, and he later explained to interviewer Morton Cooper (*Chicago Weekly Defender,* May 4, 1963):

"No, no, I'm not being facetious at all. I'm four square behind the nomination of Dick Gregory for president of the United States.

"What's strange about it? Any well-ordered society would think of him in those terms. What credentials does the job take? Tom Dewey caught crooks. What did Ike know? He knew Sherman Adams. Rockefeller's profession was inheriting money. George Romney's profession was selling automobiles. Gregory is certainly more in tune to the United States than those fellows.

"You can't help but think seriously of him. He's got a magnificent mind, he's a responsible citizen, and he has guts. More than that, he knows how to utilize his passion to improve social conditions; he's a calm, very controlled man. He never goes off half-cocked.

"One thing about Dick Gregory: no American philosopher comes close to him as far as punch is concerned. *The New York Times* was horrified some time ago when I reviewed a book for them about Will Rogers. They were horrified because I wrote that Rogers didn't deserve his speaking-out-on-the-issues reputation. He took pains to offend no one. He was a bootlicker who wanted to be loved by all.

"Gregory, on the other hand, has a roaring career going for him by saying what he damn well pleases. He's never heard of the agencies that scream, 'Don't offend anybody and you'll earn 20 billion dollars.' How can't you have respect for a guy like that?"

My threat that the 1968 Democratic convention would be held only over my dead body attracted the attention of others who were planning convention demonstrations. During the opening days of the election year, I met with representatives of the Youth International Party (YIP), a coalition which planned to bring a half-million young people to Chicago during the convention for a youth festival. Paul Krassner correctly prophesied that the initials YIP were a natural media turn-on, and in a matter of weeks, *Time*, *Newsweek*, and the other major news media would drop all reference to "hippies" and would be talking instead about "yippies."

We gathered in Art Steuer's basement in New York City. The YIP representation included Paul Krassner, Jerry Rubin, and Ed Sanders. They told me that their youth festival was going to be held in Lincoln Park on Chicago's near North Side, and they asked how their plans could be interwoven with mine. They seemed to be particularly sensitive to possible racial animosity and hostility, since most of their youthful celebrators would be white kids.

I tried to tell them how to get around any potential animosity. They had to offset the Black community's resentment toward the regular convention. I said that they ought to hold their festival in a park in the Black community rather than on the near North Side. And I pointed out the economic consideration.

The Democratic convention would be bringing millions and millions of dollars to white-owned businesses in downtown Chicago. But the yippies represented more than a million dollars a day, which could be spent in the Black community at Black-owned businesses. If there were a half-million yippies, they would each spend at least two dollars a day on food alone. That's a million dollars a day spent at Black lunch counters, restaurants, or grocery stores. If the idea was to provide a political alternative during the convention, then I felt that it was also necessary to provide an economic alternative. Yippies should buy Black just as regular convention delegates would be buying white.

By the end of our meeting, the YIP representatives had agreed with my thinking, although I could sense considerable apprehension about being in the Black community. They issued a press release which spoke of the meeting and said, "It was agreed that an important aspect of the festival would be to urge the young people coming to Chicago to shop and eat only in the black community. This will show in very concrete terms our alliance with the black people's struggle for freedom in this country."

The wording of the press release indicated to me that apprehension had prevailed. They weren't about to move the festival out of Lincoln Park. And simply "urging" young people to shop in the Black community was a bit unrealistic, since they would have to make quite a trip to the ghetto from the near North Side.

Tim Leary came through Chicago the next month for a lecture. He also urged young people to come to Chicago for the Democratic convention to "laugh and pray for LBJ." He insisted that the country had been "on a bad trip." To bring the country out of its bad trip, Tim further elaborated, "we need a young, turned-on, laughing Black man in the White House. And we have him." Thus did Tim Leary endorse my candidacy.

People had been urging me to attend the Peace and Freedom Party convention where its presidential candidate would be chosen. I had a strong contingent of young supporters among the convention delegates. So I attended the convention. I was really saddened by the divisiveness, the infighting, and the downright hatred among delegates. There was a determined group of Eldridge Cleaver supporters. I honestly feel, if I had not been Dick Gregory, whose nonviolent, civil rights record was well known, I might have been hurt at that convention. I thought to myself, "This is what America is doing to its young people."

When I addressed the convention, I pleaded with the delegates not to make my candidacy a cause for division in the ranks. I told them that I had not come to seek their nomination. I was *already* an independent write-in candidate. And I also told them that the real work of the Peace and Freedom Party would begin *after* the 1968 election—the building of a strong alternative third-party base for the 1972 election.

Eldridge was chosen as the candidate of the Peace and Freedom Party. However, many of my supporters broke away and formed the Freedom and Peace Party, thereby getting my name listed on the ballot in a number of states, including Virginia. As I look back, I'm not really disappointed that the split occurred. If the Peace and Freedom Party had stayed together and had really become a strong, organized third-party alternative, I seriously doubt that the Twenty-sixth Amendment to the Constitution, giving eighteen-year-olds the right to vote, would have passed three years later.

My college lecture tour became my campaign trail. And before long I really began to feel like a professional candidate. The campus newspaper at Vanderbilt University endorsed me as its official presidential choice, much to the consternation of the university officials. A straw ballot at the University of the Virgin Islands resulted in my being the number one choice.

I developed a political platform statement which was largely an expanded version of my Chicago platform, projected onto the national scene. The sections of my platform were: moral pollution, Vietnam, welfare and poverty, unemployment, starvation in America, voting age, Indians, foreign aid, youth, education, civil rights, gun legislation, and veterans.

In my platform, I called for:

The creation of a special unit in the Justice Department to vigorously pursue and prosecute the activities of the crime syndicate in the United States;

The immediate end to hostilities in Vietnam and recognition of the National Liberation Front and the territorial realities in that war torn country;

More realistic welfare allowances along with an increase in vocational training and expanding job opportunities, including an end to discrimination in the labor unions;

The building of industrial complexes as a job-creating mechanism;

The creation of a national advisory committee on rural disorders to thoroughly investigate the farm situation and America's food supply;

The immediate lowering of the minimum voting age to 18 years of age;

The creation of a commission on civil order, which would investigate the horrible conditions on Indian reservations, as well as probe the needs of other minorities;

The requirement that 98 percent of all foreign aid money be spent for health, education, food production, and technical assistance;

The creation of a youth commission in the federal government to serve as the focus of youth activity in this country and to be the federal agency through which youth relate to so-called adult society;

The establishment of a federally financed, twenty-four-hours-a-day educational TV channel for adult education at home, offering courses in reading, writing, English, foreign languages, child care, food preparation, history, politics, and other relevant and meaningful subjects;

An all-out campaign across the nation to implement the recommendations of the National Advisory Commission on Civil Disorders (the Kerner Report);

An immediate prohibition against the manufacture and sale of handguns and strict registration requirements for those who own shotguns or rifles; and

Federal legislation making the families of soldiers killed in action wards of the federal government for life, and families of those wounded and unable to work wards of the federal government until each child has completed college.

An expanded version of my political platform was published in June by Bantam Books under the title *Write Me In!* To my knowledge, it is the only time a presidential candidate's platform has been printed and sold by a major publisher, and I thank Bantam editor Walter Glanze for that.

I also produced a unique campaign handbill. It was a facsimile of a one-dollar bill, bearing my photograph where George Washington is supposed to be. It projected the message of one person, one independent vote. The wording on my "freedom dollar" paraphrased the inscriptions found on a real dollar bill, such as "In God We Hope," "Your vote is legal, sacred, and private," and "This country is redeemable." Instead of the signature and title of the United States treasurer, my bill read, "Dick Gregory, President," and in place of the secretary of the treasury was "Mark Lane, Vice President."

A couple of weeks before the November election, I was watching the CBS Evening News on television and was shocked to see Walter Cronkite backed by a blow-up of my dollar. He reported that the Secret Service was confiscating my campaign literature, under orders from the Treasury Department, because it too closely resembled a real dollar bill. They had been picked up in such places as Nashville, Cincinnati, and New York City. The Secret Service claimed that the bills were showing up in money-changing machines. Walter further reported that the bill was tried on a money-changing machine at CBS, and it didn't work.

I started getting calls from newspaper reporters covering the story. I told them, "Well, I'm sure my literature and my campaign is bugging the machines—the political machines all over the country! It's a heck of a commentary on technological advance, if a money-changing machine can't tell the difference between my face and George Washington's! I can't see how my face on a bill could confuse any human being or machine, until the portrait of a Black man appears on regular United States currency."

On April 4, 1968, my campaign came to a horrible halt. I was giving a lecture at Hartnel College in Salinas, California. I was riding in a car when the news came over the radio. Martin Luther King, Jr., had been shot. In Memphis.

I had been following the Memphis situation very closely and had thought many times about going down there. But the more I read, the more I thought something strange was happening in Memphis. Dr. King had been forced to flee an earlier demonstration because gunshots had been fired and violence had erupted. I knew it was not the normal pattern for gunshots to be fired by anyone but the police. And I also knew it was not Martin Luther King's style to run away. But I had usually followed a personal policy of not going into a demonstration led by someone else, unless I was called in by the leadership.

The radio report said that Dr. King was mortally wounded and that he had been shot by a white man. By now I had learned to read between the lines of assassination reports. I never doubted for a moment that Martin Luther King was the victim of a conspiracy. It didn't make sense to me that it was known and *reported* so quickly that he had been shot by a white man. Considering the potential consequences in an outraged Black community in anguish, I would have expected some reportorial stalling, at the very least saying that it was not yet known if the killer was Black or white.

I suspected a conscious governmental attempt to start riots all across the country, a declaration of martial law, and a suspension of the Constitution. I had been looking for something big to happen since the first of the year when the USS *Pueblo* had been seized by North Korean patrol boats in the Sea of Japan. President Johnson had called some 15,000 Navy and Air Force reservists into active duty and federalized thousands of National Guardsmen in case there was a showdown in Korea.

But I was aware of a white paper issued by the Chinese which received considerable attention in Europe but not a word of mention in the United States. It said that the Chinese considered the United States like a child with its hand caught in a cookie jar. They were waiting now to see where the United States would dip in next in Southeast Asia. I was quite sure that the United States would not get heavily reinvolved in Korea as long as the war in Vietnam was raging full scale. I was suspicious that the troop buildup was really related to something else—like instigated urban rioting. I called Lil and said, "This may be it. Keep your eyes open and be very careful around the house."

I began remembering Martin, his sweet innocence and his warm, gentle smile. I thought of the time I had been riding on a plane with him and he expressed concern about my personal safety. He said, "Now, Gregory, I want you to be careful. I'm just afraid they're gonna kill you." I answered, "If they do, Doc, will you preach my funeral?" He said, "I sure will." And I told him, "Now, remember, I don't want none of that whoopin' and hollerin'! Just a simple, straightforward funeral."

My thoughts also flashed to Ralph Abernathy. I wondered if he was safe, or if this terrible act was the preface to wiping out the whole top echelon of the Southern Christian Leadership Conference. And when Attorney General Ramsey Clark flew into Memphis, and immediately declared that there was no conspiracy, I became even more convinced that there was.

I never will forget the reaction of white America that night. The looks of horror, disbelief, embarrassment, and guilt. The haunting question was written on every face, "How will Black folks react?" I saw it in California Governor Ronald Reagan's face on television that night. Black folks in California saw it too, and I really believe his tearful expression of personal shock and horror was largely responsible for keeping things cool in Watts.

At my lecture that night, I realized for the first time that America was in trouble with her young white kids. I was surprised to see the effect that Martin Luther King had upon those kids. They had grown up hearing about Martin, seeing him on television, and being influenced by his national presence. No matter what J. Edgar Hoover or their own mommas and daddies had said about him, those young white kids knew Martin Luther King was not wrong, and he was not bad. Martin was a living denial of all those racist myths perpetrated in the white community about Black folks. Martin didn't lie, he didn't cut, he didn't steal, and he wasn't on welfare. Those young white kids learned the truth about Black folks from Martin Luther King, and he had made much more of an impression upon their minds and their lives than anything they had heard around the family dinner table.

I went to Atlanta for the funeral, still apprehensive about what might happen. I really felt that the Ebenezer Baptist Church might be blown up. Rioting had not been as widespread in the Black ghettos as had been expected. I thought that blowing up the church, with all the celebrated people at the funeral, was not beyond the realm of possibility.

So many superstars were gathered at the funeral, from the fields of both politics and entertainment, that it would be futile to try to recall all of them. But I do remember reading *The New York Times* account of the funeral. I was startled to see that no Black mourners were listed. I remember thinking that anyone outside the United States reading that story would have assumed that Black folks did not respect and admire Dr. King.

Martin Luther King, Jr., was laid to rest in the spirit which defined his days among us. It was a poor folks' funeral, as sad as it was beautiful. I realized that there would never be another Martin Luther King, nor did there need to be. A little bit of Dr. King resided somewhere in the heart and soul of every American, and he had awakened it and brought it out into the open. He did what he had been placed on this earth to do, and there was no need for subsequent imitations of his glorious life. America is a better place because Dr. King lived here, and his blood spilled upon American soil has hallowed and consecrated this ground.

I returned to Chicago and announced that I was calling off my demonstration plans for the Democratic convention. I said, "A peace march in the wake of frustration over Dr. King's death could easily tip off major rioting. I cannot be responsible for leading upset Black folks and white folks through the streets of this city." I felt that Black emotions were too raw, and Black pain too severe, to guarantee peaceful, nonviolent protest.

A few weeks later I was being interviewed on television, and I was asked about recent assassinations and my feelings concerning conspiracy. I said something which turned out to be tragically true. I expressed the feeling that Bobby Kennedy knew the truth about who really was involved in the killing of his brother. And I also said that I feared for Bobby's life if he won the California presidential primary election. If he won that primary, he would undoubtedly be the Democratic nominee for president and probably the next occupant of the White House. He would be in a position to finally expose the truth about his brother's death.

Shortly after midnight on June 5, I was at home in Chicago. I had been watching television and had just gotten up to go to the bathroom. I heard a voice saying, "They shot him! They shot him!" I ran back to the TV set to learn that Bobby had been shot in the kitchen of the Ambassador Hotel in Los Angeles as he was leaving the celebration of his victory in the California primary.

This time I watched the report of Bobby's assassination through eyes trained to search out conspiracy and contradiction. I knew that the most immediate eyewitness reactions would be closest to the truth. I heard a police officer being interviewd at the scene who said there were definitely two people involved. Others verified that a girl in a polka dot dress had been an accomplice. But after the excitement and shock died down, and the official story was put together, Sirhan Sirhan emerged as the lone assassin.

The day after Bobby died, my presidential campaign became a reenactment of an election nearly fifty years earlier. In 1920 Eugene V. Debs was serving time in prison because of his antiwar activity. He ran for president from his prison cell as the candidate of the Socialist party, and he received about 3 percent of the popular vote. I was soon to follow in Debs's footsteps.

I heard the news on the radio. The State Supreme Court in Washington had upheld my conviction for illegal fishing, and my lawyer, Jack Tanner, vowed to take the appeal all the way up to the United States Supreme Court.

I sat down and had a talk with Lil. We recalled together how our original idea was to focus public attention upon the plight of the Indians. I said, "Do you suppose more publicity would be attracted by my serving the time?" We agreed that it would. I called my lawyer and told him not to take the case any further.

On June 7, I submitted myself to the sheriff at the Thurston County Jail in Olympia, Washington, to be confined for a period of ninety days. As I entered my cell, I announced that I was going to fast for the entire period of my incarceration, taking only distilled water for nourishment. My decision turned out to be a financial burden on the jailhouse budget. It cost about fifty cents more per day to provide me with distilled water than to feed the other prisoners their daily food.

It was such a beautiful jail, I really wished that I was eating.

There was an Indian cook, and the food looked and smelled like the fare in a fine restaurant. From the window of my cell I could look out and see the majestic beauty of Mount Rainier as I lay on my bunk. I thought of the people who saved up their money all year to make the trip to Washington to see Mount Rainier. And I thought of all those other folks who dreamed of making the trip but could never quite get the money together. Here I was saying, "Good morning," and, "Good night," to Mount Rainier every day.

My Indian brothers and sisters were so beautiful. They visited me every day. Under the leadership of Janet McCloud, they protested my confinement by setting up tepees on the lawn of the state Capitol and camping out until Governor Daniel J. Evans ordered my release.

Others on the outside were also clamoring for my release. Sterling Tucker sent a request that I lead the Poor People's March in Washington, D.C., on June 19. The NAACP asked me to address its Fifty-ninth Annual Convocation in Atlantic City. Canon John Collins of St. Paul's Cathedral in London requested that I come to England during the month of June to address a mixed group of students. I was more in demand inside the jail than outside.

I was busy inside trying to protect both my candidacy and my life. I was constantly on the lookout for possible government "plants" among my fellow inmates. It would have been a simple matter to have me killed and to lay the blame on a prison fight. Even though it was well known that I was nonviolent, it could be said that is what caused the fight. Some inmate was checking me out to see how nonviolent I really was.

One day my intuition told me to look under a fellow prisoner's pillow. I found a pair of scissors. I suspected that I might be the scissors' intended victim. I asked him, "What are these scissors for, brother?" He broke down and started crying.

He was a disc jockey, serving time for having attacked his wife. He had caught her with a lover. His prison term was an especially maddening ordeal since he could see his house from the window of his cell. And he would see his wife's lover coming in and out of his home. So he had stolen the scissors from the prison barber and was planning to break out on the weekend when an older and more feeble guard was on duty. Then he planned to kill his wife. We talked and talked and talked. I finally convinced him that his plan was self-destructive. Nonviolence had won another victory, and I turned the scissors over to the prison guard.

Having successfully avoided that potential pre-election assassination attempt, I concentrated upon my presidential candidacy. A couple of weeks before going to jail, I had sent a telegram to Secretary of State Dean Rusk, Undersecretary Nicholas Katzenbach, and President Lyndon Baines Johnson, demanding the same foreign policy briefings accorded other presidential candidates. Six candidates had been offered such briefings—Robert F. Kennedy, Eugene McCarthy, Richard Nixon, Nelson Rockefeller, Harold Stassen, and George Wallace. Since those six candidates were white, I suggested that I was being discriminated against, and I threatened to take legal action if my foreign policy briefing was not forthcoming.

I did file a petition in the United States District Court for the District of Columbia, but to no avail. So I had to take things into my own hands. I sent yet another telegram from the jailhouse to President Johnson and Secretary of State Rusk. I said that their refusal to respond to either my personal request or my legal petition was "a racial insult not only to me personally but to Black people all over the world, as well as to Indians, Mexicans, Puerto Ricans, and other minority groups who are consistently and similarly discriminated against by a racist federal administration."

I also informed the president and the secretary that I had no alternative but to try to talk with world leaders directly and to conduct an international fact-finding mission of my own. I said that I had contacted twenty-six heads of state by telegram, requesting permission to visit their countries and discuss world problems: North Vietnam, South Vietnam, China, the People's Republic of China, Germany (East and West), France, North Korea, South Korea, India, Great Britain, Japan, Switzerland, Israel, Ireland, Ghana, Nigeria, Ethiopia, Tanzania, Russia, Mexico, Albania, Canada, Cuba, Egypt, and the Hopi Nation.

I concluded my telegram with the following note:

"Please note that I have included on my itinerary a request for hospitality from North Korea. It is my intention to apply for permission to interview the members of the crew of the USS *Pueblo* if they are not released before my arrival, so that I might ascertain the truth behind this critical incident. In my discussion with world leaders, I shall ascertain for myself the situation in their countries and explain to them American domestic issues not generally understood abroad, such as the Poor People's March, the travail of the American Indian and the Field Foundation report on starvation in the southern states of our own nation."

The longer I fasted, the more concerned prison authorities and state government officials became. And in trying to make me comfortable, they ended up landing me in the hospital. The weather was very hot, and additional fans were sent to the jail to keep me cool. On the twenty-third day of my fast, I caught a bad cold, which everyone insisted was pneumonia. I was transferred to a hospital in Tacoma, and Lillian flew in from Chicago to be at my bedside. Ironically, I was in the hospital on the Fourth of July, and I couldn't help thinking about the tyrannical sickness Thomas Jefferson had written about in the Declaration of Independence. Nearly two hundred years later I was fasting in the hospital, trying to represent those same principles.

I recovered and returned to jail. But my continued fasting was becoming more and more of a sensitive political issue. Governor Dan Evans was slated to be the keynote speaker at the Republican Party National Convention. Jack Tanner sent a telegram to Ray Bliss, Republican Party national chairman, indicating that Governor Evans's refusal to respond to a petition for my release indicated his insensitivity to the problems important to people seeking justice in this country and, for that reason, his role as keynote speaker ought to be reconsidered. Chairman Bliss responded with a letter thanking Jack Tanner "for his interest in the party and its activities."

An arrangement for my release was finally made on the fortieth day of my fast. As a matter of fact, it was actually rehearsed the night before the official day in court. A doctor testified that my health was endangered by continued fasting. The prosecutor talked about the mercy and compassion of the state of Washington.

But the next morning I gave unrehearsed testimony. After hearing the doctor's recommendation, Judge Hewitt Henry asked me how I felt. I answered, "Just fine." I also said that I would not curtail my travel plans if I were released. The court decided that I was not an authority on the actual state of my personal health and I was released as a "trusty-at-large," in the custody of Lillian. My trusty status was to remain in effect until my sentence was completed. As I left the jail, I told the waiting press, "If more people went to jail for rights, fewer would have to go for wrongs."

When it became clear that LBJ was not going to attend the Democratic convention in Chicago, I was suspicious that he knew something. I thought all hell might break loose. I expected the very worst, including the possible blowing up of Chicago's International Amphitheater where the convention was being held. I was also suspicious of CIA infiltration into the Youth International Party. Many of my Black friends and acquaintances left Chicago for the duration of the convention, but I stayed at home, firm in my resolve to sit out the convention.

I watched most of the convention activity on television. I saw the brutal beatings Chicago police were giving young demonstrators, news people, and even innocent bystanders. I did venture out on Tuesday evening of convention week. It was LBJ's birthday (which he celebrated down on the ranch) and Mobilization to End the War in Vietnam held an anti-birthday party at the Chicago Coliseum. Some 3,000 kids attended. Folksinger Phil Ochs entertained. William Burroughs, Jean Genet, and Paul Krassner spoke, and I gave the closing speech. Burroughs and Genet had referred to the Chicago police as "mad dogs." So I quipped, "I just heard that Premier Kosygin sent a telegram to Mayor Daley asking him to send over 2,000 Chicago cops immediately." As I was speaking, Jim McGraw, Steve Rose, and some other clergymen were being tear-gassed out of Lincoln Park where they were holding an outdoor worship service in defiance of the 11 P.M. curfew.

The next day I went back to Grant Park. My fellow presidential candidate, Gene McCarthy, and I spoke to a crowd of young people just across the street from the Hilton Hotel. Then I went further inside the park to a rally being held at the bandshell. The Mobilization-to-End-the-War people and the yippies had combined forces and were planning to march to the amphitheater, even though a parade permit had been refused. Norman Mailer and Allen Ginsberg were among the speakers. When my turn came to speak, I urged the young demonstrators not to blame the Chicago police for the beatings and harassment of the past couple of days.

"They're just following Mayor Daley's orders. Blame Mayor Daley for what's been happening. You know every few years the Shriners come to Chicago for their convention. And when they do, they end up tearing up the town. And the cops just look the other way. Why? Because Mayor Daley tells them to leave the Shriners alone. And why does Mayor Daley say that? Because the Shriners don't come to town to *change* anything, they just come to *buy* something! Who do you suppose spends more money on booze and prostitutes while they're in town? The hippies and the yippies or the Shriners?"

And all during the speeches, the cops were documenting my point by beating people on the fringes of the crowd. After the rally, I went back home to my television set.

That night I saw something I never thought I'd see on national television. An ad hoc line of march had gathered behind the mule-drawn wagon, which was the symbol of the Poor People's campaign. It had been stopped at Balbo and Michigan avenues in front of the Conrad Hilton Hotel. After about a half-hour standoff, the cops waded in with their billy clubs flying, mercilessly and brutally beating the predominantly white crowd. Innocent, elderly bystanders were caught in the onslaught. It was a bloody, crazed, unbelievable scene.

I knew that moment in history would be a turning point in America. For the first time white folks would understand what Black folks have been saying about police brutality. After that bloody battle on Balbo, those "Support Your Local Police" bumper stickers began disappearing. Police all over the country began to have more trouble getting raises and increased benefits. I really believe it was the result of the Chicago police having violated a cardinal rule: don't whip white folks on national TV.

But I immediately had another fear. I knew Mayor Daley and the Democratic Party would be desperate. It suddenly dawned on me that the best thing that could happen to clean up Mayor Daley's image would be for a cop to get killed. It would shift public sympathy back to the side of the police. And I knew the government was not above setting up a sacrificial cop for that purpose.

I decided to assume more of a leadership position in the streets during the remainder of the convention. I wanted to make sure that the demonstrations remained peaceful, while also keeping an eye open for government instigators. The goal all during convention week had been to march south to the amphitheater. An injunction had been issued against marching south of Eighteenth Street. I had an idea that might beat the injunction.

So I announced we were going to march south. Everyone assumed I was talking about the amphitheater. My line of march included a blend of concerned demonstrators, including some convention delegates who had been sickened by the brutal beatings of the night before. I went up and down the line and made sure everyone understood that this was a peaceful, non-violent march. We started marching south, accompanied by hordes of National Guardsmen.

At Eighteenth Street the line of march was halted. The general in command told me it was as far as I could go. I said, "Why? This is a democracy, unless democracy is suspended when the Democrats come to town." I was reminded about the injunction against marching south of Eighteenth Street. I said, "I live south of Eighteenth Street. I'm just walking home with some friends of mine I invited over for a party!" Just in case my strategy worked, I had called Mike Watley in advance to arrange a place large enough to hold all the people and to have soda and potato chips for refreshments. After all, I had promised a party!

The general said if we stepped off the sidewalk onto Eighteenth Street, we would be arrested. Again I went up and down the line of march, making sure everyone understood that this was an arrest situation. Then I took the crucial step off the sidewalk. I was followed by Murray Kempton and others willing to submit to arrest. One by one we were arrested and taken away.

After a representative group had been arrested, the cops fired tear-gas cannisters into the midst of the remaining demonstrators. The cops did not have either the facilities or the inclination to handle all the paper work involved in arresting the peaceful hundreds in the line who were willing to get arrested. So they did the next best thing. They sent them away screaming, coughing, and crying!

A week and a half later, Lillian and I were in Paris. As part of my personal fact-finding vow, I had come to meet with members of the North Vietnamese truce-negotiating team. Two days after our arrival in Paris, Lillian and I went to the residence of the representative of the Democratic Republic of Vietnam, where we met with Mr. Nguyen Minh Vy, a deputy of the National Assembly, and his secretary, Mr. Bai, and his interpreter, Mr. Yoang. We talked for two and a half hours.

It was a revealing conversation. I discovered, first of all, that there were no peace talks going on in Paris. The North Vietnamese flatly stated that no peace talks would begin until the bombing above the demilitarized zone had been stopped unconditionally. I had gone to Paris believing the press and the government and thinking that peace talks were under way.

I also learned a lot about the attitude of the North Vietnamese. I was surprised to hear that they did not consider the American *people* to be their enemy. Rather, they blamed the United States government, the military, and the industrial powers which profited from war and possible conquest. They were very much aware of the opposition to the war in the United States, and they said that the courageous acts of American young people were responsible for saving the lives of captured American pilots.

"You must understand," Mr. Vy told me, "that when a pilot is captured, he does not fall into the hands of disciplined soldiers; he is taken by ordinary people upon whom he has only a moment before been dropping bombs. The anger of these people is very great, and the only way that we have been able to persuade them not to harm the pilots is to tell them about the large number of young people in the United States who risk imprisonment and brutality in order to protest against such atrocities."

My most startling revelation was later to be realized in history. The Vietnamese genuinely believed that every day the war continued, the United States was losing and they were winning. They considered the continuation of the war a much greater problem for the United States than for themselves, even though the war was being fought on their soil. The North Vietnamese were calculating the balance sheet of the war, not in terms of casualties, but rather in terms of territory controlled, the loss of American matériel, and the drain upon the United States economy.

I asked Mr. Vy what assurances the United States would have that more American lives would not be lost if the bombing were stopped. He replied, "The only way to stop the loss of life is to end the war. The only way to end the war is to stop the bombing." It was such a simple formula, but there would be two more presidential elections before America got the message.

The real fun of my presidential campaign began after the other candidates were chosen. After I returned to Paris and started my college lecture tour again, I was actually running against Richard Nixon, Hubert Humphrey, and George Wallace. The equal time regulations turned out to be a tremendous boost to my candidacy. I would be invited on all kinds of radio and television shows in the hope that the other candidates would demand equal time! Even the most conservative stations wanted me so they might get George Wallace. And I obliged. I did every show that asked me. I soon became the hottest commodity in politics.

Tuesday, November 5, was election day. I anticipated that I might just possibly be defeated at the polls. So I held a morning rally at my campaign headquarters and announced that I was declaring myself to be the independent write-in president of the United States in exile. I was doing so as the elected representative of all those people who voted for me. I also announced that my inauguration in exile would be held in Washington, D.C., on March 4, 1969. "The number one concern of my administration in exile," I explained, "is going to be a world food program, beginning right here at home, to somehow guarantee that no human being will ever have to go to bed hungry."

At the time I made the announcement, I had really planned to open a headquarters in Washington, D.C., paint it black and call it the Black House. Those who felt disenfranchised and dispossessed by the White House could take their problems to the Black House. Unfortunately I had to abandon the idea because of a lack of financial resources. But feeding hungry people has remained my number one obsession.

Election night I gathered with my supporters in the Continental Ballroom of Chicago's Knickerbocker Hotel to watch the election returns. For the first time, all three major networks had a computer hookup to project the winners at the earliest possible moment. It represented something like a $40 million investment. I was glad to be a part of the historic new development in election night reporting.

It was such a thrill to be watching television and to see my name up there alongside the other candidates. It seemed to make the long, hard months of campaigning all worthwhile. But at twelve midnight, the computer blew out. All that money had gone down the drain, and reporters had to revert back to earlier reportorial techniques.

I was determined to be first on election night. So I called a 3 A.M. press conference and said, "At this early hour, I have the honor of being the first candidate to concede." I also released the contents of a telegram of concession which I had sent to both Richard Nixon and Hubert Humphrey. In a few more hours it became clear that the legitimate recipient was Richard Nixon.

Five years later, I found out what actually had happened to

the television computer that night. An article on computers, which appeared in the Sunday *Chicago Sun-Times*, June 10, 1973, began:

"Computer experts remember with a sense of creeping horror that election night in 1968 when the television network tote boards began blinking results from Pennsylvania.

"Dick Gregory, the Peace and Freedom (sic) candidate, had rallied some 6,500 votes at one point, and then seven minutes later, the computer told the country that Gregory now had 9.7 million votes. Because that represented 74 percent of the entire vote in Pennsylvania, it looked like quite a trend was forming.

"However, it seems there was a little error somewhere and the entire computer operation shut down at about midnight. Although the system worked well four years later, it is still not known what caused it to report the bogus Gregory landslide."

I don't know what caused it either. I have my suspicions. The sample district in Pennsylvania was heavy George Wallace territory. I have always believed that the machines were rigged so that my votes would turn up as votes for Wallace. But somehow the wires must have gotten reversed and I got all the votes!

Whatever happened, I was more a part of the new technology than I had realized on election night. During my campaign for mayor of Chicago, I dented the machine. When I ran for president, I ended up kicking the computer!

30

An Administration in Exile

My inauguration as president of the United States in exile was held in Washington, D.C., on March 4, 1969. The date had very special significance. I believe that the founding fathers, particularly Thomas Jefferson, were tuned into astrology. Consequently, I do not believe that July 4 was chosen as the birthdate of our nation by accident or coincidence. The date represents highly significant planetary configurations. Other significant dates in American tradition follow from July 4 in the astrological cycle of fours. National elections are held in November, the fourth month following July, and the original date for the inauguration of the president was March 4, the fourth month following November (see the Twelfth Amendment to the United States Constitution). Count four more months and you find yourself right back at the birthday of the United States.

So I wanted to be the president inaugurated by astrological and original constitutional design. Plans for my inauguration and for setting up an administration in exile were coordinated by the New Party, a national coalition of political independents. Dr. James P. Dixon, president of Antioch University in Yellow Springs, Ohio, and I had recently been elected co-chairmen of the New Party, succeeding Marcus Raskin. Even though the date for the inauguration was a return to earlier tradition, the inauguration itself was quite up to date. I wanted all the trimmings that the other president had—a swearing-in ceremony, an inaugural address, and two inaugural balls.

President George Williams of American University got me a lot of pre-inaugural publicity, although he didn't intend it that way. Original plans called for the entire inaugural event to be held on the campus, using the facilities of American University. President Williams refused permission. The students protested, and a week-long hassle followed. After the first confrontation in his office, President Williams promised to reconsider his decision. He did and came to the same conclusion. He said, "On a weekday thousands of students and faculty members are on the campus attending classes. Available parking and university facilities are occupied. Given these circumstances, the university simply does not have the means to accommodate a possible additional thousand or more individuals—regardless of whether the gala is said to be a student affair or not."

The students saw things differently. They were outraged by the arbitrary decision, and they had strong faculty support. The university chapter of the American Association of University Professors voted to support "the Gregory inaugural gala." Walker "Moose" Foster, chairman of the Organization of Afro-American students at the university, voiced student feeling: "In specific terms, the question is Gregory, but generally it is whether students will be trusted with themselves. This university is racist. We feel that Gregory is important to the nation. We're talking about the hunger right here in Washington. What if my people were to eat up everything in sight? To become human locusts. This time they might come up past Connecticut Avenue!"

For whatever reasons, faculty support, student power, or the prospect of Black folks eating up the university, permission was given for one of my inaugural balls to be held at American University. The confrontation was a front-page item in Washington newspapers all week, thus giving my inauguration unexpected press coverage.

I was sworn into "office" as president of the United States in exile at the Morgan School auditorium on Eighteenth and Chaplain streets, N.W. The oath of office was administered by attorney Ruby Burrows. Vice-President-in-exile Mark Lane was not able to attend the ceremony. He was busy in New Orleans helping out District Attorney Jim Garrison. The trial of Clay Shaw on charges of conspiracy in the assassination of President Kennedy was in progress. So Mark Lane was sworn into "office" by long-distance telephone. The oath of office was administered by Attorney Jean Williams. I took the same oath Richard Nixon took, with the sole substitution of the words "in exile."

Jim McGraw served as my Billy Graham by opening the ceremony with prayer. My inaugural address doubled as my state of the union message. I really caught the "presidential spirit" in the glare of the TV lights and in the presence of so many friends and supporters, some of whom had come from Chicago and New York City. That evening I was watching the news on television in my hotel room, and I was amazed to hear the reporter talking about my inauguration as though it was the real thing. Then I saw and heard my inaugural address being replayed, including the part where I focused on the words of the Declaration of Independence, "When these rights are denied over a long period of time, it is your right, it is your duty, to abolish and destroy that government."

That night, I shuttled between my inaugural balls at American University's Leonard Center and the Hotel Americana in a rented limousine. At the university my first lady, Lil, and I were greeted by a standing ovation and an acid-rock substitute for "Hail to the Chief." I told the enthusiastic student and faculty crowd, "The most morally committed force in America is you young folks. I hope you have the courage all your lives that you have displayed here over the past week. Now our biggest job is to convince that other fellow in the White House that he's *not* the one!"

Back at the Hotel Americana, another crowd of supporters was waiting patiently. I rushed to the microphone as soon as I arrived.

"I'm sorry to keep you waiting. The first lady will be along in a moment. She had to stop on the way to plant some trees. And I want to apologize for not having a big name band tonight. The only famous band available was Lawrence Welk. And for me to have Lawrence Welk playing at my inaugural ball would be like Muhammed Ali having the United States Army band play at one of his fights.

"But this has been quite a day, starting with the swearing-in ceremony this afternoon. I guess I'm the first president in about twenty years who's not disappointed Billy Graham didn't show up. I would have never believed my inauguration would get so much press coverage. I'll bet Barry Goldwater is turning over in his cave!

"And I'm pleased to tell you that the Black House is about ready. We installed the hot line today—to Alabama. The next thing I'm going to do is clean up the crime in Washington—by impeaching about one-third of the Congress."

When I finished speaking, the band began playing music for dancing. The crowd standing on the ballroom floor parted and formed a circle as Lillian and I started the first dance. It was an eerie feeling. For a split second, it seemed as though everybody in the room really believed that I was the president. The next day, when I picked up the newspaper, I became even more convinced of the astrological significance of March 4. The headline news was the attempted assassination of South Vietnamese prime minister Tran Van Huong. Underneath that headline, completely filling the front page, was a picture of Lillian and me dancing the first dance at the inaugural ball.

In less than a month I was back in jail again. It took me completely by surprise. I knew that I had a court date on April 1, but I assumed that the case would be postponed or continued as it had been many times before. It was the same old case of my allegedly kicking and biting the cop. But time had run out. I was taken from the courtroom to the Cook County jail to begin serving a five-month sentence. It was quite an April Fools' joke, only the judge wasn't fooling. Once again I began fasting as soon as I entered the jail. Even though I was faced with a possible 153-day fast, I vowed to take only distilled water for nourishment.

My stay in the Cook County jail was a turning point in my life. It is significant that it came at the close of the sixties. I had time to do a lot of thinking. In jail, a prisoner has nothing but time. A prisoner is *serving* time. The time can be used to personal advantage or it can drive a person crazy. Some prisoners come out of jail as wiser and better people; others commit suicide in their cells. Malcolm Little went into prison as Big Red of Harlem and he came out as Malcolm X. He had used his time wisely. Most prisoners, remembering the old adage that "society can imprison the body but not the mind," leave their minds outside the prison walls. Their minds are obsessed with thoughts of the outside—wife, family or sweetheart, what life will be like when the sentence has been served, fond memories, plans, strategies, resentments, regrets.

The secret to serving time in jail is learning how to make time serve you. To accomplish that, prisoners must bring their minds into the jail with their bodies. When a person enters this life, she or he is born out of the womb. When this life is ended, a person returns to the tomb. I think that the womb and the tomb have very real symbolic significance when applied to the penal system in this country. The closest a human being ever comes to entering the tomb before death is to be entombed in prison. And too often the prison experience becomes a living death for the prisoner.

If society were *really* committed to rehabilitating criminals, the prison experience would be more like reentering the womb. The whole structure of the prison and the behavior of its personnel would permit and encourage self-reflection and self-revaluation. The prison environment would be geared toward rebirth and regeneration. Prison guards would recognize and respect the need of inmates to have time to themselves and would just leave them alone. After all, an inmate isn't going anyplace. And a changed prison environment might eliminate the scheming and plotting of the few inmates who do try to break out.

When the jail becomes a womb instead of a tomb, the warden and the prison guards assume a role similar to that of parents. They have the same concern for those committed to their care as good mommas and daddies have for their children. The key to rehabilitation is the simple word "dignity." The prison environment should constantly emphasize the dignity and worth of each individual prisoner. No matter how low a prisoner's own self-esteem has fallen, the prison environment should never reinforce that loss of personal human dignity.

It makes no more sense for prison guards to curse or get angry with prisoners than it does for a doctor to cuss or yell at a patient's cancer. The doctor can curse, beat, or degrade a patient, but the doctor also knows that the patient will die if the disease is not treated. It should be the same with jailers and their "patients." A prisoner's ills can only be effectively treated by a restoration of human dignity. And if society is not willing to make prisons into wombs for true rehabilitation and rebirth, then society should stop using the word "rehabilitation" completely. Society should openly admit that prisons are tombs for social outcasts, designed merely for retribution and punishment.

During my stay in the Cook County jail, I thought back over my life, trying to identify the real turning points in my personal growth. They fell into place easily—getting involved in track in high school, making it in show business, getting involved in the civil rights movement and accepting the nonviolent philosophy, changing my diet and going on my first long fast.

I made a promise to myself as I recalled those high school and college days on the track. The pressures of a hectic schedule had made me forget those wonderful days and that good feeling of being physically fit. I promised myself that I would start running again every day. There are twenty-four hours in each day, and I vowed to reclaim one of those hours for myself, alone, on the track, or at least running somewhere.

Even though I was inside the jail, I was constantly reminded that many people on the outside were thinking about me. So many letters came to the jail from schoolchildren and college students, including a letter from a seventh grade history class at the predominantly white Central Grammar School in Gloucester, Massachusetts, which told me I had been voted the class "personality of the week." I could look through the bars of a jail window and see the members of Operation Breadbasket holding a prayer vigil outside the jail in protest of my imprisonment. I even spoke to the demonstrators through the bars.

"Even though I am in jail and I appreciate your concern, remember that the problem is still out there. So many people on the outside in Chicago are worse off than I am. They will go to bed hungry. But if I weren't fasting, I'd have three meals a day like my fellow prisoners. I have a warm place to sleep tonight, but many people in Chicago are homeless. In the Cook County jail I don't have to worry about being bitten by rats as I sleep. But many poor ghetto mothers will lie sleepless, worrying about their babies being bitten in their cribs."

On the twentieth day of my fast, my lawyers began petitioning Governor Richard B. Ogilvie to grant clemency and commute my sentence. As grounds for executive clemency, the petition cited admission by the Chicago Board of Education since my arrest that the conditions which gave rise to the protest demonstrations did exist in the schools. An August 23, 1967, Board of Education report entitled *Increasing Desegregation of Faculties, Students and Vocational Education Programs* said, "Our study of current data indicates that, beyond question, teachers in Negro schools and schools in low socioeconomic neighborhoods are younger, are less experienced, have less formal training, are less qualified in terms of the Chicago system's certification requirements, and are subject to higher turnover than is the case with their colleagues in predominatnly white schools and in schools in more favored socioeconomic areas." A February 9, 1967, report by the United States Commission on Civil Rights to the president entitled *Racial Isolation in the Public Schools* found that ninety-seven percent of the Black elementary school children in Chicago were in schools that were predominantly Black-segregated.

So two years after my arrest, both the Chicago Board of Education and the United States Civil Rights Commission documented the legitimate grounds of our protest. It took some three weeks after my petition was filed for Governor Ogilvie to respond. When he did, the commutation of my sentence was cloaked in secrecy. I was released from jail very early in the morning, while it was still dark. There were no press representatives around, nor was there any advance notice of my release. I just got out, and my forty-five day fast was over.

Even though I had served my time, the two cops continued to press their lawsuit against me for allegedly kicking and biting them. It really had me worried because I was convinced I couldn't win a case in Chicago no matter how right I was. Then I got unexpected legal aid.

Harry Moses, an old friend and television producer, asked me to appear in the pilot show he was producing, starring attorney F.

Lee Bailey. The premise of the show was to have Lee question two witnesses on the opposite sides of a social or political issue. The pilot show featured Florida Governor Claude Kirk and me testifying about law and order.

After the show, Lee and I got together. I told him about my case in Chicago with the two cops. I figured that Lee ought to be able to handle my twisting the chain around the cop's neck since he had done so well with the Boston Strangler. Lee agreed to handle the case, even though he thinks lie detector tests are the greatest invention since Kool Aid.

Irv Kupcinet ran the following item in his column on October 7, 1969: "Famed attorney F. Lee Bailey, back from Saigon where he was scheduled to represent one of the Green Berets, revealed he will help defend Dick Gregory in a case coming up here November 13. That's the charge against Gregory for allegedly biting a policeman during a demonstration in 1965." The next thing I knew, the case was dropped. And many months later, I was told that the two cops were indicted for shaking down tavern owners.

As president in exile, I continued to appear on the nightclub stage. And I talked about what would have happened if I had won the regular election.

"If I'd been elected president, my biggest worry would have been how to get from Chicago to the White House without bein' assassinated. And if I did make it, that's the last you'd have seen of me. My first lady would come out on the balcony of the White House every day and report, 'Greg's all right, folks.'

"I guess I would have had to have a tax increase. It would have been expensive to have those 150,000 Secret Service and that bubble top tank. Oh yes, I would have had me a bubble top tank. If anybody shoots at me, I'm shootin' back!

"And if I'd been elected president, you would have accused me of bein' a racist. I would have appointed an all-Black cabinet, and everybody else who worked for me would have been Black and looked just like me—beard and all. I can just see that first assassination attempt. After the shot was fired, the assassin would run back and report to his fellow conspirators, 'Well, fellas, I just shot President Gregory.' And they'd say, 'Fool, we were watching it on television. You shot his maid!'"

The highlight of that first year of my administration in exile came on October 15, 1969. It was the day of the first big Vietnam

War Moratorium in Washington, D.C. It was a cold day, and a strong wind was coming off the Potomac. But hundreds and hundreds of thousands of young people had gathered to protest the war. I sat on the speakers' platform and looked out over that sea of determined faces of those sitting on the wet grass. There were familiar faces in the crowd and on the platform—Harvey Cox, Tim Leary, Richie Havens. As I walked to the microphone, I really felt my role as president in exile. Those young people were also living in exile in their own country. They had been banished and repulsed by their country's continuing madness and brutality in Vietnam. They represented my true constituency.

"I am Dick Gregory and I am a convict. But I am not a criminal. I have been arrested, tried, found guilty, and thrown in jail. Therefore, I am a convict. I have been convicted because of my convictions. The problem in this country today is that the real criminals have not yet been convicted. But one of these days there will be enough of us convicts in this country to rise up and convict real criminals.

"Let me say this to you young people. I know what you are capable of doing. If Nixon doesn't believe that you young people are capable of changing things in this country, then I suggest that the president of the United States make a phone call to that boy down in Texas and ask him what the young people are capable of doing. You young folks ran LBJ back to his ranch!" When I finished speaking, it seemed that a tidal wave was coming toward me as row after row of those young folks rose to their feet to applaud. It was a sight I will never forget.

Although I didn't realize it at the time, I seem to have started a trend with my administration in exile. Five years later the man who defeated me at the polls in 1968 ended up in exile in San Clemente, while various members of his administration were trotted off to jail.

Richard Nixon and I took opposite approaches. I started off in jail and ended up as president in exile. Richard Nixon started off as president of the United States and chose exile to avoid going to jail.

31

The My Lai Caper

In June of 1969 Lillian and I attended the World Assembly for Peace in Berlin. The World Assembly represented some twenty international organizations and included such outstanding voices as Pastor Martin Niemoeller and the former Indian defense minister Krishna Menon. During that trip, while we were in London, we were visited by some of the North Vietnamese representatives we had met on prior trips. They told us that they had some movie film which they would like for us to view. My wife and I have always enjoyed going to the movies together, so we agreed to see the flick.

It turned out to be a home movie, and it certainly wouldn't be nominated for an Academy Award in the United States. It was filmed at a village called My Lai, and it showed American soldiers ruthlessly and heartlessly murdering North Vietnamese villagers. It was a sickening sight to see American soldiers standing on their victims, adjusting their hats for the camera before firing the fatal shots.

As I watched the film I felt a sense of outrage, not only because of what I was seeing on the screen, but also because I felt that the North Vietnamese were tricking me. I couldn't understand how they possibly could have gotten those horrible and revealing home movies out of the hands of the American soldiers who made them.

I raised that question. The North Vietnamese representatives said that when American soldiers want women and whiskey, they use money and anything else in their possession as a means of exchange. Wine, women, and *wrong!* I thanked them for showing me the film but I said I really didn't see anything I could do with it. But I assured them I would be in contact again if I figured out an appropriate strategy.

One day at home in Chicago I had an idea. I said, "Lil, I'm going to show you how to make a tapped phone pay off." She said,

"What do you mean, Greg?" I said, "I really believe if I call some friends on our phone and tell them I'm going to pick up those movies we saw in London, we can cut some time off the war."

So, knowing my phone was monitored by the government, I started calling folks and saying, "Hey, I can get my hands on some on-the-spot movies of a massacre which proves beyond a shadow of a doubt that American soldiers were involved in killing innocent women and children in Vietnam. I'm fixin' to go get 'em right now."

I made enough phone calls to make sure the government knew what I was doing. I really felt that the government itself would break the news about My Lai if I successfully got those films into this country.

In November Lil and I left for London. As we left New York City, we could tell we were being tailed. We identified a particular agent, and we started playing cloak-and-dagger games with him. We arranged a secret rendezvous with the North Vietnamese representatives. Then we went to a movie theater. Our agent followed. During the movie Lil and I slipped out a side door, met our Vietnamese contacts, and picked up the film. We walked the streets all night.

We had successfully confused our agent. He didn't know when or where we were going to pick up the film. So we continued our cloak-and-dagger strategy. We flew to Paris, and our agent followed. In Paris we were met by an old friend, Don Bourgeois, by prior arrangement. I didn't want my bags searched and the film brought forth under the watchful eyes of the agent. So I gave Don some money and asked him to deal with customs. Don combined charm with cash and got us through.

It was time to implement phase two of my caper. I introduced myself to the agent! I told him, "Look, I know who you are. You've been following us all the way from the States. But now you need *me* for protection. What you were supposed to keep us from getting, we've already got. It's already been dealt with."

Then I pointed out Don Bourgeois and made up a story. I told the agent, "See that Black cat over there. He's an agent too. I know him from Chicago. And I'll bet he's the one who's supposed to deal with you because you messed up." I convinced the agent that I would keep an eye on Don in the interests of his own personal security.

That night we all went out to dinner together. Don had made

arrangements at the restaurant in advance while I was with the agent in my hotel room and had given the maitre d' a hundred dollars, explaining to him who I was. As we left the hotel I picked up my brief case, which was not unusual, since I usually carried it everywhere. Only this time, unknown to the agent, it contained the My Lai movies.

At the restaurant, the maitre d' treated me like visiting royalty. We had dinner and left. I purposely left the briefcase under the table. After everyone had gone to their respective hotel rooms, I called the restaurant. I told the maitre d' I had left my bag. He said, "We'll send it to your hotel right away, Mr. Gregory." I said not to bother, that I'd pick it up the next day. He kept insisting that it was no trouble at all, so I had to concoct an excuse for leaving the bag in the restaurant overnight. I didn't want it in my hotel room.

I told him, "Look, I've got to confess. There are pornographic movies in that bag. I don't want my wife to know." The matire d' understood and said that he could have gotten me better pornography if he'd only known I was interested. I thought to myself, "No, baby. You'll never find anything more pornographic than those movies."

The next day Lillian and I went to the airport. A friend in Chicago had arranged for a separate ticket for Lillian, using her maiden name, Paris to Montreal, Montreal to Toronto, Toronto to Chicago. On the last leg of the return trip, Lillian would tell customs that she was just visiting in Canada. We first drove by the restaurant and picked up my bag. Lil boarded Air Canada with her truly explosive parcel, although its explosive quality would not be picked up by airline security devices.

Lil was on her way, when I saw the agent enter the terminal and look around for me. Hs spotted me and said, "I thought you were going to stick close by me." Once again I needed an excuse for being at the airport. I was standing next to a newsstand, and I looked down and saw the Sunday *New York Times!* I said, "You must know that I'm a news freak. I had to come out to get a copy of the *Times.*"

The agent asked, "Where's your wife?" I said, "Back at the hotel, I suppose." "No she ain't," the agent replied. "I went by your room." I had to take a gamble concerning how closely I had been watched and how much personal information had been re-layed.

So I said, "Didn't your people tell you that Lillian jogs every day?" He was caught off guard, "Yes, I knew that." I breathed a sigh of relief and said, "Well, I guess she must be jogging now."

I returned to the hotel, and I really sweated out that day. About two hours after Lil was due to arrive in Chicago, I received her phone call. Her plane was an hour late, but the caper was over. She had made it safely and so had the film. During that telephone conversation, I sent another message to the government. I said, "Well, fellas, you're really in trouble now. That My Lai mess has got to come out."

It was only a matter of days before the story of the My Lai massacre hit the headlines. On November 24 the Army ordered a court martial for Lieutenant William Calley. Two days later the White House described the massacre as "abhorrent" and promised strict justice for the persons involved.

32

Thanks for the Memories

I was back on the show business pages once again in the late spring of 1970. Columnists and reviewers seemed to feel that I was returning to nightclubs after a long absence. Of course, I'd never really been away. But over the past few years my name had appeared more often in the news section than in the entertainment section of the newspaper.

In May I appeared at Mister Kelly's in Chicago. I got a great review in *Variety:*

"Dick Gregory has taken a break from his civil rights activities and related college speaking dates to play a rare nitery gig at Mister Kelly's, his first there in eight years. His involvement in the rights movement and subsequent political efforts ... has cast a controversial air around the comic, so there was considerable anticipation and much interest prior to his opening.

"If there was any question about his ability to deliver a strong session, however, it certainly didn't last more than a few minutes into the show. Gregory has lost neither pitch nor timing skills during his hiatus from the boite circuit and had no difficulty producing some of the biggest laughs heard here in many months. . . . In all, his first local appearance in some three years shapes as a sock outing. Although he pretty much treats nitery work as a part-time endeavor, he has lost none of his feeling for the genre, and if the jammed opening was any indication, he will keep Mister Kelly's busy during his three-week stand."

After Mister Kelly's, I played two weeks at the Village Gate in New York City. The press coverage was unbelievable. It was due to the hard work and public relations genius of Ed Gifford of Gifford-Wallace, Inc. Ed handled publicity for Kevin Eggers and Poppy Records, with whom I had recently done two lecture albums and a comedy album. Even though I had been playing the Gate all along, Ed hit on the gimmick that this was my first *extended* appearance in New York in five years. Other appearances had been only one-night stands or weekend stints.

In the *New York Post*, Alfred G. Aronowitz devoted his "Pop Scene" column to me and entitled it "Dick Gregory, Brain Surgeon." He wrote: "A brain surgeon, as a matter of fact, is what Gregory comes the closest to being as a comic. That he is also a brilliant monologuist, a compelling storyteller and a magician of special powers also becomes quickly evident as his hour on the stage unfolds. Because even as a comic, Gregory comes on as a heroic figure. He doesn't depend on crazy hats or funny faces or ridiculous poses for his laughs but rather he speaks to us straightforwardly and in the grand manner, filtered as it is by what he'd call a Chicago nigger's accent. . . . But as a strictly commercial act, his routine is no more politically oriented than Bob Hope's."

McCandlish Phillips reviewed my act in *The New York Times*. With typical *New York Times* obsession for statistical detail, he even counted my laughs! He wrote: "There is no venom in the tone and the clown-sized smile betrays not a touch of acrimony as he fires round after satire round in his 62-minute monologue. . . . His hooded eyes are sleepy, but the lines comes fast. In a timed segment, he got eight big laughs and nine little laughs in four minutes—seventeen in 240 seconds, one every 14 seconds. That testifies not only to the rapidity of his delivery but also to the fact that, judging by audience response, he seems never to spin off a clinker."

I'm sure the press coverage, and particularly *The New York Times* review, was responsible for the two distinguished members of my audience one night. I was ready to start my act when I looked out and saw Ed Sullivan and his wife. I was overjoyed. I had never played the Ed Sullivan Show. I always figured there were two reasons why I hadn't been asked. My first big television exposure was on the Jack Paar Show. And there was a bit of a hassle between the Paar show and the Sullivan show. The Paar show paid minimum scale, whereas Ed Sullivan paid top dollar. It got to the point where performers who appeared on Jack Paar's show were not invited on the Ed Sullivan Show. Then, as I became more and more identified with the civil rights struggle, I assumed my controversial status kept me off Ed's show.

But I was determined to make Ed and his wife laugh that night!

"It's nice to see so many of you New Yorkers out tonight. Of course, I knew you'd be here. Right after I read that good review in *The New York Times*. I'll bet, if *The New York Times* reviewed a race riot, you'd want to go catch it, wouldn't you?

"I feel so sorry for John Lindsay. Can you believe that one guy can have so much bad luck with a town? Everything happens to him. I wouldn't be surprised to pick up the papers tomorrow morning and read where the Statue of Liberty got knocked up—by a Russian tugboat!

"I had a newspaper reporter interviewing me the other day. He said: 'Mr. Gregory, why do you think there were no riots in the Black community last summer?' Now how the hell do I know? Do you know Black folks in America are the only folks on the face of this earth they give a riot *season* to? July through August! And last season we didn't come out, and the whole country got uptight? They said, 'Where were you? We had the tanks waiting for you.' I'll tell you where we were. We got tired of stealin' all those bad, no-good products. So last riot season we decided to go under-ground and study the consumer report. And when the riot season opens up again next month, we ain't stealin' no more Motorolas!

"But I had to tell that newspaper reporter something. So I said, 'There were no riots in the Black community last year because all of the Black leaders were in Ireland serving as technical advisers.' They're really doing their thing·in Ireland! But have you noticed, no matter who's rioting or where the riot's being held, all cops react the same? In Ireland, the Catholics and the Protestants are fightin' like hell, and the Irish police is blaming it on outside agitators—Billy Graham and the Pope! And then they say it's Irish extremists that's causin' all the problems—like H. Rap O'Brien and Eldridge McCleaver."

I could see how much Ed Sullivan was enjoying the show, and it really made me proud. He and his wife came back to the dressing room after the show, and we had such a beautiful conversation. Ed admitted, "Dick, I don't know why I've been afraid to have you on the show all these years. But I'd like to have you on this fall." I told him just to set a date with Ralph Mann and I'd be there. It was like a dream come true.

The supreme publicity triumph came when the entire "theater" section of *Newsweek* was devoted to me. Alex Keneas wrote the piece entitled "Return of the Native Son." The opening paragraph said: "In the pantheon for black entertainers—let us for now assume separate-but-equal pantheons—Dick Gregory will have to occupy a singular and somewhat curious place. No black comedian of comparable stature or exposure in the last decade has wielded the cutting edge of social criticism as forcibly as Dick Gregory. Indeed, most widely known black comedians have stuck to the traditional show-biz antics that guarantee mass appeal. But Gregory's own career, swept up in the civil rights movement, has taken him from stand-up gigs to sit-down demonstrations and beyond.

"Now Gregory has come full circle," the review continued, "returning to the cabaret circuit at a time when we are accustomed to gauging his success, not on the laugh meter, but on an index of political and social ferment."

During my two-week engagement, I held a press conference at the Village Gate and announced that I was going on another forty-day fast. This time I was fasting to call attention to the tragic and hypocritical nature of the narcotics problem in America. I felt that law enforcement energies were being focused upon the victims of narcotics addiction rather than upon the perpetrators of it.

I explained the symbolic significance of the fast in my press conference statement: "As I am fasting, I will be cleansing my body of all impurities. I hope my action will help people to realize that the only way for the narcotics problem to be solved is for the national body also to be cleansed of all impurities."

One line from that press conference really seemed to strike a responsive chord. I saw it quoted over and over again, and television interviewers always mentioned it when I was on their show, "If a nine-year-old kid can find the Heroin Man, how come the FBI can't?"

Less than a month after Alfred Aronowitz said my act was no more "politically oriented" than Bob Hope's, Bob Hope himself contacted me, asking me to appear on his Fourth of July "Honor America Day" celebration in Washington, D.C. The giants of comedy were going to be there—not only Bob, but also Jack Benny and Red Skelton. It would be a thrill to be on the same stage with them. But it was a thrill I had to pass by. Bob Hope and I both used politically oriented material, but there was a deeper question of political orientation. I sent the following letter to Bob, in which I tried to speak from the heart, indicating my feelings both about Bob and the war in Vietnam.

I told Bob that I was honored by his invitation and admitted also that appearing with him on the same stage, in the same show, would have deep personal meaning for me. Bob Hope has had a great influence on my life and my career. In my letter, I recalled those early days in Saint Louis as a poor ghetto kid on relief. I listened to Bob on the radio, heard his pointed and incisive political satire, learned to laugh at the amusing ironies of American life, and saw the close relationship between humor and tragedy. Although I didn't realize it at the time, the hours I spent listening to Bob on the radio were the elementary education period for my later career as a comedian. And I was not alone in my appreciation of Bob's humor. So many poor Black folks came away from listening to the Bob Hope show with a lighter heart, having heard him so brilliantly satirize the social and political realities in America.

But I also told Bob that I had to decline his invitation. I felt that it was not possible for an "Honor America" show, held in Washington, D.C. on the Fourth of July, 1970, to be neutral and devoid of political overtones. After all, I had demonstrated in the nation's capital many times before to advance the causes of peace, civil rights, and human dignity. My participation itself would give the "Honor America" celebration a political flavor. So I thanked

Bob for thinking of me and passed on my kindest regards to the other performers.

A couple of years later, Bob and I did appear on the same stage together. And it was an entirely appropriate setting. We were appearing on a benefit for the victims of the flash floods which swept the eastern seaboard in the wake of hurricane Agnes. It was so beautiful being backstage with Bob, and I was so happy that we could finally be together, sharing those common bonds we both hold most dear, comedy and human compassion.

Sunday, November 15, I was scheduled as a guest on the Ed Sullivan Show. It was a big day. I was so excited, you'd have thought I was just starting out in show business. I flew into New York City, accompanied by Lillian, Jim Sanders, and two of my daughters, Lynne and Michele. We went directly to the Ed Sullivan Theater at Fifty-third and Broadway. There was an afternoon rehearsal and a live TV performance that night.

I'm sure my excitement surprised Jim Sanders and Jim McGraw. It was probably the first time they had ever seen me rehearse in the dressing room. But I wanted this show to be perfect. I had waited a long time to be on Ed's show, and I wanted to be sure my few minutes on camera were worth the wait. So I went over my lines again and again and again, with the two Jims as my dressing-room audience and critics.

That night, I waited in the wings to walk onstage for the "really big show." I heard Ed announce my name. This was it!

"First I'd like to congratulate Tom Dempsey of the New Orleans Saints for kicking that sixty-three-yard field goal. Sixty-three yards! Most athletes I know can't even see that far. But I really dig football, 'cause football is a fair sport for my people. It's the only sport in the world where a Black guy can chase a white guy, in front of 50,000 people, and it won't start no riot.

"I do a lot of traveling across the country, and I've never seen so many upset and worried people. Most people are worried about inflation, and also about France and Canada recognizing Red China. But do you realize that one out of every four persons on this earth is Chinese? So don't you think everyone ought to recognize them?

"I mean, do you realize that Red China has something like 688 million folks? I say 'folks,' 'cause people would scare the heck out of you! I mean, do you realize that Red China has more census takers than we have people? We could load up all of our nuclear bombs and drop them on Red China, and they would consider it birth control.

"Do you remember a few years ago when Red China blasted off its first nuclear bomb? And our State Department said, 'Don't worry about it, because it's primitive.' How do you have a 'primitive' nuclear blast? Then the State Department said that what was meant by that statement was that they weren't referring to the nuclear bomb as being primitive, but that it would take Red China ten to twenty years to develop a vehicle to deliver that bomb over here. And I sent the State Department a telegram to inform them that with 688 million folks, they could carry that bomb over here!

"I worry too, but I try to do constructive worrying. Like, I worry about the gold down there in Fort Knox. Now I don't mean to scare you or anything like that, but I don't believe it's there! And I base that on the fact that there are over 200 million of us Americans, and you haven't, and I haven't met anybody that's seen that gold. And I'm not taking anybody's word for it. I believe if the gold was there, they could take 'In God We Trust' off the money.

"And do you know the main reason I don't believe the gold is there? 'Cause none of the television networks has done a special on it. They showed us the moon. And do you know why? Because the moon is there!"

I did more than six minutes that night, which is a lot of time for a comic to have on The Ed Sullivan Show. The band got its cue line mixed up, so I got a band cue on the last few lines of my set. Rather than serving as a distraction, it only served to build the set to a crescendo.

When The Ed Sullivan Show went off the air, I had an empty feeling. I was writing a syndicated column at the time, which appeared in some dailies and quite a few campus newspapers. I wrote a column which tried to record my feelings about the social significance of Ed's show. I called the column "Toast of the Ghetto."

"After more than two decades of weekly national prime time television, The Ed Sullivan Show has been cancelled. The casual observer would say that the show was an inevitable casualty of changing viewing habits and the television industry's concern for both image and market.

"The ratings for The Ed Sullivan Show had dropped; more important, it was determined that the young market was no longer interested. The show had its appeal almost exclusively among the older, middle-America, rural-oriented mind-set, and the new CBS image was to be more city-oriented, urban-hip. And no Sunday evening institution is too sacred for a determined CBS change of image. In other words, the old 'Toast of the Town' had lost its urban appeal. No longer the 'toast of the city,' the Ed Sullivan Show was seen to be at best the 'taste of the expendable.'

"But there is more to evaluating a show's worth than tabulating ratings. Rather than the 'toast of the town,' I will always remember Ed Sullivan as the 'patron of the ghetto.' Of course ghetto dwellers—indeed all poor folks—do not figure highly in the decision-making processes of network studio offices. And so the social significance of The Ed Sullivan Show was probably not only never mentioned but never even realized by those who decide what TV fare the public will consume for seasons to come.

"Ed Sullivan opened a world that otherwise would have remained forever closed to poor folks in America. The very features of The Ed Sullivan Show, which made him the butt of comedians' barbs for years, were his most beautiful expressions of social service. The poor Black kid in the ghetto, and the poor white kid in Appalachia, who knew his parents could never buy him a ticket to the circus, also knew that Ed Sullivan would bring the circus into his own humble living room on Sunday evening. Ed Sullivan spread out the whole spectrum of fantasy and glamor, and for one magic moment the poor kid shared the thrills otherwise restricted to the lucky kids of parents who could afford such entertainment.

"Ed did not restrict himself to providing children's entertainment. He took poor kids' parents to the opera and the ballet. He presented the best of American ballet, Russian ballet, and African dance. He took entire poor families to the Ice Capades and gave them a front row orchestra seat to the best scenes from top Broadway musicals. Not only was Ed Sullivan the 'toast of the town,' but he took the kind of entertainment that was the special property of those who toasted New York City night life and placed it in the slums and ghettos and poverty areas of America.

"I wonder how many poor kids in this nation began to dream of a career in show business because of what they learned from Ed Sullivan? Few poor kids would ever aspire to a career in the legitimate theater if their dream could only be triggered by entering a Broadway theater. How many poor kids would ever have seen a magician or a ventriloquist if Ed Sullivan hadn't presented them? Without Ed Sullivan most Black kids in America would have assumed that show business consisted of singers and musicians.

"So Ed Sullivan defined 'show business' for poor kids in America—the business of working professionals displaying the many, many facets of the art of entertaining people. The appearance of more and more young Blacks, for example, in the heretofore white-dominated areas of show business—legitimate theater, the dance, concert orchestras and the like—is as much a monument to the social service of Ed Sullivan as it is to the breaking down of the walls of discrimination and prejudice.

"Now The Ed Sullivan Show is gone. It will be replaced in the fall by a new series with a law and order theme, a sheriff at work in a contemporary setting; and the social justice which Ed Sullivan brought to the television screen in his selection of entertainment is past history.

"It is a sad commentary upon both the television industry and America that the shoot-em-up series, programs which feature that unique excitement that only violence can bring, continue to enjoy top ratings and network sponsorship. Poor kids in the ghettos and slums of America will continue to receive Matt Dillon's instruction that it is a virtue to shoot straight. And Americans will continue to bemoan the increase of violence in the streets.

"Perhaps the cancellation of the 'toast of the town' is the supreme symbol that America has given up on her cities."

I was later told that of all the many, many tributes Ed received when he went off the air, mine was among those which touched him most deeply. And I'm glad, because I meant every word. As Brother Bob's theme song says, "Thanks for the memories."

Talking to the National Guard at the Democratic convention,
Chicago (1968).

Politics

With Gene McCarthy under the shade of the old rabble tree,
Grant Park, Chicago (1968).

Above: Inauguration as
president-in-exile,
Washington, D.C. (1969).

Left: Following Mahatma Gan
with Jim McGraw at the
Taj Mahal (1970).

Above: After roadwork with Muhammed Ali, Detroit (1974).

Right: With our shining ebony ambassador, Ossie Davis (1974).

Below: Running with the heavyweights, Rev. Ralph Abernathy of SCLC and world champion Muhammed Ali.

Up from Nigger.

33

Around the World in Twenty-Six Days

During the latter part of July and August in 1970, I rented a house in Toronto, Canada, to complete my fast against narcotics. It was the first time I had gotten away from the pressures of my daily schedule during a fast, other than those times when I was fasting in jail. This time I was removing myself by choice. The summer in Toronto came as close to the ideal conditions for fasting I had ever experienced. Since very few people knew where I was, my time was my own. I could lie in the backyard, soaking in the sun, getting the proper amount of rest, and being completely quiet and contemplative. As a result, I felt the spiritual and cleansing powers of the fast as never before. I had announced a forty-day fast, but I ended up fasting for eighty days.

After the first couple of weeks, I began to get lonely. I began calling folks on the phone and inviting them up for a visit. Soon I had a steady stream of visitors: my brother Garland; Sally Wales, a psychic and spiritual adviser from Chicago; Dr. Fulton; Kevin Eggers; Jim McGraw; and Michael X Malik, founder and director of the Black House in London, England. I hadn't seen my younger brother for a long time, and I really appreciated our days together. I taught him about natural foods, and he became an enthusiastic devotee of freshly squeezed juices. And I got to know Sally Wales in a way I had never known her before. Once again I was impressed and inspired by the wisdom of old Black folks, and I could sit and listen to Sally talk and tell stories for hours, just as I had listened to the old folks as a kid.

In September a summit conference of nonaligned nations was being held in Lusaka, Zambia, in Africa. All my life I had wanted to visit Africa, and I particularly wanted to attend the conference.

Bob Lecky, who was then editor of the newspaper *American Report*, arranged a speaking tour for me in Australia during the third week in September. Bob is a Methodist minister and is originally from Australia. The speaking tour was to be sponsored by the Aquarian Foundation, an organization of Australian student groups.

The Australian tour provided the perfect opportunity to get to Africa and the conference. As part of my lecture fee, I included two round-the-world tickets, which were not much more in price than round-trip tickets to Australia. Jim McGraw and I planned to circle the globe together. We sent our passports to an agency in New York City, Visa Center, Inc., along with our proposed itinerary. Jim McGraw was to bring the passports with him to Chicago at the beginning of the trip.

When Jim called Visa Center, Inc., he discovered a problem with the Australian Consulate in New York City. He was told that our visas to Australia were being delayed. Everything had seemed to be all right when the man at the visa center first contacted the consulate, but over the past couple of days, he was getting the run-around. I told McGraw to pick up the passports anyway and that we would get the remaining visas at the Australian Embassy in London.

We left Chicago for London on September 1, checked into the Churchill Hotel, and started making some visits. We visited Canon John Collins at St. Paul's Cathedral, and I talked with him about using the church for a Christmas fast to dramatize the problems of South Africa and Vietnam. That night I spoke to a gathering at the Black House, although Michael X had not yet returned to England.

The next day we were getting ready to go over to the Australian Embassy, Australia House, when I started getting calls from newspaper, radio, and television reporters. They wanted to know what time I would arrive at Australia House. As we entered the downstairs lobby of Australia House, a whole crowd of reporters were waiting. I still didn't know what was happening. I gave my name at the desk and was told that the ambassador was waiting in his upstairs office.

When Jim and I sat down in the ambassador's office and I told him we had come to apply for a visa, he looked at me as though I was putting him on. He said, "Do you mean to say that you really don't know what has been going on in Australia?" I didn't. So he said, "Well, the best thing I can do is show you the latest cable. Here, read this."

A debate had been raging on the floor of the Australian Parliament for several days. The government was insisting that our visas be denied. The liberal opposition, led by Gough Whitlam, who was later to become prime minster, was insisting that our visas be granted. It was a big liberal-versus-conservative fight, and the conservatives had the votes.

The government insisted that our presence in Australia would be disruptive. My anti-war views were cited as disruptive because Australia had fighting forces in Vietnam. The minister of immigration, whose last name appropriately was Lynch, insisted that I had been deliberately deceptive and dishonest in applying for a visa. I had said that I was coming as a tourist, but it had been widely publicized that I was going to be speaking at anti-war moratorium demonstrations at various colleges.

I really didn't know what to say. Visa Center, Inc., had filled out the application and had automatically listed "tourist" for all the countries we were planning to visit. But my visit had become such a big political issue that a simple explanation just wouldn't do. Our visas were denied.

I went back downstairs to talk to the press. "I really don't blame the Australian government for this," I said. "I blame the American government. I can understand my visa being denied. My views about the war in Vietnam are known all over the world. But Jim McGraw was also denied a visa. His views about the war could only come from information supplied by the CIA and the United States State Department." I said that we would continue to apply for visas in every Australian Embassy along our journey.

We flew from London to Paris. Paris is certainly one of the most beautiful cities in the world. The beauty of the city does not depend upon the people populating it. All Parisians could disappear, and it would remain one of the beauty spots of the world. Walking through the streets of Paris once again, I remembered that even though Adolph Hitler ordered the city destroyed, some of his underlings declined to carry out the order. And I also remembered hearing that Hanoi was even more beautiful than Paris. It took the United States to bomb Hanoi in a display of disregard for beauty which even the mad regime of Nazi Germany would not tolerate.

The Australian Embassy in Paris gave us the expected refusal.

From Paris, we flew to Rome. I looked down on the Alps from the airplane window and marveled at the accomplishment of that Black soul brother General Hannibal. I thought, "Wow! He got across with all those elephants. That's Black Power!"

I had never visited Rome before. I found it to be the opposite of Paris. The real beauty of the city is its people and their life style. Some of Hannibal's "soul" must have rubbed off on the Romans. People in Rome seemed to have learned how to live and had established a sensible pace for life. But if the people disappeared, there would be nothing left but ruins, reminding visitors of ancient Roman imperialism. I was particularly disappointed when I visited the Vatican. I told Jim McGraw, "Man, I sure thought the Pope would have better housing than this!"

Even though our airline schedules had been arranged far in advance, we lost our reservations in Rome. The delegates to the conference of nonaligned nations included monarchs, emperors, and other heads of state. They commanded extra reservations for their entourages, and it's difficult for a ticket agent to say no to a king. We were laid over an extra day in Rome. When we did get a flight out, our reservations were guaranteed only as far as Nairobi, Kenya.

I was both excited and apprehensive about landing in Africa. Africa was the continent of my heritage, but I only knew it from the Tarzan movies. Having been born and raised in America, I identified more with the white man as I watched those movies than I did with the Africans. The Africans were always portrayed as ignorant savages. As a kid sitting in the movie theater, I thought they were real Africans. I didn't realize they were some California Black folks who got a temporary movie gig as extras. As the plane approached African soil, I felt like a kid from a broken home whose parents were separated before his birth. I was going to see my momma for the first time—Mother Africa.

All the flights were full going to Lusaka, Zambia. East Africa airlines put us up for the night in Nairobi until reservations opened up to Lusaka. We checked into the Nairobi Hilton, and I was right back home. The room-service menu was the same as any Hilton menu in the United States. No matter where I went, Conrad Hilton had been there first! The next morning, I went outside and thought I was in Memphis, Saint Louis, or the Black community anywhere. It was the same down-home atmosphere. Folks even dressed like Black folks in a little southern town. I saw more dashikis in one block on the West Side of Chicago than I saw in all of Africa.

But the attitude of the people was different from back home. Folks were so open and friendly. I began to understand the origin of true "soul." Everyone spoke to you on the street, not yelling from across the street, but politely crossing over to engage in conversation. Men walked along together holding hands as an expression of friendship. They didn't have the hangups men had in the United States.

I was overwhelmed by the respect African folks displayed toward each other. Once again I realized the terrible destructiveness of an American system which forced Black folks to despise their Blackness. Black folks in America have always shown respect toward those in authority rather than respecting each other. They have said "yes, sir," "no, ma'am" and even "massa" to white folks in authority. Yet the "kill rate" in the Black community is a continuing reminder that the same respect is not displayed at home in the Black neighborhood. Black folks kill more Black folks in a month in the ghettos of America than the Ku Klux Klan has killed in its entire infamous history.

The next day I was sitting in the observers' gallery in the new conference hall in Lusaka, Zambia. I had my zoom-lens camera, and I had a ball zooming in on world leaders such as Indira Gandhi, prime minister of India; Haile Selassie, emperor of Ethiopia; President Tito of Yugoslavia; and conference host Kenneth Kaunda, president of Zambia. I thought of all the potential power represented in that room. The delegates were the representatives of the majority of the world's population, and their countries contained most of the world's natural resources.

While in Lusaka we were taken on a tour by representatives of the Zambian government. We went to visit some new housing developments. On the way we heard about some of the thrilling accomplishments of the Zambians during their first six years of independence. When the British got out of Zambia, they left the new nation with only a half dozen schools. Six years later the Zambians had a school system of well over a hundred schools. The Zambian oil pipeline was laid in less than a year and a half. The Lusaka conference center was constructed in only two months. Those Tarzan movies were wrong. Those "savages" didn't need white folks to build a truly humane and civilized nation.

But there were still painful reminders of former colonization.

At the housing development, an area of simple, modern bungalows which only months before had been filled with grass huts, we were permitted to walk through one person's home. There were no pictures on the walls until we got to the last bedroom. There, smiling down from the wall, was an album-cover picture of Elvis Presley!

In downtown Lusaka I walked past a record store, and the entire window was filled with copies of a new album by Dean Martin. More recordings by white artists were being sold in Africa than those by Black artists. On the talent agency, distribution, and promotional levels of show business, white folks are still in the overwhelming majority. Black artists must make it their personal business to see that their records and books are readily available on the African market. It is their duty to themselves as well as to their African brothers and sisters.

From Lusaka, we returned to Nairobi. I had been calling Australia every night. My Australian contacts had been trying to find a way to circumvent the government's refusal to give us visas. They first suggested picking us up in a private plane and landing in some remote area of Australia without governmental permission. I refused to have anything to do with those plans. I didn't want to become the victim of an Australian "kangaroo" court!

Then it was suggested that we fly to Sydney, Australia, where we would be met in the waiting room of the terminal by an Australian film crew. We wouldn't officially enter the country. Then we would fly to New Zealand where my college lectures would be filmed and brought back for use in Australia. I agreed to that strategy. But the Australian government got wind of our plans. The CIA must have given them a course in how to tap telephones. A worldwide bulletin went out from the Australian government to all airlines, insisting that we not be allowed to board any flight headed for Australia.

With the Australian part of our trip definitely canceled, we had some time to fill. We substituted visits to Ethiopia, India, and Thailand. In Ethiopia we stayed at the Addis Ababa Hilton, across the street from the palace residence of Emperor Haile Selassie, Lion of Judah and direct descendant of the Queen of Sheba. Through a government contact, I arranged an audience.

I had heard about Haile Selassie all my life. He was the Black emperor, the symbol of ancient, regal Blackness. He was also the symbol of ancient wisdom and the knowledge of the secret mysteries of the past. In recent years I had become more involved in the occult. I noticed Emperor Selassie at the Lusaka conference, sitting with his thumbs and forefingers formed in the shape of a pyramid. I knew it was not accidental, and that he was aware of the mysterious power of the pyramid.

So I was really looking forward to rapping with the emperor. I went across the street only a few minutes before my appointment and was told by a guard that I had come to the wrong place. I had gone to the emperor's residence. His office was in the Old Palace some distance away.

By the time I got to his office, I was quite late for my appointment. Walking through the Old Palace grounds, I saw lions lying on the grass. I can't deal with dogs, let alone *lions!* But then I noticed the lions were chained to stakes driven in the ground. I still kept my distance. There was a whole crowd of folks in the waiting room outside the office. One guy had been coming back day after day for several days, hoping to get a couple of minutes with the emperor. I was ushered in immediately.

I was never more disappointed in my life. Although I knew that Haile Selassie spoke English fluently, he talked to me through an interpreter. Instead of being the wise, occult statesman I had expected, he sounded like any other politician. I came back to the hotel. Jim McGraw asked, "How did it go? What was the emperor like?" I answered, "Just a chump." I didn't elaborate because I didn't know if recording devices were hidden in the room. If so, I'd let his interpreter try to translate "chump" into Amharic!

I saw a lot of poor folks in Ethiopia and later in India. So many American tourists return from around-the-world trips, talking about the horrible conditions of poverty in other countries and saying how fortunate we are to live in America. But I had a different reaction. Poverty is more *visible* in other countries than it is in America. The typical American tourist is quite ignorant of the depths and extent of poverty in the United States. The American tourist who can afford to travel abroad is in a privileged income bracket. Yet those tourists compare themselves to poverty-ridden people in every country they visit. But the same American tourists would never think of comparing themselves to poor folks at home. As a matter of fact, they seldom see enough poor folks to do any comparing.

In Ethiopia and India the poor are everywhere. As soon as you step outside the hotel, you see poor people on the street, begging or simply standing and staring at you with wide-eyed curiosity. Poor people surround the finest restaurants and hotels, government buildings, and tourist attractions. In the United States poor people are not as visible. They are carefully shut up in their own special neighborhoods, called slums and ghettos.

Vagrancy laws in the United States protect tourists from seeing America's poor, just as they protect American citizens from having their privileged neighborhoods invaded by poor folks A poor person in the United States is seldom arrested for standing around on a slum or ghetto street corner or for panhandling from fellow poor folks. But the same person who dares to stand outside a prestigious hotel in any American city, or outside the White House, will quickly be found in violation of vagrancy laws.

We arrived in New Delhi at night. Our hotel reservations in New Delhi had gotten mixed up, so we took a cab to the Oberoi Maiden's Hotel in Old Delhi. Driving through the streets from New to Old Delhi, I saw another popular tourist myth exploded. I saw many bodies lying at the side or in the grass mall in the middle of the street. I automatically thought of all the stories I had heard about people starving to death in the streets of India.

But then I realized that these people were sleeping outdoors. Many held the religious belief that God was in the air, and they would not sleep indoors. Others found it more comfortable to sleep outside than to swelter indoors without air conditioning. Consequently, people who died in their sleep, for whatever reason, died in the street. I wondered how many dead bodies would be found in a densely populated American city each morning if everyone slept in the street.

As we were leaving for Bangkok, Thailand, I made another startling discovery at the New Delhi airport. I went to the men's room and put my money into a coin-operated stall. I opened the door and thought there had been a burglary. There was no toilet stool. Just a hole in the floor! I thought, "When in Rome, do as the Romans do. But this is ridiculous!" You'd be surprised how quickly you can lose the urge.

In Bangkok we visited a number of Buddhist temples. In one of them I found the answer to something that had been bothering me ever since I first became heavily involved in fasting. I had become convinced that there were no truly wise fat folks. But then I thought about Buddha and his supposedly roly-poly self. I just couldn't figure him out. At the Buddhist temple in Bangkok, a series of statues depicted the stages of Buddha's life. The first statue was the fat, cross-legged form that is a familiar incense burner in the United States. But then I came to a statue that was the skinny, scrawny form of a fasting Buddha. You could count every rib in his body. I had found the real Buddha.

From Bangkok, we stopped in Hong Kong and Tokyo. As I stood registering at the desk of the Tokyo Hilton, I was surprised to hear someone call my name. I looked around, and there was Carmen MacRae. She had been in Japan for some time, performing at military bases. Being with Carmen in Tokyo was like a touch of home before I actually got back.

When I did get home and reflected back upon the trip, I thought of the irony of America's enemies and her friends. I had been welcome in Hanoi, but I couldn't get into Australia. With allies like that, who needs enemies?

34

Freeing the Army

My lecture schedule had included some military bases, such as Fort Carson, Colorado, and the Air Force Academy at Colorado Springs. I was amazed at how well I was received. Social and political awareness seemed to be as strong among young GIs as it was on the college campus.

So when I was contacted by Jane Fonda to participate in the Free-the-Army shows she was putting together, I jumped at the opportunity. The shows were sponsored by the United States Servicemen's Fund, a nonprofit organization concerned with the welfare of persons who have served or are serving in the military. Our performances were offered as alternative entertainment, presenting a different point of view from the usual USO shows.

I felt that the Free-the-Army shows had tremendous potential. Not all young people had fled to Canada or Sweden, or been imprisoned for refusing induction. Some had accepted being drafted, entered the military service, and were engaged in the lonely, difficult, and courageous task of working on the inside. Others had volunteered to serve their country, but had a change of heart when they realized the truth about the Vietnam War. They represented the forgotten, neglected element in the anti-war movement. I felt there was a great need to establish a relationship with those in military service whose opposition to the war in Vietnam was no less strong just because they were wearing the uniform.

I had appeared on anti-war programs with Jane and I was impressed by her energy, determination, and the wide range of information she had at her fingertips. And Jane worked so hard on the Free-the-Army shows. I can't think of anyone else who could have pulled the project off. She was in constant telephone contact, giving progress reports on planned performances and checking individual schedule details.

Our first performance was a fund-raiser at Philharmonic Hall in New York City. A number of stars appeared on the bill, many more than I remember. Ossie Davis was the emcee. Nina Simone was on the show, as were Jane, Donald Sutherland, Faye Dunaway and Eli Wallach.

Then the Free-the-Army troupe went to Fayetteville, North Carolina. We had hoped to give our performances on the base at Fort Bragg. But Lieutenant General John J. Tolson refused to let us perform because it would be "detrimental to the morale and discipline of the troops." Negotiations were made to use a large auditorium outside of town. The request was initially refused, but the court later ruled that our request was completely legitimate. The ruling came too late, a day before the show, and we performed instead at the Haymarket Square coffee house in Fayetteville. It was a gathering place for the *real* "new army"— those active-duty GIs who were opposed to the militarism and oppression which defined America's image all over the world.

The Haymarket Square coffee house really shook that Friday and Saturday. I wish Lieutenant General Tolson had been there. He would have learned something about "morale" and true "discipline." The spirits of the troops couldn't have been higher. And imagine what personal discipline it takes to wear the army uniform, but to refuse to permit it to either cover or diminish your convictions.

Our troupe gave the troops quite a show. It was a blend of solo performances and sketches. The sketches were primarily the work of cartoonist-playwright Jules Feiffer. Folk singer Barbara Dane opened the show, and she had the whole room stomping and clapping during her rousing rendition of "Insubordination." The entire audience joined in singing the lyric, "I don't want nobody o–v–e–r, I don't want nobody u–n–d–e–r, ME!"

Soul rock singer Swamp Dogg was next. He sang his song, "God Bless America For What?" As incredible as it sounds to anybody who wasn't there, the irresistible beat of the backup music and Swamp Dogg's down-home rap about what America *could* and *should* be had every voice in the room joining in at the end to sing "God Bless America."

I only remember a couple of the sketches. In one sketch, Donald Sutherland and another actor I didn't know reported a battle in Vietnam as though it were a Monday night football game on television. The play-by-play sportscaster reported "twelve water buffalo down and kicking on the field." Donald came in with the color commentary, "The American team is really up for this one, but you have to say that the Vietcong team has had a beautiful season, no matter whom they've been up against." Donald also promised a post-game interview with the maimed and the survivors and reported that President Nixon would have liked to be present "to throw out the first grenade."

In another sketch an actor was introduced as the president of the United States. Greeted by boos and hisses from the audience, the president said, "Thank you, men of Fort Bragg, for that warm reception." The president announced that he was going to take a referendum on the war in Southeast Asia. "All those in favor of withdrawing our troops immediately, say aye," the president instructed. The whole room chorused, "Aye!" "Now, those in favor of our troops staying where they are," the president asked. Dead silence prevailed in the room. "Carried," said the president, "by the silent majority!" Stage blackout.

Midway through the sketches, Donald Sutherland gave a moving reading of a portion of Father Dan Berrigan's final statement at the Catonsville Nine Trial. He held the room spellbound in silence. It was the only silent majority that counted—those with tears in their eyes, too choked with human compassion and sensitivity to suffering to utter a word.

It was my turn to do a monologue. I cut loose on Nixon and Agnew.

"You know, President Nixon's a funny lookin' cat. Did you ever take a good look at Nixon? Ever check out that right jaw? That's what his problem is. How can you trust a cat whose jaws be movin' and he ain't even talking? Nixon missed his calling. He's in the wrong occupation. With them jaws, he should have been a shoplifter. He's the only cat I ever saw who could go into a music store and walk out with a piano in his jaw.

"And Nixon keeps bringin' funny lookin' people into his family. Did you ever take a good look at little David Eisenhower? Next time you see little David, take a good look at him. Who does he remind you of? That cat on the cover of *Mad Magazine!*

"But funny lookin' as he is, I still get upset every time Nixon leaves the country. First of all, I figure he might know something we don't. And second, when Nixon leaves the country, Agnew becomes the number one boy in charge. Now that really scares me. I mean, Agnew reminds me of the type of cat who'd make a crank call to the Russians on the hot line. Agnew's so dumb, he'd probably hijack a train and tell the conductor to take him to Cuba.

"I met a cat the other day who used to room with Agnew in college. And he said Agnew was really a dumb cat. One night, everybody in the dormitory went out on a panty raid. And Agnew was the only one who came back with a jockstrap!"

And I also did lines on the military and the war in Vietnam. Those beautiful GIs ate it up.

"You know, anything Nixon does, Black folks are suspicious of. Like one day, Nixon announced that he was appointing three Black cats as generals in the Army. Remember that? All in one day, man! That really got us uptight. We figured if the Nixon administration was appointing three Black generals in one day, they must be planning on pulling out all the white soldiers and leaving us. Nixon is the only president in the history of America that don't *no* Black folks trust. I mean, you can walk into a room full of Uncle Toms and just mention Nixon's name, and those cats start talking militant.

"I wish I'd have won the election when I ran for president. None of you folks would have had to go to Vietnam. I'd have gone to all the prisons and got all the sex maniacs and given them some LSD and tennis shoes and sent them to Vietnam. It would have been a hell of a war. It would have been better than those headlines we read now: FIVE THOUSAND VIETCONG KILLED, AMERICAN CASUALTIES LIGHT—which is buggin' the hell out of the NAACP! If I had my sex maniacs in Vietnam, you'd pick up the paper and read: TWELVE VIETCONG AND 99 TREES ATTACKED!

"And do you realize it would have ended the war? When them plant lovers read that the trees were being attacked, they would have marched on the White House and demanded an end to the war. That's the crazy kind of country we're living in. Nobody gives a damn about a mother's son losing his life. But don't molest a tree!

"But I wish I'd have talked to you young GIs before you got your induction notices. I could have told you how to avoid the draft. And you wouldn't have had to go to jail or split for Canada. All you'd have had to do is, when you were filling out your induction form and you got to the place that said 'occupation,' just write in 'murderer!'

"Do you realize we have laws in this country which would not permit drafting a murderer into the Army? No, you got to be nonviolent. Then they take you into the Army and teach you how to kill. If that ain't a waste of tax money, I don't know what is!"

Over and over again during my performance, I was greeted with the clenched-fist salute. I never saw so many white clenched fists, not even on the Arm & Hammer baking soda shelf in the supermarket.

After the show was over, and everybody was pitching in to help clean up the coffee house, Jim Sanders, Jim McGraw, and I huddled in the corner for a postmortem on the show. I said, "Weren't Jane and Donald beautiful? And who was that other cat?"

Jim McGraw answered, "Gary Goodrow. He's with an improvisational group called The Committee." And he pointed out the guy he was talking about.

I said, "No, I mean that bald-headed cat that played the president and the sports announcer."

The two Jims looked at each other and shook their heads. I realized I had done it again! I said, "All right, tell me who he is."

Jim McGraw explained, "Greg, for over a year you've been telling everybody to be sure and not miss the movie *Joe.* That's Joe, man. Peter Boyle!"

As we left the coffee house, I noticed a bit of graffiti scrawled on the wall that said it all. It read: "War is NOT hell—hell has a purpose."

The spirit of that coffee house stayed with me. A month later, I was speaking at a huge, outdoor anti-war rally in San Francisco. I really got turned on by both the spirit and the size of the crowd. I knew that this was the kind of commitment and dedication that would finally end the war.

The next thing I knew, I heard myself saying, "I pledge to you this day, that from this moment until the end of the war, I will not eat another bite of solid food." There was a thunderous ovation from the crowd.

As I left the platform, I fully realized what I'd just done. I ran to a telephone and called Dr. Fulton in Chicago. I told her what I had done and said, "How long can I make it?" She assured me it could be done.

That's all I needed to hear. If it could be done, I'd do it with ease. It's those things that can't be done which cause me a little more difficulty.

35

The Last Mile

I returned to my first love in 1972. I decided to enter the Boston Marathon. I did it for two reasons. I knew that my participation in the event would attract a lot of publicity and would call attention to my continuing protest against the war in Vietnam. And I also wanted to explode the persisting myths about American dietary habits. I wanted to prove that it was possible for me to run the twenty-five mile distance, even though I had not eaten any solid food for more than a year.

I began training hard for the event. I ran five or ten miles every day. Every campus I visited, I headed straight for the track before my lecture. I even went to Haiti so I could build up my legs by running up the hills. My training for the Boston Marathon took me back to my high school days in Saint Louis. I was reliving those wonderful moments of my youth.

Running has always been so important to me. Through running I first became aware of what it meant to *be* somebody. When I was a kid running track in high school, I found that running wiped out everything. It wiped out the conditions of poverty, a racist system, the humiliation and frustration of second-class citizenship.

The race track became the great equalizer, a kind of laboratory of true democracy. On the track the Declaration of Independence became a living reality for a moment—all competitors were created equal. They were created through hard training. They were in the meet because they had obeyed the rules of physical fitness. They weren't there because they had money or because they knew somebody or because they came from a certain neighborhood. Nor were they there because some good soul said, "Hey, he's just a poor little Black kid. Let's give him a break."

A kid might be kept *out* of the big meet because he was Black and poor. But if he fought his way up and made it into topflight competition, he was there because he deserved to be, because he had trained to be, because he was physically fit.

For months I built my body and psyched my mind. Everywhere I went on the college lecture tour, I announced that I would be running in the Boston Marathon. I scoffed at those who doubted that I could make it to the finish line. I'd say, "Twenty-five miles? That's no big thing. Just watch me." And all the time, I was saying to myself, "Remember, Greg, that's twenty-five miles. You've got to make it!"

The day of the Boston Marathon arrived. It was a beautiful day for running. It seemed as though everybody I knew was in the crowd of spectators. Lillian, Jim Sanders, and Dr. Fulton were there, and so many other close friends and associates: Don Bourgeois; Steve Jaffe, from Los Angeles; Warren St. James, my high school track coach; Dr. Roland J. Sidney, our family naprapath from Chicago; astrologer and seer Lillian Cosby, from Philadelphia; and my personal spiritual adviser and friend, Mother Gibson, from Chicago.

I started running, and it was that old magic feeling once again. I was surprised and touched by how many of my fellow runners slowed down as they ran past me and said, "Thanks so much for what you're doing." My participation had also brought out many spectators who wouldn't ordinarily have gone to the Boston Marathon, especially those who shared my opposition to the Vietnam War.

I ran and ran, until my legs began to cramp! The finish line was still up ahead, and I tried too hard to make it. But I just couldn't. I finally collapsed. Other runners stopped to lift me up and help me to the sidelines. I was completely exhausted, and I'll always believe that I might have died if Dr. Sidney had not been there. He is a doctor of the natural healing arts, and he began massaging my body and restoring my strength.

Then one of the officials came up and said something which really startled me. "Well, Mr. Gregory, if you're through running, I just wanted you to know that you collapsed at the twenty-five mile mark." For the first time I realized that the Boston Marathon was *not* a twenty-five mile race. It was twenty-*six* miles and a few extra yards. I also realized the power of the mind over the body. For months, I had been psyching myself to run a twenty-five mile race. And I did! Only my mind and the finish line were a mile apart.

I thought of those old movies with James Cagney on death row. Your head really has to be in the right place to be able to make that last mile!

36

Chasing After Famine

In 1973, a decade after the Emancipation Proclamation reception, I was back at the White House again. This time I showed up without an invitation from the president. I had been invited instead by Mitch Snyder, coordinator of many antiwar demonstrations. Earlier in the week, a group of nuns had been arrested for kneeling and praying in protest against the mining of North Vietnamese ports and the increased bombing of the Hanoi-Haiphong area. All week long other demonstrators had joined the daily White House tours and had been arrested for kneeling and praying.

I arrived outside the White House gate and got in line with the other tourists. The two-block-long line included nuns and others who intended to conduct a pray-in. As we got inside the gate and the tour was beginning, my fellow demonstrators and I stepped out of the line, knelt on the steps of the White House, and started praying. A White House policeman interrupted our prayers of intercession to read the law. We would be arrested if we didn't get back in the line. We continued to pray.

An elderly White House guard, who seemed to be a religious man, was upset by the arrest of folks whose only "criminal" offense was prayer. He knelt down beside me and said, "Mr. Gregory, I want you to know that you're not being arrested because you're praying." I answered, "Then what am I being arrested for? Throwin' watermelons at the White House? You've got to be arresting me for praying because that's all I'm doing!"

The White House police escorted us to the back of the White House to be searched and picked up by a paddy wagon. I said to that same White House guard, "Wow! President Nixon must have changed. He must be getting ready to appoint me to the cabinet." The old fellow looked bewildered, so I explained my reasoning. "I always figured if Nixon appointed a Black to the cabinet, he'd bring him in through the back door of the White House."

Our case was tried by Judge Charles W. Halleck, son of the late Republican congressman from Indiana and former House minority whip. Judge Halleck was so beautiful. The prosecution introduced pictures in evidence. The pictures showed the arresting officer kneeling down with us to read the law we were violating. Judge Halleck asked the prosecutor, "Is this gentleman also praying?" The prosecutor answered, "No, your honor, he is the arresting officer." Judge Halleck said, "You brought the pictures. As far as I can see, he's doing the same thing the defendants are doing." Case dismissed.

On July 25, 1973, the Gregory family became an even dozen with the birth of my youngest son, Yohance. We had definitely outgrown our Chicago apartment. While I was playing an engagement at Paul's Mall in Boston, I used most of my free time to look at real estate. One day I went to see the four-hundred-acre Tower Hill Farm on Long Pond Road outside Plymouth, Massachusetts. It appeared to be the ideal place for relocating the Gregory family. The property fronted a pond, which looked like a lake to me. There were six houses on the property, including a twelve-room main house and a six-room boat house. The boat house was an ideal residence for Mike Watley and had ample space to accommodate visitors. I decided to take it. With ten times my forty acres, I could overlook the fact that Tower Hill Farm didn't have a mule!

We packed our belongings and moved to the country. With the help of my good friend George O'Hare, who works for the Sears Company in Chicago, I got prompt delivery of enough new furniture to fill the much larger home. But the first night on the farm was one I'll never forget. I was more unpopular with my wife and kids than the original Plymouth Rock settlers were with the Indians. It was such a drastic change from the environment and life style we had known in Chicago. The kids missed their friends and playmates. Lillian missed the convenient shopping center. And evidently I had missed the boat by making the move.

My unpopularity at home didn't last very long. Lillian and the kids soon came to love Tower Hill Farm. It was close enough to town to get the necessary goods and services. But it was far enough removed to really get close to nature. The kids could lie on the grass and look up at the stars, communicating with the earth while viewing the mystery of the heavens, listening to the quiet rustling of the leaves on the trees. For the first time in their lives, my kids got to know the true momma of all humanity, Mother Nature. I loved the natural setting even more than the kids did. My change in diet and my long periods of fasting had heightened and deepened my spiritual awareness. I pitched a tent up on the hill and began spending more time at home in prayer and meditation.

There was no question about public-school busing in my new neighborhood. All the kids were bused to school. You either put your kids on the school bus or taught them at home. Even though there were no antibusing demonstrations, the school bus became a classroom in American racism for my five-year-old son, Christian. Christian came home from school one day and told his mother, "Mommy, I really feel sorry for that little boy on the bus."

"Why, Christian?"

"Because, mommy, he told me he really liked me, but his mommy and daddy said he can't play with me."

"But why does that make you feel sorry for him, Christian?"

"Because for all his life he won't be able to play with people he likes." Little Christian had pretty well summarized the folly of racist thinking in America.

Gregory was eight years old when he came home from school with a problem of a different sort. Most of his classmates are white. Gregory told his mother, "Mommy, I want my hair to look like them other guys."

"What guys?"

"Them guys in school."

"Gregory, your hair can't look like theirs."

"Yes it can. I watched 'em. All they do is put water on theirs."

Lillian told me the story. It took me back to my own childhood. All of my movie heroes were white and had straight hair. I remember trying to get my hair to look like Clark Gable's hair, including the little cowlick over his forehead which he would flip back in place with a toss of his head. Like so many other Black folks, I was ashamed of my nappy hair. Now my son was experiencing the same feelings in his integrated classroom. I decided it was time for a father-and-son talk.

"Gregory, what's wrong with your hair?"

"Nothin'."

"Your mother told me you wanted your hair to be like them guys in school."

"I do."

"Are you talking about those white kids?"

"Yes. I want my hair to be like theirs."

"Well, son. Let's talk about it. What color are those other kids?"

"They're white."

"And what color are you?"

"I'm black."

"Do you think white people might have one type of hair and Black people might have another type of hair for a reason?"

"I don't know."

I saw my big opportunity to teach my son. I intended to tell him about Mother Africa, the difference in climate, the physical differences which resulted, including our nappy hair, to protect us from the hot sun. So I said, "Son, do you know where Black folks come from?"

"Sure I do."

"Where do Black folks come from?"

"Chicago."

As the summer of 1974 approached, I began planning my own

marathon, an eight-hundred-mile run from Chicago to Washington, D.C. The run was intended to be a dramatic personal witness, focusing national public attention upon the food crisis in this nation and the world over. It was the greatest challenge of my life. Two things were necessary to make the run successful. I had to be in shape physically, and I had to have some money. In order for the run to successfully focus public attention upon the world food crisis, press conferences would have to be held all along the way, and an advance party would have to accompany me to handle the necessary arrangements and details.

Raising money for the run was very difficult. On the surface the run appeared to be a solitary witness, which shouldn't cost a penny. Just Dick Gregory, running alone alongside the highway. Potential financial investors had a hard time understanding the need for a support staff, salaries, and other expenses. I went to California to talk with Steve Jaffe about getting some financial assistance from people in the show-business community. Steve told me that Barbra Streisand and her boyfriend, Jon Peters, wanted to talk with me about food, diet, and health. I also wanted to talk to them about the run. So we drove out to Barbra's house.

Since I was hoping to begin the run in a few weeks, I couldn't afford to miss a day of training. So I took my track equipment along. Barbra, Jon, and I talked for a long time about health food and proper diet. As the day wore on, I remembered that I still had twelve miles of jogging to do. Jon pointed out a jogging route, from the house down to the ocean and back. I changed into my track clothes, grabbed my can of Halt dog repellent spray, and started jogging.

Right away, two medium-sized dogs came after me. I really didn't want to spray them, because the owner was one of Barbra's neighbors. So instead of using my Halt, I halted myself. It was a standoff until the owner came and took his pets home. I looked ahead and saw two Great Danes coming toward me. I didn't see any fence to prevent them from reaching their obvious target. So I changed direction and started running back to Barbra's house, with the Great Danes in pursuit. As I was running, I turned around, raised my spray can, and missed both dogs twice. The dogs' owner heard me shouting and called off his Great Danes. I was embarrassed and humiliated. All the way back to Barbra's house, dogs kept barking at me and occasionally one of them would pick up the chase.

I told Jon Peters what had happened. He suggested that I might try running up a small mountain path nearby. Jon evidently assumed that I would only run up to the first plateau. But I kept running up and up and up. All along the steep path I noticed holes in the ground, and I heard hissing noises. But I kept running. The next thing I knew I was at the top. It had been a steep run, but it was the best possible conditioner. On the way back down, I met Jon Peters riding a horse. He looked at me in startled disbelief. He said, "Didn't you hear all those rattlesnakes while you were running?" I said, "Yeah, but as long as they weren't barkin' they didn't bother me."

I had intended to see if Barbra was interested in helping me finance the Chicago-to-Washington run. But after I came down from that mountain, I wasn't even interested in the run myself! I showered, changed, returned to my hotel, and flopped into bed. The next morning I ached all over, and I was really tempted to skip running that day. But a massage relieved the ache, and I jogged over to a nearby park. As I was jogging back to the hotel, my ankle started bothering me. I stopped jogging, coincidentally, right in front of the United Artists building. United Artists had produced my last comedy album "Caught In the Act." So I went inside to see if United Artists' vice president, Mike Stewart, was there. George Butler, who had supervised the taping and editing of my album, took me into Mike's office. In my track clothes, I was hardly dressed for a business meeting. But Mike Stewart is the kind of person who realizes that the cause rather than the clothes make the man. He loaned me $20,000 so I could begin the run. My run against hunger would never have happened without the help of Mike Stewart.

The first few days of the run were exciting and glamorous. I ran from Chicago to Gary, Indiana, where I received a warm reception from Mayor Dick Hatcher. From Gary I headed toward Detroit. Since I couldn't run on the highway, I ran on the shoulder at the side of the road, which meant I was running on loose gravel. Just outside Sturgis, Michigan, the loneliness and pain of my ordeal began to set in. The temperature was over a hundred degress. The loose stones underfoot were killing me, and the road ahead seemed to be growing longer with each stride. To keep myself going, I concentrated upon the meaning of this run.

As I thought about it, it seemed as though I had been running all my life. Running from poverty. Running to get a medal.

Running to beat somebody. Running for recognition. Running to be the fastest in the group. Running in high school. Running in college. Running in the Boston Marathon. Running for mayor. Even running for president. But now, for the first time in my life, I was running for somebody else. Everybody else, really.

This run was different. I was no longer running to call attention to Dick Gregory. This wasn't Flagpole Gregory, the grandstand favorite of the high school track meets in Saint Louis, who used to salute the flag in the homestretch. This was Dick Gregory, running to call attention to the world's number one problem—hungry, starving folks the world over. This was Dick Gregory, running against famine, against hunger, against time.

As I looked back, I realized that I had been training for this run all my life. This was the "big meet." I used to run against opponents I could see, guys from another school, another town, another state. No matter whether I won or lost, there was always another meet, another week. But this race was bigger than a game. There was nothing "sporting" about this event. I was running against a whole system—a system which dared to decide that food is a weapon. The stakes were higher now. It was more than medals, more than recognition, more than endurance, more than crossing the finish line. Every step of the way on this run, someone, somewhere, was dying.

I tried to visualize the starving, dying millions in my mind's eye. I thought it would help me to keep going. I re-created mental pictures of starving kids in Africa, India, and right here in the United States, with the bloated bellies, the bald heads, and the wide, staring eyes. I tried to envision people lying alongside the road up ahead, dying from starvation. To my surprise, those mental pictures didn't bolster me at all. So I changed my mental strategy. Instead of visualizing starving millions, I pictured them being fed, their tears of anguish changing into smiles. Mothers feeding their babies. Folks getting up and walking to their dinner. The new image gave me the mental and spiritual lift I needed. I realized that I had been trying to counteract a negative reality with another negative image. Once I changed to a positive image I was able to continue my struggle against the negative reality of world starvation. I realized the truth of my bumper sticker slogan: DICK GREGORY ON THE RUN: FIGHT FAMINE WITH FOOD.

On July 11, I interrupted my run to attend the ceremony for

the unveiling of the Mary McLeod Bethune Memorial in Washington, D.C. I had originally intended to end my run at the Washington Monument. But after attending the unveiling ceremony, I changed my final destination to the statue of Mary McLeod Bethune. I had spoken at Bethune-Cookman College in Daytona Beach, Florida, and had visited Mrs. Bethune's home on the campus. When I resumed my run, I thought of her lifelong dedication to providing educational opportunity for Black youth and the moving words of her "Last Will and Testament to My People." Mary McLeod Bethune pulled me toward my final goal in a way George Washington could never have done.

After the ceremony I met with Dorothy Height, president of the National Council of Negro Women. She agreed to provide the necessary follow-up and substance for the run. Her organization set up a mini-conference which provided a thorough analysis of the world food crisis, especially probing the political dynamics involved. Mrs. Height kept the run from being viewed as a Dick Gregory ego trip. Instead, it became a relay race, with the National Council of Negro Women taking the baton of hunger from my hands.

While I was in Washington, D.C., I ran the same number of miles as I did each day of the Chicago-to-Washington run. I felt somewhat guilty because funeral services were being held for former Surpeme Court Chief Justice Earl Warren at the same time that I was jogging. Ordinarily I would have attended the funeral, even though I had mixed feelings about Earl Warren. The Warren Court handed down the historic 1954 decision on public school desegregation. But the Warren Commission handed down what I consider to be a cover up concerning the assassination of John F. Kennedy. I believe that Earl Warren knew that the Warren Commission report was a cover up but that he felt it was his patriotic duty to allay the fears and suspicions which could have torn the country apart. So I felt gratitude toward the Warren Court and outrage toward the Warren Commission.

My jogging route took me into Arlington Cemetery. As I was jogging along the path, I ran smack into the Earl Warren funeral procession. I was really embarrassed. A number of Black leaders and friends recognized me and were waving from limousine windows. I had no intention of being at the funeral, let alone in track clothes! A Secret Service agent yelled, "Get out of here. You can't be on this path." I shouted back, "And I don't want to be here either!" I turned and ran away as fast as I could. After I had run a respectable distance, I stopped and thought about the incident. It was really weird. Either I should have been at the funeral, or else I had chased Earl Warren all the way to his grave.

I was back in Washington, D.C., on August 4, the final miles of the long run which began in Chicago. Mayor Walter Washington met me at the city limits. I ran to the Capitol building where I was met by Congressmen Andrew Young, Louis Stokes, and Walter Fauntroy. They joined me in running to the Bethune Memorial. My arrival in Washington, D.C., was a beautiful day of personal triumph and satisfaction, but it could have been a disaster if I had followed the advice of my friends and medical advisers. I had developed bad foot trouble during the run and was urged to lay off for a few days. But I had to open an engagement at the Apollo Theater in New York City on August 9. I couldn't afford the time off. If it hadn't been for that Apollo gig, I would have been running into town at the same time that Richard M. Nixon was running out!

At the Apollo Theater my run against famine was fresh in the minds of the audiences. I included lines about food, food prices, and Secretary of Agriculture Earl Butz in my act.

"Secretary Butz is something else. I'd say his popularity in America is about equivalent to that of the Grim Reaper. Earl Butz is the only man in America who makes us miss Herbert Hoover. He's the type of friend you invite over to dinner when you're having leftovers. Or during a fast.

"Sometimes I think we've gone completely crazy in this country. We process enough fertilizer in America to plant and grow enough crops to rid the world of starvation. But there's a fertilizer shortage because we all want kelly green lawns, so our dogs, cats, and neighborhood squirrels will have something pretty to pee on.

"We even feed our pets better than we feed ourselves. And we show more feelings toward our pets than we do for our own kids. Walk into the average American home at dinnertime, and you'll hear something like this from a parent: 'Boy, if you don't eat that liver, you're going to bed without dessert.' But at that same house, if the family dog won't eat his Liver Snaps, they rush to the supermarket and buy eighty different kinds of dog food, trying to find something the dog will eat! And to really prove we're crazy, 90 percent of the dog owners will tell you they never feed their dogs table scraps. They're afraid they might make their dogs sick. Now that's got to tell us something! I've seen stray dogs eat grass, snakes, rocks, and snails and not get sick. But if he eats your left-over filet mignon, he might die!

"Can you believe we give away guns, bombs, and bullets to some countries, yet we can't give food to starving nations? But I'll tell you one thing. We'd give food to starving nations if they struck oil. If those starving countries struck oil, we'd be sending planes full of food every second on the second—with Colonel Sanders leading them.

"It looks like quite a few heroin dealers have gone into a more profitable business. Pushing sugar! 'Cause with sugar prices so high, you'd be surprised at the number of people walking around hooked on sugar, who can't afford to buy it. They call them 'sugar junkies.' And a lot of police departments are worried about all the sugar smuggling going on. I understand that in some airports, the cops have trained cockroaches to sniff out the sugar. So if you see a guy in the airline terminal with a can of Black Flag in his hip pocket, he's probably a sugar pusher!

"But sugar prices are ridiculous. I was in the supermarket the other day when a stock boy accidentally dropped a five-pound bag of sugar, and it burst open on the floor. One hundred and fifty customers volunteered to clean it up—with their tongues! But we deserve our high sugar prices, the way we let those nuts run things in Washington. Do you realize we can sell wheat to Russia, but we can't buy sugar from Cuba? Like we can trust the Russians, but we can't trust the Cubans! Let me ask you, which one of those countries do you think has a 900,000 megaton hydrogen bomb—aimed at President Ford's swimming pool?"

The United Nations World Food Conference was held in Rome, Italy, during the month of November 1974. I wanted to attend, not as a delegate nor even as an official observer, but merely as a concerned citizen of the world. But I was committed to a full month's schedule of college lecture dates. After the conference opened and I began reading newspaper reports from Rome, I decided that I had to find a way to go. So I rescheduled a lecture commitment at the University of Wyoming.

Newspaper and television reports from Rome had indicated that the United States was unwilling to make a definite commitment as to how much food it would send to starving nations. On the other hand, Canada had announced a twenty percent increase in its food aid to a hungry world. I sent a telegram to Canadian Prime Minister Pierre Trudeau commending him for making such a commitment and stating further that his example had inspired me to leave for Rome immediately to try to influence United States policy at the food conference.

Before leaving for Rome on Sunday night, November 10, I held a press conference in Boston. I told the representatives of the press, "Whenever a government supported by the United States is threatened by military attack, the United States is quick to send increased supplies of planes, bombs and ammunition. But when Third World people are attacked by famine and starvation, the United States government is unwilling to give a definite answer to how much food we are going to provide. That's an outrage! The United States has always tried to solve problems by shooting. It's time we learned to solve problems by sharing."

I also said that I hoped to enlist interest at the Rome conference in utilizing abundant existing food resources. I pointed out that the only nourishment I took during my nine-hundred-mile run was a kelp-based liquid formula. "That ought to call into question the old American habit of three square meals a day," I explained. "Kelp is one of nature's most nourishing foods. It's very ironic that everyone talks about the fish supply being inadequate to feed hungry people. We're so busy worrying about eating the fish that we overlook the nutritional value of what the fish eat! After looking at Watergate for more than a year, we ought to start looking *underwater* for nourishment."

I arrived in Rome on Monday, November 11. Some 1200 representatives of the press were in Rome to cover the World Food Conference. Actor Eddie Albert had also come to Rome as a concerned citizen, along with a determined group from Pennsylvania, which prodded the United States delegation with hard and demanding questions. As soon as I stepped off the plane, I was greeted by members of the press.

"Why are you here, Mr. Gregory?"

"Because I couldn't in good conscience remain at home while the starving people of the world hungrily awaited word from the United States government about specific commitments of food aid. I'm outraged to live in a country that can send tanks around the world, but can't send turnips; a country that can supply nations with napalm, but not with fertilizer. And I think I represent other decent, thinking Americans who feel the United States should have sent humanitarians to deal with world hunger rather than politicians."

"What are you going to do about it?"

"I'm going to call the president at the White House to see if we can get a definite commitment of increased food aid. If we don't get that commitment, I will lead a twenty-four-hour vigil outside the conference."

The press wouldn't let me forget my off-the-cuff promise. Reporters kept asking me, "Have you called the president yet?" After being asked several times, I answered, "No, I haven't called yet. I'm really looking for a phone." A reporter said, "Come up to the press room. We've got a phone you can use." I followed the reporter to the press room, and all the newspeople gathered around while I placed a credit-card call to the White House.

The overseas operator asked, "What number are you calling?"

"This is Dick Gregory, and I want to call the president of the United States, Gerald R. Ford, at the White House in Washington, D.C."

"Do you have the number?"

"No, but I'm sure it's listed."

Then I heard the overseas operator talking to a White House operator. "We have a call for President Gerald R. Ford from Dick Gregory in Rome." The White House operator asked, "Is the call paid for?"

The president was not available, so I was connected with Norman E. Ross, Jr., assistant director of the Domestic Council. I told him that I felt it was very important for the United States to make a definite food commitment, because other nations of the world tend to follow our lead in foreign policy matters. For example, when the United States decided to boycott Cuba, other nations followed suit. Mr. Ross said that the Domestic Council was discussing the possibility of committing $660 million in emergency food aid, even though Secretary Butz had recommended only $33 million. I asked when the emergency food aid decision would be announced. Mr. Ross answered, "Sometime soon."

I hung up the phone and relayed the information to the press. I thought "sometime soon" would mean in a matter of hours. When I realized that Mr. Ross had a very different timetable in mind, I went ahead with the twenty-four-hour vigil outside the conference center. During the vigil, I promised my fellow demonstrators that I would be at the White House on Thanksgiving Day if the United States food aid pledge was not upheld.

On Monday of Thanksgiving week, I released a Thanksgiving Proclamation to the press. I quoted Edwin M. Martin, deputy chairman of the United States delegation to the World Food Conference, who said: "This conference was not called to get food to people tomorrow but to lay out a plan of action to prevent the crisis we have now from recurring." And I also quoted the often repeated statement by Secretary of Agriculture Earl Butz that food is a "tool in the kit of American diplomacy." My proclamation suggested that neither quote reflected the attitude of the American people or the original pilgrim spirit. I invited all Americans who wanted to see starving people fed immediately to join me in the White House Thanksgiving Day demonstration to call upon President Ford to announce in specific detail the amount of foreign food aid to be supplied by the United States government.

On Thanksgiving Day I arrived at the White House at ten-thirty in the morning. A handful of other demonstrators were with me. I was carrying a picket sign made by Willie Beal, a very clever artist. It was a cartoon of a turkey with the head of Earl Butz. The caption read: "While Millions Starve, Are You Going to Swallow This?" Since it was Thanksgiving Day, the only reporters around were the White House press corps holiday shift. President Ford had held his press conference earlier in the morning on the White House lawn. He appeared with teammates from his old high school football team.

The Washington police were waiting for me with their paddy wagons. I was told that I couldn't march around the White House without a permit and that we would be arrested if we didn't leave. I said, "I think you're making a mistake. This demonstration is bigger than the few people you see here. On November 21, hundreds of thousands of people fasted and contributed the money they would have spent on meals to food programs for starving people. Before you arrest me, I think you'd better check with the White House."

The police checked inside. They came back out with new orders. "Mr. Gregory, you can picket, but you'll have to picket alone and you can't carry that sign." I answered, "No way! I'm carrying my sign, and anyone who shows up is welcome to picket with me." We started picketing the White House, and the Washington police watched. Some members of the White House press corps came out on the way home to their Thanksgiving dinner. When they saw the Earl Butz cartoon, they postponed their dinner plans and ran back inside to file their stories.

As the day wore on, the White House demonstration became the hottest Thanksgiving Day attraction in Washington, D.C. Mayor Walter Washington drove by, honked the horn of his automobile, and waved greetings. A lady drove up in a limousine and got out to join the picket line. She told me that her son had heard me speak at his college and had phoned home with the instructions, "Whatever else you do on Thanksgiving Day, be sure to walk in Dick Gregory's picket line." She walked for more than two hours.

Other folks joined the line after they had finished their own Thanksgiving dinners. We ended up with some 200 picketers. About ten o'clock that night, I went to make a phone call. When I returned, I saw that the picket line had become disorganized in my absence. I asked everybody to straighten up the line. I noticed three Black guys fall to the back of the line, and I wondered who they were. I went to check them out.

"Hey, brothers, when did you get here?"

"Just after you left, Brother Greg."

"How long you going to stay?"

"Oh, we can't stay too long. We got to get back to work. We're bus drivers, and we left our buses parked across the street. We just wanted to show you that we're with you. And tell the folks that as long as we're here, they can warm up inside the buses."

We picketed until Thanksgiving Day ended at midnight. Many newspapers and television news reports carried the picture of Earl Butz as a turkey. And a few days later, the government announced $110 million of emergency food aid to Bangladesh and India.

37

Comedy and Conspiracy

One night, after a college lecture in New Jersey, I stopped by Ralph Schoenman's house. Ralph, who had been Bertrand Russell's secretary, was now living and teaching in the United States. Ralph showed me a copy of the autopsy report on Bobby Kennedy. It raised very serious questions about Sirhan Sirhan being the lone assassin, considering the angle and location of the shots which entered Bobby's head. Ralph also showed me a photograph taken in Dallas on the day of Jack Kennedy's assassination and later published by A. J. Weberman in an underground newspaper.

The picture showed three men being taken into custody shortly after the president was shot. They had been discovered by the police behind the bushes on the grassy knoll in front of the president's motorcade. The Dallas police decided that the three men were tramps who had jumped off a freight train and were only coincidentally on the grassy knoll at that fateful moment. But two of the so-called tramps bore a striking resemblance to E. Howard Hunt and Frank Sturgis, both of whom were involved in the Watergate break-in. Hunt was a known CIA agent. Sturgis admitted participating in several "adventures" in Cuba, which he believed were organized and financed by the CIA.

I was determined to bring the tramp photos to the attention of my fellow Americans. My first idea was to rent a billboard in a key location, reproducing the tramp photo, with closeups of Hunt and Sturgis, and raising the question of CIA involvement in President Kennedy's assassination. I asked George O'Hare to check out billboard possibilities in Chicago. George located an excellent billboard, but the reproduction process would have required painting in the photograph. So Ralph Schoenman started checking out billboards in New York City. He found one in Times Square, and he also found someone who could reproduce the photo without touching it up. But the cost of the billboard was $42,000. It was definitely out of my price range.

I decided to go to the White House on Christmas Day with Mike Watley dressed as Santa Claus, carrying a bagful of goodies for the press—copies of the tramp photo. But for some reason on the day before Christmas, I didn't feel right about the White House demonstration. On Christmas Eve, I was still apprehensive. I couldn't figure out why, but something didn't feel right. About one o'clock Christmas morning, I told Mike Watley, "We're not going."

When I read the newspaper on Christmas morning, I realized that I must have had some ESP going for me. The headlines told of a Black guy who had smashed through the White House gate with a carload of dynamite. The Secret Service later said that they had been watching him for two days. I couldn't quite understand how a guy could have planned well enough to get within a few feet of where the president slept with a carload of dynamite and yet not realize that President Ford was on vacation, skiing in Vail, Colorado. Nor could I understand how anyone could crash down the White House gate with the Secret Service watching. Whatever it all meant, I was glad I had cancelled my demonstration plans!

Instead of that White House demonstration, I sent a telegram to the president on Christmas Day. Just before Christmas, the Seymour Hirsch exposé of clandestine CIA domestic surveillance activities had appeared in *The New York Times*. CIA Director William Colby flew to Colorado with a special report to the president. Vice President Nelson Rockefeller was asked to head a commission to investigate CIA activities. In my Christmas Day telegram, I raised the following questions:

"What are the sources of CIA financing beyond the governmental appropriations by Congress? Is there a link between CIA financing and some of the illicit activities it is involved in? To what extent is the CIA involved in the training of police in this country? To what degree is law enforcement controlled and directed by the CIA?

To what extent has the CIA infiltrated labor unions and the American press? Can the CIA be linked to illicit activities designed to destroy the youth of our nation, such as drug traffic and weapons made so readily available to juvenile gang members? Can the CIA be linked to the assassinations of John and Robert

Kennedy and Dr. Martin Luther King, Jr.? What is the working relationship and coordination between the CIA and the FBI?"

I closed my telegram by telling the president that I had evidence in my possession which suggested that prominent Watergate figures may have been in Dallas on the day of President Kennedy's assassination and which called into question Sirhan Sirhan's lone role in the assassination of Bobby Kennedy. I offered to turn my evidence over to any representative the president might select. I told the president, "I would view my providing you with that evidence as the most sincere and heartfelt Christmas present I could possibly give at this critical hour."

Nelson Rockefeller answered my telegram. In his letter the vice president insisted that there would be a thorough investigation of the CIA and that no stone would be left unturned. But he didn't ask for my information. So I took the issue to the public. Each night during my college lectures, I read my telegram to President Ford and held up the letter from Nelson Rockefeller. I showed the tramp photos and the autopsy report. Then I would say, "I want you agents in the audience to get a message back to the White House. The CIA commission is going to have to deal with this information."

I also held a press conference in Chicago. Evidently a number of newspaper editors thought that Hunt and Sturgis were the tramps in the photo, because they ran the pictures in their newspapers. Right after my press conference, I got a call from the Rockefeller Commission inviting me to present my evidence. I flew to Washington the next day and turned over my information to Rockefeller Commission counsel Robert B. Olsen.

When it came out in June 1975, the *Report to the President by the Commission on CIA Activities Within the United States* concluded, "It cannot be determined with certainty where Hunt and Sturgis actually were on the day of the assassination. However, no credible evidence was found which would contradict their testimony that they were in Washington, D.C., and Miami, Florida, respectively."

With regard to the tramp photos, the Rockefeller Commission report said, "The photographs of the 'derelicts' in Dallas have been displayed in various newspapers in the United States, on national television programs, and in the April 28, 1975, issue of *Newsweek* magazine. But no witnesses have provided testimony that either of the 'derelicts' was personally known to be Hunt or Sturgis—and no qualified expert was offered to make such identification."

In January 1975, I attended the First Annual Comedy Awards Show in Los Angeles, California. It was sponsored by a new organization for comedians headed by Alan King. Lillian had been filling out forms and returning them on my behalf. One day I called home while I was on the road. Lil said, "You got two tickets for the comedy awards show. You have this Friday off." I assumed that Lil was really saying that she wanted to go. So I said, "OK, I'll make airline reservations to Los Angeles. What time shall we leave?" She said, "What do you mean 'we'? I'm not going. I just think you ought to be there." I asked Lillian to send the tickets to Steve Jaffe. Steve answered the R.S.V.P.

I flew to Los Angeles, rented a tuxedo, and Steve and I went to the show. I was so grateful to Lil for insisting that I attend. It was a funny, funny night. Bill Cosby was brilliant doing a routine about how people in the street treat comedians. Mel Brooks broke up everyone as he accepted the award for his movie *Blazing Saddles*. But the funniest portions of the evening didn't appear on film when the show was later aired on television. The ad lib banter from the audience, especially from Buddy Hackett, Totie Fields, and Don Rickles, was side-splitting but not entirely suited for family viewing.

Sitting in the audience that night, I became aware as never before that I was part of a very special fellowship. I realized that whatever else I've done or will yet do in my life, I'm first and foremost a comic. I was proud to be a comedian that night, proud of my profession, and proud of whatever contribution I've made to comedy. When Anthony Newley sang his moving song about the funny man, it brought tears to my eyes. He was singing about me and my life, as well as the lives of all those comedy colleagues sitting around me. And he dramatized that song as only Tony can.

At the close of the show, Alan King began calling people up to the stage from the audience. Brock Peters was sitting on the other side of the room, and I heard him shout, "Dick Gregory's here." Alan looked up and said, "Dick Gregory? Dick Gregory's here? Dick, where are you? Come up here." I got up to answer Alan's call, and my colleagues gave me a standing ovation. It was one of the most moving and beautiful moments of my life. I walked down the line, shaking hands with my colleagues assembled on the stage, stopping to hug Jonathan Winters. Then we all turned to face a portrait of Jack Benny, who had just passed away, and paid tribute to one of the true giants of our profession.

After the show Marty Feldman came up and told me about the many times he had come to see me perform in London. And I had never known he was there. I walked over to greet Red Buttons, who was talking to a group of people. Red told the other folks, "This man is a prophet. We sat on a plane together one day and talked about all kinds of things that were happening in this country. And everything Dick predicted has come true." I smiled and said, "Red, aren't all comics prophets?" And I remembered Red's television show years ago. Maybe Red was saying more than he realized when he hopped on stage, with his hand to his ear, and sang, "Ho ho, he he, strange things are happening."

Soon after the comedy break, I was back on the case, tracking down conspiracy. I attended an assassination convention in Boston that turned out to be old home week. So many of those who had been tirelessly researching the assassination of John F. Kennedy, and other conspiracy-related matters were there—Mark Lane, Mae Brussels, Sherman Skolnick, and many others whom I'd never met. But I was saddened to see all of the infighting among assassination buffs. Their efforts had been ridiculed and rejected for so long that they didn't trust anybody, including each other.

When I arrived at the Boston convention, everybody was talking about Robert Grodin and his film. He had a "first generation" copy of the Zapruder film, which heretofore had been exclusively in the possession of Time-Life, Inc. The film sequence seemed to indicate clearly that one of the shots had hit President Kenndy from the front. When I saw the film, I knew that I had to find a way to get it shown to the general public. But convincing Bob Grodin to make his film available to others was no easy matter. He was justifiably very protective of his explosive property. He carried it around with the film case handcuffed to his wrist.

When I first approached Bob Grodin about trying to get the film on national television, his associates insisted upon a minimum of $100,000 to cover time and expenses already put into the film, and insurance coverage in case of a lawsuit. Of course, I didn't have that kind of money. But on the second day of the convention,

I talked for hours with Robert Grodin and his wife. I told them over and over again, "What you have in your possession could save this country." After considerable mental anguish, Bob agreed to go public with the film.

We held several press conferences, showing the film to representatives of the press as Bob explained the apparent contradictions with the conclusions of the Warren Commission report. Our press conferences paid off. I got a phone call from Geraldo Rivera, inquiring about possibly using the film on his Good Night, America show. I was overjoyed because I felt Geraldo's show would be the perfect forum. He is a very dedicated, fair-minded, and trusted person. In the hope of prodding Geraldo to make an immediate and definite decision to use the film, I made up a story. I told him that Peter Jennings was thinking about using it, so I had to know what to tell Peter when he called me back. Geraldo said he was definitely scheduling the film. When I hung up the phone, I suddenly realized that Peter and Geraldo worked for ABC. I began desperately trying to contact Peter Jennings to ask him to back up my story.

Before I could make telephone contact with Peter Jennings, I was back at the White House for yet another demonstration. A demonstration had been called to protest American policy in Cambodia, to demand the release of political prisoners in South Vietnam and to insist upon amnesty rather than clemency for Vietnam War resisters. The demonstration took place on a Saturday morning, and I almost missed it. All morning long demonstrators had taken the White House tour and refused to leave the White House grounds when the tour was over. There would be no arrests until early afternoon when the last White House tour was over.

I lined up for the noon tour. A White House guard was standing at the end of the line. I stood behind him. He said, "I'm sorry, but this is the end of the line. Nobody behind me will be allowed to take the tour." I said, "That's all right. I'll just stand here and watch you." As we got up to the gate, the guard repeated the regulations, "I'm telling you, you won't be able to take the tour." I answered, "OK, I'll just follow you up to the gate and watch you lock it."

The guard locked the gate in my face and I stood outside looking in. I could see the demonstrators assembled on the other side of the White House, awaiting arrest. Another White House guard recognized me. "Dick Gregory, what are you doing out there?" He unlocked the gate and let me in.

"Do you want to take the tour?"

"Not really. Can't I just cut across the lawn and join those other folks?"

"I can't let you do that. If you want to join them, you'll have to take the tour."

So I spent the next hour looking at all the White House relics. I decided that the first thing I would have done if I had been elected president was to call Sears Roebuck and have them send some new continental furniture. At the end of the tour, I joined the other demonstrators. The announcement was made that the gate was being locked and that anybody remaining on the White House grounds would be arrested. Remembering earlier White House demonstrations, I suggested that we all kneel while I led the group in prayer. After I finished praying, we were taken to the police station and booked. The cop at the desk said, "You folks sure know how to mess up a guy's Saturday." I told him, "The tragedy is that every one of our names will be reported to the president, but none of you cops who had to work overtime on Saturday will get an honorable mention." We were released on our own recognizance.

The following Saturday I returned to the nation's capital for the premiere of Barbra Streisand's movie *Funny Lady*. It was also a live television benefit, sponsored by the Kennedy family, to raise money for the Olympics for mentally retarded children. I checked into the same hotel where Barbra, Jon Peters, and Steve Jaffe were staying—the Watergate! That night Steve and I went to the Kennedy Center for the benefit premiere. I went backstage to say hello to Barbra and Muhammed Ali. Just before the show, we all stood as President Ford entered the concert hall. There is a truly beautiful potential in America when someone can be arrested at the White House and be sitting with the president enjoying a show the following week. Dick Cavett opened the show with a timely line, "A live television show is very rare these days. But here in Washington, after Watergate, everybody is afraid to tape."

Intermission was like "who's who in Washington." I chatted with Jack Valenti, Douglas Kiker, Mayor Walter Washington, Cliff Alexander, Rafer Johnson, and Peter Jennings. I finally had a chance to explain my conversation with Geraldo Rivera. Peter is a friend of many years, and he understood completely.

Douglas Kiker introduced me to White House Press Secretary Ron Nessen and his wife. I asked Ron, "Would you get a message to your boss's secretary for me? Tell her I came to town to pick up my apples, and I hope I don't have to come back again." Then I explained the bet I had made one day in Grand Rapids, Michigan. Gerald Ford had been nominated as vice president, but not yet confirmed. His secretary and I were together at a press conference. I said that when her boss was confirmed, it would be the confirmation of our next president. She didn't believe it. So I bet her a case of Michigan apples against a case of Massachusetts cranberries. Ron said he would relay the message on Monday morning, but I still haven't received my apples.

Geraldo ran the Zapruder film on two different Good Night, America shows. The second time was as a preface to an hour-and-and-a-half probe of the lingering questions about the assassination of John F. Kennedy. That show was like a decade-long dream come true for me. It included Mark Lane; Haverford College professor Josiah Thompson; and Dr. Cyril Wecht, one of the nation's leading forensic pathologists and former president of the American Academy of Forensic Sciences. Dr. Wecht is one of the few people who have seen the assassination evidence in the National Archives, and he was very critical of the autopsy. From his own study, Dr. Wecht said he was convinced that more than one person was firing at the president that day. Former Senator Ralph Yarborough, who was riding in the presidential motorcade that fateful day in Dallas, called for a reopening of the JFK assassination investigation.

During the taping of the show, I kept thinking of that day in my Chicago apartment when I shut off all my tape recorders because I didn't want to record a lie. Thank God a man named Zapruder kept his camera rolling. Now the whole nation has seen what his lens recorded. The camera is still rolling, and one day the record will be set straight.

38

Skipping Christmas Dinner

During Christmas week 1975, I was fasting again. This time I was not fasting alone. One hundred and twenty fellow fasters had come from all over the country to join me in a Christmas-to-New Year's-Day fast at the West Hunter Street Baptist Church, Atlanta, Georgia, where the Reverend Ralph Abernathy serves as pastor. Since Thanksgiving Day, when Ralph Abernathy and I marched together in front of the White House to call for a new investigation of the assassination of Martin Luther King, Jr., I had been inviting people to join me in Atlanta on Christmas Day for the week-long fast. I held press conferences, issued invitations during my college lectures and on television talk shows, and sent out a notice to the large mailing list I have compiled from the college campuses.

The West Hunter Street Baptist Church is a huge structure, with more than ninety classrooms and a large gymnasium. The gym was converted into a makeshift dormitory for the fast. It was ironic that the church was originally built as a "separate-but-equal" alternative to public school integration. Now it is pastored by one of the leading spokesmen for integration in the nation. And our group of fasters was a model of integration—Black and white, young and old, male and female.

The purpose of our fast was to focus public attention upon the food crisis at home and abroad. As I explained in press conferences and on television shows, "When you consider the worldwide problem, food shortage is a matter of scarcity. But in this country, the food shortage is a matter of price. People just can't afford to eat anymore. Old people are shoplifting in the supermarkets. Poor people are eating dog food. You just have to look around all those housing developments where no pets are allowed and count the empty dog-food cans, to realize that folks are eating Alpo. The food situation in this country will soon be worse than it was in the 1930s. Then, at least, if you could get hold of a dime you could buy your family some substantial food. I'm convinced that if we don't take immediate action, there will be food riots in 1976. And that will be some Bicentennial!"

Dr. Alvenia Fulton came to Atlanta to supervise the fast. Ox-Fam America provided the necessary funds for staff and expenses, including the salary for fast coordinator Melissa Lawson. Mayor Maynard Jackson proclaimed Christmas to New Year's Day "Dick Gregory Food-Fast Week." And the mayor also came to the church to visit the fasters and demonstrate his support. We received telegrams and messages from so many good people, including Cesar Chavez, Barbra Streisand, Eugene McCarthy, John and Yoko Lennon, Freddie Prinze, and Ryan O'Neal. Eddie Benson, an Indian brother whom I had met during the Wounded Knee demonstrations, phoned and said that a group of Indians on the reservation were joining us in prayer and fasting.

On the sixth day of the fast, we received three phone calls that really lifted our spirits. A conference-call hookup had been arranged so that the entire group could hear the callers and talk to them. Newspaper reporters were also invited to sit in on the conference phone calls. The first call was from actor Richard Dreyfus. Richard had planned to join us in Atlanta, but the tragic bombing at New York's La Guardia Airport forced him to change his plans. So he gave his testimonial by phone.

"When Dick Gregory says that eating is not a privilege, it's a right, he knows what he's talking about. It is obvious to me that everyone in this world should have the necessities of life without having to pay for them. There should be no such thing as a profit or a loss in living. We have the gift of life, and we should not take it away from other people simply because they have no food.

"It's really hard to rap about it over the phone. And obviously you people down there are doing more about the problem than I am doing up here. But I wanted to call to say that to let one person starve is a disgrace, to say nothing of letting millions of people starve. Anything that can be done to alleviate that is all to the good. And I wish you all well."

I told Richard that I was making plans for a cross-country run against hunger from Los Angeles to New York City. And I asked if he would want to jog a few miles with me. "For the good it will do my heart," Richard answered, "and the good it will do me to be with you, I'll jog with you all the way down the San Bernadino Freeway."

The next call was from Stevie Wonder. Stevie had been fasting at home in support of our Atlanta fast. He spoke to us as a faster addressing his fellow fasters:

"I basically just wanted to ask, how good can any of us feel this holiday season? Are we reflecting upon those who are so weak from starvation that they cannot even open their hands? How good can the rich man feel who, when asked to help the poor from his riches, anwers, 'People should pull themselves up by their own bootstraps'?

"We fast this length of time because we're protesting something which shouldn't exist. How much pain do you think those people feel who must fast, whether they want to or not, because they are unable to get what everyone rightfully deserves? . . . .

"If we are going to have a war against starvation, we have to do something about it and not just talk about it. I will sing my happiest song when the day comes that we know we are actually making a move to solve the problem of starvation throughout the world and throughout this country. Let's write a song about that."

The last phone call was from the heavyweight champion of the world, Muhammed Ali. Ali was in training for his fight with Jean Pierre Coopman and made a rare exception to interrupt his training schedule to call Atlanta.

"The reason I cancelled my training program today, Dick, was because what you are doing is so worthwhile and so great. People don't realize how far ahead of them you are. You mentioned you all have been fasting since Christmas. In reality, probably only you have been fasting since Christmas. The rest of them told you they have been fasting. You have to condition yourself for that kind of suffering. I just can't believe the average person came and fasted for that length of time with no prior training. But if they did, God bless them.

"Most of us are so intoxicated with wealth and our style of life that we no longer see the condition of the people around us. But if you can get that hungry, and realize how other people feel, you move far beyond the average person's understanding. I'll do everything I can to help your program. If it weren't for this serious fight I have coming up, and being fifteen pounds overweight, I would be there. But I'm with you in everything you want to do."

I told Ali that his suspicions that some of the fasters were cheating was really a tribute to them. I reminded him that he had accused me of sneaking food during my first long fast.

"It's hard to believe, Dick," Ali admitted. "I'm in training for a fight where they're going to pay me a million dollars. And I won't fast three days to get that million dollars. And you fast for twenty-nine days, and forty days, and now you tell me you're gonna run across the world!

"You're a miracle man. The more I hear about you and watch you and think about things you do, if you're really telling the truth, you've got to be one of the greatest men in America today. Just keep out of the boxing ring."

I told the group about the time Ali decided to put me to the test in Detroit. He joined me as I was passing through Detroit during my run against hunger. Ali took up the story from there.

"I met you in Detroit, and I knew I was good for five miles. Five miles is about forty-five minutes, and anybody who knows anything about jogging knows that five miles is a long way. I said to myself, 'I'm gonna take this chump for five miles and see what he can do.' We went four miles and you weren't breathin' hard, so I stepped it up another mile, real fast. You followed me, and then you got faster. At five miles I said, 'Doggone him, he can't go much farther.' So I jumped into a car and followed you fifteen more miles! I said, 'This man's crazy!' "

One of the fasters asked Ali how he got fifteen pounds overweight. He used the question as an opportunity to remind us of food. "I like sweets too much—cake, pie, ice cream. I come down to the kitchen in the training camp, and the cook has a big piece of chocolate cake, with ice cream melting down all over it, and a big dish of peach cobbler—" By that time, Ali's words were drowned out by the groans his food images had created among the fasters. I told him, "Man, you sure are dirty. If you don't stop, we're gonna tell you about barbecued ribs, Muslim! Which reminds me of a question I've been wanting to ask you. In the Black community, we call Cadillacs 'hogs.' Can Muslims own Cadillacs?" I could mentally visualize Ali shaking his head as I heard him say, "Oh, Lord!"

On the final day of the fast, we had a steady stream of visitors— Mrs. Coretta King, "Daddy" Martin Luther King, Sr., Congressman Andy Young, Georgia State Representative Hosea Williams. At the stroke of midnight, we broke our fast, as the Bicentennial year began. All week long, as I looked into the eyes of my fellow fasters, I saw in their expressions and in their self-sacrificing dedication those qualities which inspired the original settling of this land. Like the Pilgrims, my fellow fasters willingly endured hardship and suffering and deprivation because they saw the hope and promise of new life in a new land.

This Bicentennial year, I hope all Americans will recapture that pilgrim spirit. The gloriously dissatisfied pilgrim spirit is a necessary corrective for an America which has become settled and complacent. It calls us to an ongoing process of resettlement, to a yearning for a better life in a better land. The pilgrim spirit finds no hardship or suffering too unbearable, no immediate obstacle too insurmountable, to silence the longing for a new life of true human freedom and dignity. The pilgrim spirit unsettles complacency, apathy, and greed, in order to settle *finally* the most basic human problems.

The pilgrim spirit should and must be the eternal soul of America.

Epilogue

Up from Nigger

In my first autobiography, *Nigger,* written in collaboration with Robert Lipsyte, I talked a lot about the monster inside me, which drove me to outwit, outsmart, and outlast the obstacles and barriers in life. In a later article for *Esquire* magazine, Bob Lipsyte described my monster as "a combination of ego and ambition" which all men have but which drove me "harder than most men." And I guess Bob was right. The life blood of the monster inside me was adrenaline, which filled my veins when there was a race to win, an audience to turn on, a civil rights struggle to engage in. My monster grew right along with the poor ghetto kid on welfare, and it too became a state champion in track, overcame poverty, fought discrimination, and climbed to the top echelons of show business.

Now the monster has been subdued. I used to think my monster was a good thing. It gave me the drive to climb to the top. But now I realize that the monster was created within me by an oppressive and unjust social and political system. Mine was a two-headed monster, representing both my frustrations and my ambitions, the positive and the negative aspects of my life. The monster would rise up and take control of me. But since the system created the monster, the system was still in control.

As I came to understand my monster's creator better, the monster itself began to disappear. I now clearly see and understand the system of injustice and oppression which creates such monstrous conditions in the lives of the poor. The system is very real to me; there are faces to it. As I have matured in spiritual awareness and understanding, I have outgrown the monster. Now I am driven by a commitment to the laws of Mother Nature and the moral demands of the universal order.

In their young innocence, my kids seem instinctively to understand what took me four decades to learn. Before going to bed at night, my younger kids will often come to me and say, "Daddy, let's play monster." If the weather permits, we go outside and I am the monster, looking for the kids hiding in the bushes or behind trees. The kids scream and fake being scared, but it's just a game. They're not really afraid of the monster; he's fun to play with.

But my kids would never ask their daddy to play Dr. Frankenstein. They seem to understand instinctively that the monster's creator is truly terrifying. The cold, calculating freak who reactivated the dead to create the monster is certainly not a desirable playmate. The social and political system in the United States is Dr. Frankenstein, and it has created monsters in slums, ghettos, and other pockets of poverty all over this land. Like Dr. Frankenstein, the system creates the living dead.

When I was driven by the monster, I struggled against a system which called me "nigger." When devotion to the universal order of life replaced obsession with the system, I moved "up from nigger." The system no longer controls my actions or my reactions. Having ridden myself of the monster, I now see personal witness and human service as providing all the drive I ever needed.

I'll always be grateful to show business and to comedy for giving me the opportunities and experiences which have molded my life. I doubt that I would have been able to move "up from nigger" if it hadn't been for show business. My involvement in the struggle for human dignity, so many of the people I have met along the way, the opportunity to travel, to lecture, and to learn are all the direct result of having made a name for myself in show business. And those old show business ties happily reappear in the strangest circumstances.

Over the past two years I've spent considerable time outside the gates of the White House. Inside, my former joke writer and old friend Bob Orben serves as head speech writer for President Gerald R. Ford. Bob wrote so many of my lines when I was running for president in 1968, so I can claim some credit for giving him his start in writing presidential material! Eight years have produced a strange turn of events. Bob Orben made it into the Oval Office, and I'm still outside looking in.

But that's show business!

Index